Memoirs of a Pro-American; A Trilogy.

Brotherly Enemies

by Elie Nakouzi

Table of Contents

To my uncle, Joseph, who's chosen his little couch over the entire 'outer' world... How wise!

Some names and identifying details have been changed to protect the security of individuals.

0
My Friend Is The CIA Director

July 2011.
Penguin Place, Virginia.

There is obviously a good story behind Al's "hello" today.

"David Petraeus, your friend, was officially appointed the director of the CIA," he says with no introduction.

"Wow," I think about it for a second. "Then, I guess I was wrong," I say. "I always predicted that he would be elected the president one day, but this is even more interesting, if not more powerful," I half joke.

"Exactly," Al chuckles, and he hangs up.

Like usual, every time Petraeus gets a new promotion, I send him a greeting e-mail. And there have been many promotions since I first met him.

Last time, when he was appointed to head the central command, my message was, "I don't know whether to congratulate you on getting the new position, or congratulate the new position on getting you." I guess he liked that.

What am I going to write now that he's the head of the CIA? I think it over and over in my head.

"Congratulations, Sir. And happy Fourth of July. Best, Elie." That's the best I come up with this time. It looks empty and simple, I know; however, I push 'send' quickly before I change my mind and persuade myself to elaborate. I wait 5 minutes and reload my page to check for his reply. Nope.

I wait for another five minutes. Nothing. In half an hour, I reload my page at least 25 times. Still Nothing. "I am sure he's got 18,000 e-mails in his inbox now; it's gonna take him sometime to answer all these," I remind myself.

Forty-eight hours later, there are still no messages from my friend; it's weird.

"He's in a very delicate position now," Al justifies. He also sent a congratulation message and has had no reply from David. "He's got to think 110 times before he sends an e-mail to anyone; every word he says to anyone counts now," he explains. "Yeah," I agree with him.

I am totally not convinced with Al's explanation, but I pretend I am.

However, it turns out, just 24 hours later, that Al is completely wrong. Sadi, one of Petraeus' senior advisors and a good friend of ours, contacts Al while he's having dinner with his boss. "Petraeus had no idea that Elie has moved to the U.S.; he wants you both to join us now if you can," he tells Al. He asks him to pick me up and meet them at the Fairmont Hotel's restaurant in Washington, D.C.

...And here I am, sitting at the same table with the CIA director, chitchatting and catching up on stories from the old days. It sounds like they happened long time ago, these stories, although they only took place 3 years ago.

Truth is, I have been accused of being a CIA agent--a collaborator to be more precise, many, many times throughout my journey, but I have truly never met a CIA agent in my entire life, except for now, believe it or not.

Anyway, here I sit, not with just a normal agent, but the head of all agents. And it feels pretty good.

At the table with Sadi, Al, and me sits an elegant, classy Paula Broadwell, who David introduces as his biographer.

She isn't bored with our conversation, even though it's all about terrorism, violence and the madness in the Middle East. She shows interest in every word we say, especially when Petraeus says something.

Because it's all off the record, she isn't taking notes. But she might be taking notes in her head, just like I do, I think to myself.

David looks very cheerful. I don't know, perhaps it is the suit and necktie he's wearing that's making him look that way. I rarely see him without his uniform on, which makes him look a little different to me.

It only takes me one second to vote for the uniform in my head, perhaps, because I am used to it, but probably it is just the tie, which doesn't fit with the suit in my opinion. I have no idea.

Yet, it is amazing to see that nothing has really changed with David. He has the same warmth, the same shy smile, the same hair, the same politeness, and the same modesty... But he looks younger now.

He asks me about what I am doing in Virginia. I brief him without going into much detail. *It's inappropriate to talk business with him in this particular meeting*, I remind myself. "What do you prefer that I call you now?" I ask him. "General, Chief..."

"This is funny," he answers. "I just received an email from the agency today asking me what I would like them to call me," he chuckles. "I told them to call me whatever they usually call their boss," he explains. "And what is that?" I ask. "Are we even allowed to ask such questions?" I half joke. "Director," says David. "Hmm, I like it," I say, impressed. “Can I ask another question?" I shoot again. “Go ahead,” he gives me a polite smile. “Are you thinking you will run for president in the future?" I say bluntly.

"Absolutely not. My answer will not change just because you ask the question again and again," he chuckles. "Not now, and not in the future," he says with a decisive tone.

"But why?" I press on. "You have what it takes; you're an excellent strategist, an economic expert, and a hero who's compared with Eisenhower... just, why not?"

Sadi, Al, and Paula don't seem to disagree with me, especially Paula. I can see how her eyes sparkle when I ask the question. In fact, I think she's enjoying that I am following up on this.

Petraeus looks at the table to see if we are all done. "Let's take a walk and breathe some fresh air while I answer your question." He points to his bodyguards to settle the check.

We get up and head outside the restaurant. "When you have the time, there's a great speech by Theodore Roosevelt that I'd like you to read, the 'Man in the Arena,'" Petraeus says as soon as we hit the street. "Once you read it, you'll have your answer."

Before he finishes his sentence, Paula, who is walking right next to us, has already pulled up the speech on her i-Pad. She starts reading the speech in quick words; however, in the second sentence, she slows down a little and shifts her tone to be poetic. She is obviously affected by the strong words:

"It is not the critic who counts; not the man who points out how the strong man stumbles, or where the doer of deeds could have done them better. The credit belongs to the man who is actually in the arena, whose face is marred by dust and sweat and blood; who strives valiantly; who errs, who comes short again and again, because there is no effort without error and shortcoming; but who does actually strive to do the deeds; who knows great enthusiasms, the great devotions; who spends himself in a worthy cause; who at the best knows in the end the triumph of high achievement, and who at the worst, if he fails, at least fails while daring greatly, so that his place shall never be with those cold and timid souls who neither know victory nor defeat."

"I understand," I say, after thinking a little about those words.

I get his point. I also love being in the arena. Not that I am comparing mine to his, of course; the man has been just appointed to protect 300 million Americans. *Regardless of the size of the arena and regardless of who wins and who loses, arenas have always charmed me*, I think to myself, as we walk around the Fairmont Hotel down the streets of D.C.

Petraeus' head must be overcrowded with plans, with arenas, perhaps, and I am sure the Middle East is an essential part of them. The good news for me is that this is where I think I thrive the most--the Middle East.

Petraeus' men inform him that his car is ready. He gives me a warm, quick hug, and then does the same with Sadi and Al. He slips a medal in my hand with little discretion. I look at it very quickly and thank him gratefully for it. It's a medal of excellence that I am familiar with; I already have nine.

He promises that we'll be meeting again soon. Then he joins Paula in the back seat of his car. He looks at Sadi and informs him that he will be calling him in the next morning to follow up on something.

And they leave the three of us to figure out how to finish the rest of the night. Sadi suggests that we walk to the nearest bar, just for a quick celebration. Of course, the 'quick celebration' ends up by finishing a bottle of Patron Tequila.

Sadi is jumping for joy with pride in his boss. He has every right, I guess.

Just 10 years ago, he was a taxi driver in New York, as he

always announces proudly. And look at him now; he's one of the closest people to the most powerful man on the planet, perhaps. He knew Petraeus when he was a two-star general, and even regarding that time, he described him as a genius who could change America. He simply worships him. And now that David is what he is, Sadi knows very well that there will be many assignments for him in the near future. He just loves these assignments, especially when they include having meetings with presidents and leaders or kings and princes. He truly believes he can change history through these meetings.

Al also looks very cheerful tonight, and he also has every right. Petraeus knows him very well and has always complemented his extraordinary skills. However, when David was in Afghanistan, Al lost direct touch with him for a couple of years, like I had. In the meantime, he applied to nine different jobs. Some are with the state department and others with the pentagon, and he is still filling out paperwork and going through security clearance procedures. It is normal for him to think that it will all change now. Petraeus will surely recommend him; it goes without saying.

As for me, my story is a little more complicated than this.

Before I go to sleep, I remind myself, again, with whom I was dining tonight. It is still big in my head.

"My friend is the CIA director," I tell Mr. T, my 160 pounds St Bernard. He’s big, but perhaps the friendliest dog ever. "How many people on earth can say this sentence?" I ask him, with great enthusiasm in my tone. Mr. T doesn’t look to understand how important it is to have such an influential friend, at this particular moment. He stares at me. I take him for a long, long walk. That’s how he usually likes to celebrate big events.

Is it coincidence? Is it luck? How on earth did this happen? I ask myself. Just when I thought that it is perhaps time to surrender and quit my stupid battles, a friend, a partner and an ally got appointed in the most powerful position on earth. It's just what I needed to renew my hopes. I sleep with a big smile on my face.

I wake up grumpy the next morning, though. It suddenly occurs to me; "Why didn't you talk with him about business, you idiot?" I blame myself. "What is wrong in talking business?" I shake my head in regret, "he's American, and Americans love to talk business. *Oh! I am such an idiot*," I conclude. "*Now I have to wait, or even create another occasion to meet again with him. I should have grabbed this opportunity*."

****

I am a journalist. I fell in love with question marks when I was very little, and since then, it has been a hell of a love story. Those little questions have brought trouble to my life, though, and many headaches. But some people just love headaches. I guess I am one of them.

And where I come from, when I say headaches, I mean serious headaches, not the "I lost my job" kind of headaches, which I already did three times, by the way. No! I mean much more serious headaches!

I have been warned, threatened, arrested at times, almost kidnapped by a terrorist group, and luckily survived an assault from a suicide bomber. He killed seven and injured 19 of my colleagues. His "sponsors," the terrorist group, who took responsibility, accused me of being a "Mouthpiece for the Americans." I hope he was raped by 72 snakes instead of those 72 virgins he was promised he could fuck after he blew up into a thousand pieces. That's all I can say.

Truth is, that idiot was wrong. I was never a mouthpiece. But yes, I am pro-American, from my toes up to the last hair on my head. In fact, I have never hidden my pro-Americanism, although it's perhaps as dangerous as being homosexual in some places. And if there's truly an American conspiracy, I'll blindly embrace it, whatever it is, because no matter how ugly it might look, it is still gonna look better than what my nation looks like now.

I have been living here, in the land of my dreams, for more than two years, but our love story, America's and mine, goes way back before that. I had my first crush when I wore my first pair of Levi's. I was around ten years old then. Amidst all the miseries that surrounded us, at least there was something comfortable to wear. That made my life much easier.

The second crush came with Olivia Newton John in *Grease*; I had more than twenty pictures of her hidden under my bed. And it went on and on. Al Pacino? The entire neighborhood fell under his charm in the *Godfather*. What a movie! What an actor!

I wish you had seen my infatuation when I first saw a real American soldier. He looked even more powerful than those little toy soldiers my mother used to buy for me.

Coca Cola, Tom and Jerry, Mc Donald's... and then it became more serious--Mark Twain, Ernest Hemingway--and it just kept escalating.

Every time I felt that I'd seen it all, America would knock me over again. When I thought going to the moon was the greatest achievement of mankind, America topped it with the Internet, a magic cloud in the sky with the answers to everything.

And when I thought nothing could top that, America chose Barack Obama as its President. Well, you can like him or not, but if you think electing an African-American, whose middle name is Hussein, to be the President of the United States means less than landing on the moon and inventing the Internet, then you simply don't get it. Choosing him as the first Black president carries equal glory for Barack Obama, himself, and for those who voted for him, in my modest opinion. It was a moment that made everything I ever heard about the melting pot and dreams of equality come true.

"If there were a hundred Americas, I would live in them all. And if America didn't exist, I would have likely created one in my head and moved there." I tell my elder son, Gio, and it always makes him laugh. "That's crazy, Dad," he says. "Even Americans don't love America that much."

"That's probably because they don't fully realize what they have," I say. "Perhaps we should take them on a trip to our land."

"Oh, yeah! They will get it then," he laughs.

I am aware there's greater safety in Sweden, employment rates are higher in Norway, healthcare is better in Iceland, and the wine is superior in France. But life is just a little more than all that, especially for those who chase big dreams and pursue crazy battles.

And dreams, at least for me, are not just about money, success, and luxury; I had money, success, fame and a lot of luxury whenever I wanted them. Private boats, private jets, fancy cars, extravagant hotels, caviar, champagne, and a lot stunning women--I had it all for years. I left it all behind, with no regrets whatsoever, and got back to what I always dreamed of being: a journalist.

Yet, being a journalist -- I mean a real journalist -- is not really the safest choice if you live in the Middle East. Facts and truths don't appeal to many over there. So, I came here, where no one can intimidate me, scare me, or kill me because of my words. I can finally spit out all those questions and conclusions that were stuck in my throat for years and years. To me, this is more orgasmic than being with a supermodel on a private boat in Ibiza. Sometimes, I can't even believe what I'm saying, but this is how it feels. Anyway, I am here now, and it'd be hard to shut me up.

Among many other adjectives, I have been called naive, reckless, stupid, idiot, a pain in the ass, and a troublemaker, which I can't say I'm not, frankly. I have been all these... sometimes altogether. But they don't kill people for this in America, I hope.

Here, you can be Bill Maher and still get away with it, and I have always wanted this right and privilege to screw governments, dictators, intelligence, secret services, royalties, ministers, politicians, big companies, big banks and every other hypocrite you could think of with the truth right in their faces and go back to sleep in the safety of my home, without having someone with a gun at my front door or spending my life in jail for it. I want to have the right to tell my people how brainwashed, ignorant, manipulated, and stupid they are without having to deactivate a bomb in my car.

In my journey, I have had the chance to be close to some historical events, impressive leaders, and powerful decision makers. I have witnessed scandals, wrongdoings, manipulation, and hypocrisy-- oh! A lot of hypocrisy, which is, perhaps, a war in itself.

I don't believe in neutrality. To me, only walls are neutral. And I simply refuse to be just another wall that watches events passing by.

Objectivity? Well, I've always tried my best; however, I don't think I have often succeeded. It is so hard to be objective when you live under tyranny, oppression, dictatorship, ignorance, hatred, backwardness, violence, and terrorism. And in my homeland, these are rampant on every highway and every street. Is there actually an objective description for a gas chamber? No, there's not. Ask any Jew to describe a gas chamber objectively and you'll find out that you'll either get a punch in your face or, in best case scenario, you'll see yourself in court.

My nation is like a big, slow gas chamber, and it's practically impossible to describe it objectively. So, I admit, I sometimes lack objectivity in my career, as I probably will in this book, when I describe some of the "jungles" I have seen.

Something else I don't believe in: the off-record concept, or in other words, when a journalist conspires with hypocrite politicians to hide the real story from the public. That's what the off-record concept is really about: hiding information. Well, I understand when a Mafioso goes off record, but a journalist, really?

Journalism, at least for me since many do not agree, is not just to inform the masses about how many people were killed today. Any camera can do that. Real journalism is to name the killers, expose them, and fight them. Yes, fight them! Not with guns naturally, but with every truth that one's throat can carry.

And, although I promised myself to put my previous life and fuck-ups behind me and start a whole new beginning, that is not as easy as they make it seem in the movies.

First, there needs to be closure, an ending to the previous beginning.

My name is Elie Nakouzi. And this is my closure, and my new beginning.

I
Brotherhood

I was born in East Beirut, Lebanon on July 14, 1969. It's the same day peasants stormed the Bastille in 1789, leading to a French Revolution that toppled a corrupt and inept monarchy.

As it happens, in 1969, Beirut's nickname is "the Paris of the Middle East." It's the region's entertainment capital, packed with concert halls, nightclubs, discos, casinos, and other attractions that the Muslim countries surrounding it are forbidden by law to enjoy. Beirut has an extraordinarily pleasant climate, friendly natives, delicious food, and unforgettably sexy women. Plus, it's an economic center for finance and trade.

It also has one other thing its Arab neighbors lack: freedom. Lebanon is touted as a model for religious tolerance and diversity. It's the only country ruled more-or-less equally by Christians—the group to which my family belongs—and Muslims. Of Lebanon's four million Arabs, an estimated 41% are Maronite Christians, 27% Sunni Muslims, and 27% Shia Muslims. (The remaining 5% consist of followers of other religions and non-believers.)

Along with acceptance of religious choice come other types of openness. Lebanon is the only Arab country that holds free elections, strongly supports freedom of the press, and actively cultivates the arts. Writers, painters, singers, actors, and other talents found Lebanon the ideal place to express themselves in ways that elsewhere in the

Middle East might get them censored, imprisoned, or even killed.

Furthermore, it is fair to say that I am actually a lucky sperm!

But this paradise is not to last.

I don't recall a thing from my first five years on earth. But there's a day in April 1975 that I won't ever be able to forget.

It's Sunday in our calm, small town of Furn el Chebbak (population 17,000). Out of nowhere, my family and I hear a barrage of gunshots. They're so loud that it feels to me as if the shooting is happening in our living room. It lasts for a couple of minutes. Then, there's a horrible silence.

My mother is hysterically worried, holding my two-year-old brother, Dany, and me under her arms. My father, along with all the other men in our building, hurries to the street to find out what happened.

Ten minutes later, he's back. His face looks paler than I've ever seen it. "The Palestinians shot four people in front of the church," he says, without being asked. "Sheikh Pierre Gemayel is wounded, and Joseph Abu Assi has been killed."

"Sheikh Pierre! Oh, Jesus," My mother slaps her face. "The Phalangists will burn the town tonight."

She is essentially right. Mere hours later, the Phalangists, a political and paramilitary group of Maronite Christians, take their revenge by slaughtering 27 Palestinians who were riding a bus back to their refugee camp.

Nothing is calm after the bus incident.

In the weeks that follow, the loud gunshots escalate to the explosive sound of bombs.

Abruptly our second-floor apartment, which is the smallest in the six-story building we live in, becomes very popular. It's the only apartment lacking a balcony for overlooking the street, and that greatly lowers its risk of being targeted. Our home turns into a safe haven for our neighbors.

My mother shifts to an unprecedented emergency mode. She puts mattresses all over the floor. Our front door is open 24 hours a day for any of our relatives and friends who are scared... especially those who live on higher floors, which are the most likely to be struck by shelling.

For me, it's far from all bad. The schools are closed, and it's heaven to have all my friends around for what's effectively an eternal play date.

At the same time, we're forbidden from even thinking about going out to play on the street. And the bombs we hear at night are extremely scary; particularly the ones that land close to our building and wake everybody up at 3:00 in the morning.

When the latter happens, no one can sleep afterwards, so our parents analyze the current political situation until the sun comes up. They use big words that I don't yet fully understand, such as Muslims, Palestinians, Jews, Zionists, Phalangists, civil war, and conspiracy.

These discussions end with clear optimism. Almost everyone agrees it's only a matter of weeks before things return to normal.

The lone dissenter is my mother's eldest brother, Uncle Joseph, a man that our entire family and neighborhood hugely respect. "The dark tunnel that we have entered has no light at the end," he says. I don't know what tunnel he's talking about, but it doesn't sound good. Coming out from my uncle Joseph makes it sound scary and credible at the same time.

Over the next few months, the battles grow fiercer. Whenever I ask what's going on, I get the same rote answer: "The Palestinians are trying to kick us out of our homes. And the Phalangists are fighting to defend our country." That's what all kids my age are told.

We are strictly forbidden from political discussions, especially when questions tackle taboos, like, "Why would the Muslims in my country help the Palestinians to do that?" or "Why would Muslims want to kill us?"

These kinds of questions get the same rehearsed answer: "Christians and Muslims are brothers. We've lived together in peace for hundreds of years. Soon the dark cloud will pass, and everything will go back to normal." I'm told this almost every day.

But the fake bubble of peaceful coexistence my people hold before them explodes in their faces. In no time, long-time neighbors turn into fierce enemies.

Muslims and Christians start killing each other in the streets of Beirut like barbarians. The whole bundle of unity, coexistence, and partnership collapses rapidly, and the symphony of brotherhood and solidarity falls apart entirely.

My first direct encounter with war occurs in February 1978, when I'm nine years old.

On a cold morning an ambulance drives into the middle of the street. Three men in green military uniforms burst out of the back holding aloft a wooden box.

Their leader, named John, begins to shout into a white megaphone, "Do you know what this is?"

People in the neighborhood walk out to their balconies overlooking the street to quietly watch what's going on. My mother and I go to a neighbor's apartment to do the same.

John starts to cry bitterly.

Everyone on the block is silent and riveted, wondering what could cause a grown man to break down so publicly.

John points to the wooden box. "This is Antoun! Look how they sent Antoun back to us. In pieces!! He's in pieces!!!"

Antoun was a handsome young man from a respected family. He quit college to join the Christian militia. The first time he showed up wearing his green Guevara-style beret, the neighborhood girls swooned.

After digesting John's words, people begin to shout. They rush down to the street, creating angry voices all around him.

John resumes shouting, directing his comments to the crowd. Everyone stops talking so they don't miss a word.

"People of Furn el Chebbak, hear me. Antoun, who sought to protect our dear town, was brutally murdered today. The Palestinians cut him into little pieces to fit in this small box. And they sent it to his mother with a note engraved in his own blood."

Now, his face wet with tears, he continues. "I promise you that before Antoun is buried, I will behead two Muslim Palestinian fuckers and play soccer with their heads. Those terrorists will be brought to justice very soon."

"I hate Muslims," I whisper in my mother's ear.

"Shut your mouth," my mother, crying bitterly, replies immediately. She wipes her tears and adds, "We are Christians. We can't hate."

We later learn that Antoun was captured while sneaking behind enemy lines to plant a bomb.

I wish this had been the end of it. But it was only the beginning.

About a week later, and while my mother and I are visiting our next door's neighbors, we hear some fire shots in the street and some loud noises. We all run to the balcony to watch, like usual. However, before I could watch anything, my mother who has already seen something, shouts hysterically and shuts my eyes tightly with both her hands.

“Go home right now,” she orders very decisively.

I pretend to leave, but I sneak inside the neighbor’s bedroom discretely, where I can watch clearly what is going on from the window.

I will never forget the horrible scene as long as I live.

John, who promised to play soccer with two Palestinian heads, has actually found something scarier to revenge. He simply tied two Palestinian young men to the trunk of his military car, naked, and decided to drag them slowly in the street so that the entire neighborhood can witness that he fulfilled his promise.

The scene is merely a horror movie. It is simply a sight that you don’t even want to describe to an enemy. So, I will spare my readers -and my memory- the full details.

One of the two victims is howling like a fatally wounded animal as, inch-by-inch, his flesh is torn apart. The other is still able to scream, "Allahu Akbar, Allahu Akbar," he shouts.

Every time John reaches the end of the block, he makes a U-turn, and repeats the whole scene again.

Finally, the two men are obviously dead. They don't show any sign of pain anymore.

It's at this point that my mother, who's been frantically searching for me, finally finds me in the neighbor's bedroom, shocked to hell. Her eyes are full of tears. She looks pale and scared to death.

"I think I hate Christians, too," I look up at her and whisper.

She holds me close to her heart. "Listen to me, sweetheart, this is not what's normal. It's a nightmare. And the only way to defeat a nightmare is to forget it. I want you to try, as hard as you can, to forget all the madness you've just seen." She wipes her tears and walks me home. But she can't stop them from falling again the whole way.

I try to follow my mother's advice and banish the nightmare. But, it is unbelievably hard to remove those pictures from my brain. It's just impossible!

It doesn't help that what directly follows is a heated, insane night. Shelling begins as soon as the sunsets, and it keeps going until dawn. I squat in a little corner and hope none of the bombs land on top of me.

Beirut is split into two halves by barricades. On the east side are the Christians and their militias. On the west side are Muslims, Muslim militias, and the

Palestinian Liberation Organization (PLO).

One of my best friends is Randa, a Muslim girl I adore. Her parents now take her away from me, moving to the west side of the barricade in the belief it's no longer safe for them to be living with Christians.

I'm very upset. It's hard to accept that Randa's parents are right.

To me, the only difference between Randa and me is that her prayer starts with "In the name of Allah" and mine starts with "In the name of the Father." How could this tiny difference of just one word change everything?

I ask my mother, "Are Muslims and Christians not supposed to play and laugh together anymore?" She offers the standard response about the dark cloud soon passing. She adds, "Think about Tom; think about Jerry. Don't fill your mind with questions about Christians and Muslims." Then she smiles and pats my shoulder, ending the conversation.

It's the first time it occurs to me that my mother may be as confused as I am, perhaps even more.

Things turn more dramatic, though...

There are funerals, funerals, and more funerals; that's what I see the most, every time there is a little truce between the fighters and we are allowed to see the outer world.

The ceasefire is actually the only time we can practice the small things that human beings usually do, like playing, buying groceries, or walking in the street. The rest of the time, we are obliged to hide in our shelters.

The ceasefires may be as short as a few hours or as long as a couple of weeks. Our lives must happen in between these unpredictable truces.

The walls of my little town are always continually filled with new photographs of young men who lost their lives in the battles. Often, they are literally "the guy next door."

We lose a neighbor, a friend, or a relative almost every week.

Everyone looks either angry or heartbroken.

Military cars circle in our narrow, chaotic streets, filled with young amateur fighters who quit college to join the militia. Before the war ignited, those young men were called "Foufous and Nounous" by the Palestinians and their allies, as my neighbors tell me.

"The Palestinians are supported and financed by most Arab governments. Their soldiers are highly trained and have a terrifying reputation in battle. They thought it would be only a matter of days before they crushed us, occupied our country, and kicked us out of our homes," my mother explains.

Her tone becomes enthusiastically patriotic. "Somehow, the 'Foufous and Nounous' have been able to defend their small towns against all the attackers and to give them hell in return."

While I haven't forgotten the night when John played soccer with an apparently innocent man's head, overall, I agree with my mother. Our town is right on the boarder that separates Christians from Muslims. Our protectors are outnumbered and lack expertise and weapons, but they continue to fight and persevere against all odds.

The stories of their heroism in the battlefield are on everyone's lips. Like all the kids in my neighborhood, I'm fascinated by them—at how cool they look in their rebel-style berets and at how they refuse to surrender no matter how unequal the fight is. "Without these heroes, we would have been collectively kicked out to Canada in ships," everyone says.

I love to hear the stories of those rebels. The idea of the small guy, who stands up to the big guy and eventually beats him, merely fascinates me.

The will shown by our everyday townspeople is also incredible. Eventually the schools reopen and people return to work. Those whose houses or shops are hit by bombs start rebuilding within a few hours, as if all they suffered was a passing storm. My mother says, "We now have the skin of crocodiles. We don't feel anything and can endure anything."

I fear my mother's words will be put to the test in ways we can't even yet imagine.

II
They Have America; We Have France!

Four years after the bus incident, my Christian side of Beirut is fighting not only with the PLO, but also with Muslim regimes throughout the Middle East. Some finance and arm the Palestinians, while others take a direct role. The neighboring Syrians enter Lebanon under the pretext of being a neutral force to separate the combatants, but it quickly becomes apparent they're an occupying force supporting the PLO and may be scheming to take over Lebanon themselves.

There are only 1.5 million Arab Christians in Lebanon, and it feels like we're battling all of the 300 million Arab Muslims around us. How did this happen?

As I grow, so does my hunger for answers to such questions.

My father is seldom home, as he works long, hard hours at his shop making neon signs for store owners; my mother is usually busy doing chores and tending to my younger brother, who was born with a weak pancreas. She's busy 24/7 finding doctors who are familiar with his case to treat the sudden sugar level drops in his blood, which cause him to faint sometimes.

So, I wander into the apartments of neighbors and bother them instead. (The people of our small town tend to keep their doors open to everyone, especially children.)

I especially enjoy visiting our retired neighbor Uncle Maurice (it is very common for children in my country to call all elderly people Uncle, even if they were not blood related), who's considered well educated, as he relaxes in his favorite chair reading the newspaper. I like to see his eyes appear really big behind his glasses, with a contented look on his face. This is his favorite part of the day. But that doesn't stop me from interrupting it.

"Uncle Maurice," I once blurt out of nowhere, "why is everyone against us?"

"It's not really us," he tells me. "All this trouble started when Israel declared itself a state in 1948."

"Israel?" I ask, surprised to hear that this country is involved in our struggles.

"Yes. Israel took over Arab land and threw its people out. It wasn't fair, and it's our duty as part of the Arab nation to sympathize with our fellow Arabs until they regain their land and their rights."

I take a few moments to digest this. Then I ask, "Why are Palestinians killing Christians? If they're mad at Jews, shouldn't they be killing them?"

"They tried to liberate their country a couple of years before you were born, but Israel was way stronger. Plus, Israel created a conspiracy with the most powerful country on earth, America. That's why Arab armies were defeated and we lost the war."

"We?" I ask. "What has all that got to do with us?"

"We are part of this Arab nation," he says. "We are Arabs."

"But if we are Arabs and the Palestinians are Arabs, why are they killing us?"

Uncle Maurice shifts uneasily in his chair. This

clearly isn't fun for him, but he makes an effort to explain. "They think we aren't really sincere in supporting their cause. They believe Lebanese Christians are conspiring with the West, in that—well, that our loyalty is suspect because—Oh! It is very complicated."

I try to take all that in. Then I ask, "So, do I have to hate Jews?"

Uncle Maurice doesn't hesitate. "Yes."

"Really?" I ask, surprised from his answer. This is Uncle Maurice, the man who attends more than two churches every Sunday, so he doesn't skip anything from the Sunday Mass.

He realizes he just said a horrible thing—and to a child!

He makes the sign of the cross. "No, no, son," he backpedals. "What I just told you was awful. You shouldn't hate anyone."

"Okay," I say.

"You should just pretend to," he adds.

"What do you mean?"

"If you're asked by a Muslim how you feel about Jews, say that you hate them. That's the safe answer."

"Are you telling me to lie?"

He is getting really annoyed now. "Come on! I didn't say you should lie."

"So, what should I do?"

"Just pretend."

I stare at him, utterly confused.

"Look," he says, "this is a war waged by others, but it's happening in our land. Sometimes we have to play along to avoid angering these Arabs."

"Do you mean we're not really Arabs?"

"Of course we are!" he almost shouts. "Being an Arab is the only path available to us. We are not capable of swimming in a different ocean, even if we might prefer its waters," he says, with a hint of regret.

And with that, Uncle Maurice ends the discussion and picks up his newspaper again so he can continue enlightening himself with world events.

****

For weeks afterward, I turn over the conversation in my mind.

The priority for all Arabs is supposed to be to liberate Palestine. That's why our local politicians sympathize with the Palestinians and support their cause in all their public speeches, even while the PLO is killing us daily.

But the more our politicians are blatantly irrational and hypocritical on this issue, the more Muslims accuse us of conspiring with the West against them.

Even before we are born, we're supposed to hate the Jews and want to kill them, just to be loyal to our fellow Arabs.

The more I think about it, the less I can stomach it.

"Fuck that," I surprise myself one day by saying out loud. "I'm not going to hate somebody who's never attacked me."

At the same time, I'm supposed to sympathize with Palestinians who are murdering my neighbors and trying to drive us from *our* land. "Fuck that, too," I say.

I decide that hating, or even *pretending* to hate, an entire country of people I've never met just to prove my loyalty to people tossing bombs at my family, my friends, and me makes no sense.

Now, I have a new set of questions. Why can't we, Christians, follow in Israel's footsteps? Why not build a strong army, declare our own state, and protect it if anyone tries to attack us? Why not divide our country into two—one for those who want war and another for those who want peace?

****

"Interesting questions," says Dr. Haddad, my history teacher. "There are a number of reasons we can't do this, but the main one is our country is too small to be divided."

"Isn't it better to divide it than burn it all?" I ask.

"That's a good point, too, Nakouzi. These are strong words," he admits. "Why don't you sit down?" He gestures to a chair in his office. He's taking me seriously, and I just love being taken seriously. I sit.

"Lebanon is more than a country," he continues in a gentle tone. "It represents the ideal of all religious beliefs being able to coexist. It's an experiment that should not be allowed to fail."

I shake my head. "Is it reasonable for the world to count on us, one of the smallest countries on earth, to teach religious coexistence?"

"Yes," Dr. Haddad replies. "Because if it fails here, it fails everywhere."

"But it's already failed," I say.

"History doesn't happen in a couple of weeks. It's a course of events, Nakouzi, and it's too soon to judge. So, we must try harder to make it work. Otherwise, what will happen to eight million Christians in Egypt, the three million Christians in Syria, the two millions in Iraq, and so on? What if they all demand the same solution?"

"So what? If they want their own states, let them have them."

"Then the Arab world could end up divided into 25 countries," Dr. Haddad says, smiling.

"Why does that matter, as long as we can all live happily?"

"It's more complicated than that. Politics is the art of the possible, and what you're saying is practically impossible—"

"Why was it doable for Israel but not for us?" I ask, returning to my original question.

"Because America supports it, which makes almost anything possible," he says.

"But, we're America's friends, too. Why wouldn't it help us?"

"It's national interests that drive a country, Nakouzi, not friendly feelings. And your proposition doesn't further U.S. interests."

"So, how can we convince them?" I ask in a very serious tone.

"I don't know. Perhaps you should talk to Jimmy Carter," he says, laughing again. "Do you know who Jimmy Carter is?" he asks.

"Of course, I know who Jimmy Carter is. I see him on the news almost every night," I smile and leave the room, with some new ideas and questions planted in the back of my little brain.

What was meant by my teacher as a little joke becomes my mission. For weeks I try to find out how to obtain the exact address of the U.S. president so I can send him a letter. I have a lot to tell him. I have some big questions for him, too.

"There are millions of people who want to talk to the president," Dr. Haddad says when I return to ask for his help. "You have to *be* a world leader to speak with one."

"Really? He speaks only to other presidents?" That doesn't sound right to me.

"Yes," my teacher says. "Or big journalists," he remembers to add just before he shoos me from his office. "Big journalists speak to presidents all the time, so perhaps you should study to become a reporter. You'll be a good one, by the way."

****

On reflection, I like Dr. Haddad's advice. I feel it'll be easier to become a journalist than get elected president.

As a trial run, I take a tape recorder into my bathroom and conduct an imaginary interview with the president of the United States.

I pound the most powerful man on earth with tough questions: "Why don't you send your Marines to protect us, like you did for Europe? Why don't you help us Christians the same way you helped the Jews? Why do you let the thuggish Syrian army occupy us?" By the time I'm done, Jimmy Carter is completely grilled.

Actually, most people I hammer with my non-stop questions say I'd make a good journalist. My family says it's in my blood, as my uncle Adel Malek is one of the most respected and popular journalists in Beirut.

My mother goes further: "He's *too* good a journalist. He made so many people want to shut him up that two armed men were sent to his apartment to assassinate him. They would've succeeded, but his building's power went out while they were in the elevator, trapping them. The outage saved his life and the lives of his wife and two children. When he realized what almost happened, he and his family quickly moved to London."

My mother adores her youngest brother and so hates it when others encourage me to follow in Uncle Adel's footsteps. She feels journalism took him away from her and exiled him in the UK.

She believes I'm a genius and should be the president, or a brain surgeon at least. But she also thinks I'm the most handsome young man her eyes have ever seen, so my every glance in a mirror reminds me that she lacks some objectivity, my mother.

Despite her wishes, I become obsessed with the idea of working as a journalist. My favorite hobby shifts from playing soccer to recording my own talk shows on Maxell audio tapes.

I spend hours trying to add a musical background for my voice so what I'm creating sounds more like an actual radio show, but I can't figure out how without generating a lot of distortion. It doesn't really matter because my cousin Nicolas and I are the only listeners.

****

At age 13, I have one other obsession: a 12-year-old girl named Carol, for whom I harbor an enormous crush.

On weekdays, I frequently walk by Carol's building at 3:00 pm just to watch her return from school. Each time I intend to go up and talk to her. But at the critical moment, nothing I can think of seems adequate, so I keep my silent distance.

Sometimes we accidentally make eye contact. I quickly look away, pretending that I'm waiting for a friend.

Since I never speak a word to her, I have no idea whether Carol is aware I even exist.

Making matters worse, Carol isn't my goddess exclusively. Almost every boy in town is attracted to her. This adds to my reluctance to reveal my feelings.

My quiet stalking goes on for several weeks. Then one afternoon, the school bus arrives at 3:00, but Carol doesn't emerge from it. I must appear frantic, because I hear someone ask, "Do you need any help, son?"

I look up and see a man 65 years old, with a white beard and glasses that make him look like an intellectual. He's the owner of the portable kiosk directly across from Carol's building, where he sells newspapers, magazines, books, coffee, and pastries.

"No," I say, "I'm just waiting for a friend. But he didn't show up yet."

The man chuckles. "Perhaps your *friend* had an awful toothache all night. Maybe that's why your *friend* missed school today."

I blush. This guy is too sharp for my absurd lies. "Really?" I ask.

"Come over here, kid," he says, pulling over a chair for me. "Take a seat."

I do. Mr. Suleiman fills his mug with boiling black coffee and then looks me in the eye. "A wise man named Victor Hugo said 'The first symptom of love in a young man is shyness. The first symptom in a woman is boldness.'"

"What does that mean?" I ask.

"That you shouldn't be embarrassed if you're too shy to talk to her. It's only a sign of love."

I like the way he speaks to me, as if I'm a grownup.

The man introduces himself as Mr. Suleiman, and he reveals that Carol comes by his kiosk almost every day at 4:00 pm to pick up her father's newspapers.

I, therefore, begin a daily habit of visiting the kiosk at 4:00, pretending that I'm also buying newspapers for my dad.

While spending time with Mr. Suleiman, I learn he has very different views from Uncle Maurice. "Arabs are 1,000 years behind modern civilization," he tells me, "but they are too retarded to recognize it."

He also says, "The cancer of the Middle East isn't Israel. It's the corruption of its Arab leaders." Mr. Suleiman believes Lebanon's miseries are the result of deliberate choices made by the governments of the other Arab countries: Syria, Libya, Egypt, Jordan, and so on. But, he especially blames the oil-rich Saudis. He calls Saudi Arabia "the head of the snake."

I love Mr. Suleiman's straightforward talk, which is unlike that of any other adult I know.

I also appreciate his patience with me. I still can't bring myself to speak with Carol. But being able to watch her say "hello" and "thank you" when she makes her purchases is enough. Mr. Suleiman notices all my blushes, but he never makes fun of me.

And beyond his kindness, I grow to admire his love of knowledge. Mr. Suleiman knows something about every writer a customer can name, whether Arab, French, Russian, or American. I often see him hook customers on his favorite translated authors, such as Twain, Faulkner, and Hemingway, pushing a book at them and saying,

"Read this and thank me for it later."

If a customer hesitates over a book Mr. Suleiman admires, he recites paragraphs he's memorized. One day, a beautiful woman is thinking twice about Steinbeck's *East of Eden*, and Mr. Suleiman recites, "And this I believe: that the free, exploring mind of the individual human is the most valuable thing in the world. And this I would fight for: the freedom of the mind to take any direction it wishes, undirected. And this I must fight against: any religion or government which limits or destroys the individual. This is what I am and what I am about." She buys the book immediately.

When she leaves, I ask, "Mr. Suleiman, are you a Communist?"

He explodes with laughter. "Who says so?"

"Some neighbors."

"I am exactly the opposite of what they told you, kid. I am someone who believes America is the greatest nation on Earth, which no communist does. However, I do have a soft spot for Karl Marx saying 'Religion is the opium of the people.' I'm amazed how he was able to fit into one simple phrase two of the most dangerous words in the dictionary: religion and opium... And in a sentence of three words only." He chuckles and then asks, "What else do the neighbors say?"

"That you're an atheist."

He laughs again. "People so crave labels. No, kid, I'm no atheist. I believe in God, but I name him differently."

"Can someone create his own god, just like that?"

"Of course," he exclaims, laughing, "if He's a better God!"

With some bashfulness, I admit, "For a long time I've wanted to change my religion."

"Oh?" he asks. "Do you want to turn Muslim?"

"No!" I quickly reply.

"What, then? Do you want to convert to Judaism?"

I laugh. "No, not that either."

"Then what?"

"I'd like to become an American."

Mr. Suleiman bursts with laughter. "I see! Well, at first I was going to say America isn't a religion. But, on thinking it over, you're right. Looked at correctly, it could be a religion."

I nod shyly.

"Do you have more questions? Go ahead, I'm in a good mood," he says, offering me a free cupcake from his kiosk. "Hit me, what else have you got?"

I happily accept. "Uncle Maurice told me it's safest to pretend that we hate the Jews. Do you agree?"

"That's fear talking, kid, not the brain. Uncle Maurice is reading too many newspapers that his head is entirely screwed up now," he explodes with laughter again. "Forget such hypocrisy," he adds in a serious tone. "You can love, hate, and believe whatever you like."

"Then what do you think about the Jews?" I ask.

"They're like us: normal people fighting for their existence. Except they're smarter, stronger, and more united than we are; they've been rewarded for it with a homeland. That's the bare truth, and anything else you'll hear is empty words."

"Then why don't we do what they do? Why don't we Christians get our own homeland?"

Mr. Suleiman sighs deeply and then echoes my

teacher. "Because they have America and we have France," he explodes with a louder laughter.

At this moment, Carol arrives to pick up her father's newspapers. As usual, I'm mesmerized. But Mr. Suleiman welcomes her warmly with a little poem he improvises: "Carol, oh Carol! You'll give the young boys heartaches, and I will comfort them with Tylenol."

Carol and I both laugh at his little jingle. As usual, Mr. Suleiman folds her father's newspapers in a neat way. She smiles gently and hurries back home. Oh! She's so effortlessly cute. She completely charms me, even when she's absolutely doing nothing at all!

****

One day, I decide to ask Mr. Suleiman the biggest question I'm carrying around: "What does it take to make a great journalist?"

"If riches are what you're looking for, then you should open a supermarket or a nightclub," Mr. Suleiman replies. "There are no rewards available for those who dig for the truth in our country, kid. The big money is only available for those willing to fake the truth and bury reality underground; that's what Arabs have money for," he sighs. "Look son," he looks at me seriously. "There are journalists and there are pimps!" he throws the word with a smile on the face.

I giggle.

He rattles off the names of journalists who he considers pimps. I've never heard of any of them.

Then he tells me the much shorter list of names of those who do honor to the profession of journalism. "Your uncle is one of them, kid," he says, sounding very sincere.

I've never heard of the other names that he mentioned, though.

Mr. Suleiman adds something that grabs my attention. "A real journalist has to be brave and clever enough to uncover the truth. He's gotta get closer, much closer than everyone else... But that's not enough. He also needs to have the balls to actually *tell* the truth, even when it's inconvenient. That's the really hard part."

Being a journalist who never compromises the truth is captivating. I definitely want to be that kind of reporter, not the pimp kind.

Despite my shyness with Carol, for some reason, I feel confident that I have the balls for the job. I'm just not sure what is the truth that I should dig for?

Then I have an idea.

III
Truths & Sugar

After thinking it over, I conclude the biggest issue that's occupying my mind is the war—it affects me and everyone around me. This is the truth I want to get closer to; this is the only truth that matters to me nowadays. So, what kind of reporter am I if I have never gotten a close look at the field of battle?

I become determined to do something about that.

In my neighborhood, there are a number of Christian soldiers. I approach George, a handsome 22-year-old with black hair and dark eyes wearing a militia uniform. He's heading into his jeep, but I walk in front and block him.

"What is it, kid?" he asks.

"I want you to take me with you. I want to see how it goes, the war!"

"Are you crazy? Where I'm going is no place for a boy."

I don't waver. "I'm not a boy. I'm a journalist."

"Yeah, right. Go watch a movie, kid. I've got to go." George gently tries to push me out of the way.

"Listen," I say. "If you take me with you, just once, I'll put in a good word for you with Rita. I know you're in love with her."

George's eyes sparkle at the mention of Rita's name. She's one of the sexiest women on our block, and I've seen his expression every time she walks by. Having grabbed his attention, I press on.

"Are you going to wait forever to speak to her?

You know our families are very close. I could easily tell Rita something about you, it you'd like me to help."

George hesitates. He points to his weapon. "This is a real rifle, kid, not a toy. And a real war is nothing like what you may have imagined. Where I'm headed is very dangerous."

I stand my ground. "It's dangerous everywhere in our country. People are getting killed in their own beds. Yesterday on the news they were talking about a mother, father, and three children fried in their car while they were trying to escape the shelling. The mother died hugging her kids while they burned to death. And what about the Khoury family, who—"

"All right, all right, I got it." George considers. "What would you tell Rita about me?" He whispers, as if she's listening to us.

"I'd describe how smart and polite you are. And that you're handsome." I whisper back. I feel like we're buddies now.

"And brave. Don't forget to say brave."

I smile. "Of course."

George gestures for me to enter the passenger side of his jeep. He looks uncomfortable about it, but he gets behind the wheel and starts driving us to Ain el-Rammaneh where the action is.

As we approach the area separating Christians and Muslims, I see an increasing number of buildings that look deserted and partially destroyed.

"How many Muslims have you killed so far?" I ask.

"A lot," George says. "Maybe a hundred. More, I think."

"How do you know for sure?" I ask. "Did you actually see them die?"

"Usually I did. Or I heard their screams after I shot them."

"Aren't you scared?" I ask. "Even a bit?"

"They should be scared, not me," George replies. "I'm fighting for my country. What are they fighting for, the fuckers? This isn't their land. They should be warring in Israel, not here."

George points to his rifle's handle, which—like John's—has a picture of Jesus on it. "As long as He's on our side, no one can defeat us." He kisses the picture and places it before my lips. I hate this habit of kissing Jesus and Mary's pictures... Not wanting to cause trouble, I kiss it, too.

A little later, George drives to a narrow street and parks in front of a building that's clearly seen combat. At the entrance are four soldiers. They're all in their 20s, with black beards, and are playing cards and laughing.

George greets them with, "Fuck you, and everyone else! How are you?"

"Fuck you, too, buddy," Tony replies. "What's the little boy doing here?"

"The kid wants to watch us killing some Palestinian and Muslim fuckers," George says.

"Really? I hate to disappoint you, kid, but it's been calm all day. You might not see any action."

"I can still show him around," George responds, and turns to me. "Come on."

We go up the stairs. I can see traces of fierce battles on the half-standing walls. George keeps a hand behind me and bends my head down every time we pass a window or an opening in a wall. "Never show your head," he tells me. "The enemy is in the building across from us."

When we arrive on the first floor, I see five armed men sitting behind sand barricades. Four of them are gathered around a small radio listening to the news. The toughest looking is a 25-year-old who stands apart cleaning his rifle. The other men call him "Butcher."

"Sit," George tells me, pointing to a remote corner of the room. "It's safe there." He starts to boil water on a gas stove for coffee and then turns to the men. "No action today?"

"Absolutely nothing!" Butcher replies, sounding disappointed.

"Let me try to shake things up a little," George says. He stands and shouts at the building across the way, "I will fuck your Mohammed tonight! I will fuck him so hard!"

Five seconds later, a Palestinian fighter shouts back, "I have to finish fucking your Virgin Mary and your little Jesus. Then I will come after you, asshole."

"Yeah? Just show yourself, you coward. I'll rip the skin off your face and stick it in your mother's ass." George lifts his rifle and begins shooting at the building. When he's done, there's nothing but a long silence; the other side doesn't respond.

I'm shocked by how close the enemy is. I move to one of the windows overlooking the other building.

"Be careful, moron!" George shouts. "They have a sniper just waiting for a mosquito to fly past that he can shoot. I don't want to send you back to your mother in a small box. Sit down and keep your fucking head low."

"What the hell is he doing here, anyway?" asks Butcher. "Shouldn't a boy his age be at home watching Bugs Bunny?"

"I wanted to see a real battle," I say. "I keep hearing stories about how you guys are the Palestinians' worst nightmare. They say you're even better than Israeli soldiers."

Butcher looks flattered. "You give me the weapons the Israeli soldiers have and I will show you something. But with this?" He points to his AK-47 rifle. "It will be more difficult."

"Why do they call you Butcher?" I ask.

"Because I am a very soft person," he says, chuckling.

"It doesn't look like a good day to show you how soft Butcher is," George says. "The guys on the other side don't want to play with us."

"Let's see about that," Butcher says. From his pocket he takes a small bag full of white powder. He carefully pours two long lines of the powder and sniffs them into his nose with a rolled paper. Then he stands in front of an open window and shouts, "What's going on with you bastards? We've got a kid who came to see some action. Aren't we going to show him war, you fuckers?"

Butcher begins shooting at the other building, fast and fierce. It's so loud that I put both hands over my ears. When he's done, there's still no response. "Is it a holiday?" he asks. "This is starting to worry me."

Butcher reloads his rifle, sticks some extra rounds in his pockets, and grabs several grenades. Speaking only to the air, he says, "What are you setting up for me, Mohammed? Why are you so calm today, Mohammed?"

Suddenly moving to the stairs, Butcher announces, "You know what? I'm going to find out."

He arrives at the ground entrance and tells the soldiers there, "Cover me." Then he crosses the street to the other building. Shooting comes chaotically from multiple windows. Ignoring the bullets, Butcher disappears inside.

Seconds later, the sounds of grenade explosions come from the other building, along with screaming and shouting. The hellish sounds last for about 10 minutes. Then everything goes silent again.

Butcher appears out of the smoke, limping slowly back to us. His uniform is covered in blood. The men at the entrance run toward him. He assures them he's all right, aside from a bullet that's grazed his foot.

When he returns to the first floor, one of his comrades brings him a large pot of water. Butcher washes his face and changes out of his bloody uniform. Someone fixes up two more lines of powder for him. Everyone else gathers around him, eager to hear what happened.

Butcher first looks at the picture of Jesus on the wall and reverently intones, "In the name of the Father, the Son, and of the Holy Spirit, amen." Everyone—including me—joins him by drawing the cross.

Butcher heads over to the two lines and sniffs them up lustfully, making me think of a wild beast. Then he sits on the floor and lights a cigarette, inhaling the smoke deeply. Finally, he smiles. "Now that I ripped off that motherfucker's face, I will have to find his mother's ass to stick it in."

Everyone laughs. Things appear to have returned to normal. Butcher is about to tell his story, but then I interrupt. "What is that white thing you keep smelling?"

"It is sugar," says Butcher. "Don't you love sugar and chocolate? This is my chocolate."

George comes over and gently bats me on the shoulder before I can ask more questions. "Time to go home," he says. "It will probably be a hot night."

We both return to the jeep. Just as we drive away, explosions begin to sound behind us.

****

I have trouble sleeping for the next couple of weeks.

Surprisingly, it isn't the scenes of shooting and blood that keep coming into my head but of Butcher sniffing his *sugar*. I have no idea what it really is, but I find it creepier than the combat. The whole experience gives me a very different perspective on the Christians fighting for my country.

I have to talk to someone about what I've witnessed to avoid going crazy. My parents and relatives aren't remotely candidates; their finding out what I've done would result in a series of severe punishments.

So, I tell Mr. Suleiman.

After I finish, for the first time ever, I watch him rendered speechless.

He's very upset at the risk I took. He also feels guilty about how I interpreted his advice to become a journalist.

I calm him a little by swearing on a Bible he finds on one of his shelves that I'll never again do something so reckless.

At this point, he allows me to ask my question: "What was that white powder?"

Mr. Suleiman is blunt. "It was cocaine, an illegal drug." He shakes his head and adds, "I often wonder which addiction is worse: cocaine or religion."

"What's so bad about cocaine?" I ask.

"It crushes its victims like cockroaches." He tells me stories about very successful people who ended up destroyed by drugs. "Cocaine can bring a mountain down to its knees," he concludes, using a dramatic tone to hammer his point home.

After meeting Butcher, it's not that hard to convince me.

Of course, Butcher doesn't represent every Christian soldier. Some of our warriors in the 1970s war are thorough heroes.

And one of them is working on a miracle that will make him a legend.

IV
And The Winner Is

It's 1982, and nothing has really changed from last year or the year before. I have gotten used to war, and it doesn't scare me anymore. It's just another habit, like eating or drinking.

In the last couple of years, I have seen my mother crying more than a hundred times while listening to the heartbreaking stories of innocent kids or entire families who lost their lives in the safety of their beds.

She has her own ways to pretend that she's always strong in front of everyone, but her tricks never pass on me. I know her so well that she can't even fake one smile without me catching her bluff.

"It's when one feels hungry the most that he should show the world that he's full!" That's one of her slogans about pride. And pride... she has a lot of it.

In our family, everyone refers to her as the godmother—the leader.

"If you were born in America, you would have been definitely elected a mayor or a governor," many neighbors joke with her.

She simply has the time to listen to everyone, but most importantly, she also finds the time to endure with them. I can see my cousins, all of them, one after the other, coming to our house to speak to her about a problem here and an issue there. They always leave with a smile on the face. She has this magic of calming things down, especially when there's a fight or a misunderstanding within our family.

She and I have this extremely close relationship. We sit for hours and chat and talk about everything. All it takes us is a large pot of coffee, and the session would go on for hours. We gossip, we laugh, and we make jokes about the entire universe. She has a big sense of humor and she can be really sarcastic when she wants to be.

Everyone calls her Dadou instead of Daad—an Arab name that she hates so much. I have many unique nicknames that I call her with, though. Dadoushka, for example, or Dadoukietta, and some other crazy stuff that I keep on coming up with to make her smile... or if I wanted something big from her, of course.

People always accuse her of *melting down* every time my name is mentioned. She never tries to hide her weakness anyway. I am her weakness, and I know how to use my charm to get almost anything I really want. Well... almost!

No guns, no drugs, and recently, she added one more thing to her list: no motorcycles. "Listen," she warns me seriously, "if I ever see you holding a gun, or doing drugs, or riding a motorcycle, then realize immediately that our friendship is over." She nods her head, all seriously. And the rules apply to all my cousins, naturally. They love her so much that no one dares to break her heart. She's there for every one of them, and she embraces a policy of 24 hours open doors. You can knock anytime, without a phone call or a warning, at 10 in the morning or at 2 am, and you'll get the exact same smile no matter what. Privacy, and everything related to this expression, just doesn't exist in her dictionary.

If she's also known for something else, it's her

unforgettable Christmas parties. Despite the war and the crazy situations, she never skips *the* Christmas party. Every year, she insists on gathering all the kids of our family, and some lucky kids whom she likes in our neighborhood, all in our little apartment. She organizes a party that keeps us talking for months. Nothing makes her happier than the scene of the entire family gathered.

Christmas, Easter, and other special occasions are her alibis to bring us all together, and she never misses one. Sometimes, she just invents some events, just to get us together in one room. And when we're all in one room, we look like a mini militia. We're more than 20 cousins in total, and if someone is in trouble, it is like we're all in trouble. I like how close our family is; it somehow makes me feel a little bit safer when things get really crazy.

And if it weren't for Dadou, my mother, it would have been so hard to get us altogether this frequently. She uses every bit of her incredible energy to make us forget the war, and perhaps, it is her way also to overcome all the worries that come along with it.

Anyway, we are still lucky we're all alive, and according to my mother, we shall be grateful to Jesus and Mary—who are both doing a great job in protecting our family. She counts on Jesus and Mary a lot for this task.

"How come they don't protect the other families, too?" I challenge her. "Shut your mouth immediately," she interrupts angrily. No one is allowed to argue about Jesus and Mary in her house. She lights some extra candles and talks to Mary's picture in our living room. Mary is holding the little Jesus and she looks incredibly peaceful. "Please don't listen to him," my mother begs her. "You're a mother, and you understand that kids say stupid things sometimes."

She talks to the Virgin Mary as if they were very close friends. She prays on my behalf.

Usually, she asks her *friends* to protect the family, her siblings, our close relatives, and some very close friends; however, recently there's a new guy that she added to her prayer list; Bashir Gemayel.

His name is already occupying every tongue—literally everyone around me is speaking about him. He's no one but the younger son of Pierre Gemayel, the founder of the Phalangists and one of the heroes of our independence from the French colonialism in 1943.

Pierre, the father, had always opposed the idea of detaching Lebanon from its natural habitat, the Arab world. For him, and many other politicians of the same political school, the Christians "should find a solution for their problem through the United Nations and seek for protection through the international community." Palestine, as everyone knows, is much more than just a patriotic cause for Arabs; it's a holy mission.

Therefore, Pierre Gemayel strongly believes that the continuous fighting with the PLO would open the *gates of hell* on Christians, who count less than 1 million already.

In contrast, his son Bashir sounds completely different. Bashir realizes that all of us could be exterminated before the international community intervenes. He feels the Christians in Lebanon should make the same choice the Jews in Israel did: fight.

Against his father's wishes, Bashir forms an armed group named with his initials: BG. It has the sole mission of defending Christian areas from attack. BG quickly became famous for its heroic battles against the PLO's seasoned soldiers. Bashir's reputation grows, as well, and the inspirational young leader attracts many new followers. Therefore, he forms the Lebanese Forces, which quickly grows into a well-organized militia, equipped with the latest weapons and arms.

"How did Bashir do this?" I ask our young neighbor, Dimitri.

Dimitri and his twin brother, Antoine, were both high-ranked fighters in the Lebanese Forces. They're both very polite and amazingly calm. One can hardly believe that these two always-smiley faces are actually real fighters.

The rumor in the building says Dimitri is very close to Bashir. He's one of his trusted men. He has no problem in answering my question in explicit words. "Bashir is a genius," he replies.

"Yeah, I know; but how did he build this strong army? Where did he get all these weapons from?" I insist.

"From Israel," he answers bluntly.

"You're joking, right?" I laugh.

"No, not at all," he explains. "Bashir doesn't believe that Israel is our enemy. Actually, he thinks that it could be the opposite. He thinks that we can be very good friends, the Jews and us," he goes on. "A couple of years ago, he headed to Israel secretly on a small boat and convinced the Israeli army to give us advanced weapons," he clarifies.

"Ah! That's why Arabs and Muslims hate him so much," I say, hoping to prove that I am already aware of the crisis. I like this conversation.

"It did drive them crazy actually, but Bashir turned

his back on them," he chuckles. "Well, they watched us for many years getting killed, the Arabs... And had we counted on them, we would have ended up in refugee camps."

I am starting to love this Bashir, I think to myself. At least he's not a hypocrite like all those politicians who screw our heads with their speeches about Arabism and the destruction of Israel.

Bashir Gemayel is on the news everyday now. Dimitri, who's now a very close friend to our family, promises that something very big will happen soon. He keeps promising of the *big* thing, but he never reveals what it is. My mother begs him to speak; "I really can't," he replies very gently. "It's a military secret," he whispers. "But trust me, it will change our lives forever," he concludes.

Bashir, in almost every speech, declares that Lebanon shall take a neutral stand in the Arab-Israeli conflict. His intentions to sign a peace treaty with Israel are very clear; he's breaking the taboo. He calls for a democratic, independent, and sovereign state, and if Muslims don't like it, let's ally with Israel and declare our own Christian state.

Everyone in my town just adores him. He's young, handsome, and decisive. Every time he shows up in a new speech, people start to look fresh again. He gives us hope and he looks very certain that he can accomplish what he's promising. He's in his early 30s, and he's the talk of not just my town, but also every other town.

Anyway, what Dimitri promises has finally come true, apparently. He calls us this one day in June, just 30 days after he made the promise, and says, "Take your family and get out immediately of Beirut," he tells my father. He doesn't add a single word. "Just get out of Beirut because it will be hell soon." That's it.

My parents trust him a lot. We pack our luggage and leave to a relatively safer area 30 kilometers away from our town. We rent a small Chalet on the coast that my father had to borrow money from his friend to pay for it. We wait for a week. Nothing happens.

And then, it all becomes clear.

Miraculously, Bashir was able to convince the Israeli leaders of a wide invasion to liberate Lebanon after years of brutal battles with the PLO and their allies. What seemed as an absolute fantasy in the minds of the Christians from a couple of years is turning into reality.

Now, the invincible Israeli army is involved. Christians are already celebrating victory. There's no chance for the PLO and the Syrian army to defeat the Israeli Defense Army, as everyone confirms.

Per the agreement, Israel attacks PLO-occupied areas, such as Southern Lebanon and West Beirut; in a mere 30 days, it thoroughly defeats the Palestinians. Around 6,000 PLO fighters surrender. Many Arab countries refuse to take them, but they're eventually deported to Tunisia.

Bashir Gemayel, Ariel Sharon, and Israeli troops walk together on the streets of Beirut. From their balconies, Christian citizens throw flowers, rice, and champagne.

Most of the Middle East is outraged at an Arab country welcoming Israel into its borders. We Christians don't care. We feel strong and protected in our new alliance.

Seeing the Israeli troops is a revelation for me. I expected ugly red devils, like they were always described. However, the Israeli soldiers not only look as good as us, they even look better.

Just a glance at their sharp uniforms and advanced equipment makes me understand how they could win a war against virtually the whole Arab armies in six days.

As for Bashir, he becomes not only the most popular man among Christians; he's worshiped as a savior. People compare him sometimes to JFK, and everybody is in love with JFK, of course.

Internationally, he's recognized as a statesman able to bring new solutions to the Arab-Israeli struggle. Bashir is even received warmly in Washington DC, where he promises Lebanon as a second major democratic ally in the region. For the first time since the 1975 civil war began, Christians feel not only secure, but also triumphant.

When Lebanon holds its elections for president on August 23, 1982, no one has any doubt that Bashir will win. Still, my neighbors are on edge as each vote is counted; when Bashir's victory becomes definite, everybody jumps up and kisses each other. Amidst many popping bottles of champagne, one woman holds her glass high and says, "Bashir is our president. The war is over; the nightmare is over." Then she bursts into tears of joy. Many others join her.

East Beirut celebrates with continual fireworks for three consecutive nights.

The checkpoints are now spreading champagne and candies instead of checking identity papers. The party keeps going on. "We have won the war," people shout.

It has been 15 days since he was elected and, still, some people find it hard to believe. Everyone is crazy about him; some think he's a saint that has been sent from God to help us.

Our family, especially my mother, can't stop her smile from drawing itself on her lips. I have never seen her enthusiastic like this before. Life has turned back to her eyes.

My father finds it hard to express his feelings. Every time he mentions Bashir, he stutters and tries very hard to hide his tears. He fails every time, though, and we make fun about how sensitive he is. It's such a great mood all around me. Everyone is so happy that even Georges and Youssef, two neighbors who stopped talking to each other a long time ago, have reconciled and even hugged this week. It's magic.

The war is over. We win.

On the west side of Beirut, however, the election of Bashir is treated as a funeral for the cause of a Palestinian state, and the presence of the Israeli army is a grievous humiliation. Bashir is considered a traitor who's brought shame to the Arab nation.

People like Bashir are usually called conspirers, agents, and collaborators in the Arab world. Traitors like him should be hanged on gallows, not elected president.

A thick explosion interrupts our dream, though.

A mere 20 days after the election, on September 14, 1982, Bashir is at the Beirut headquarters of his Phalange Party giving a speech advocating a new brotherhood between Christians and Muslims.

Habib Chartouni, a member of a pro-Syrian party,

has wired the building with explosives. When the bombs are detonated at 4:10 pm, Bashir and 26 others are killed.

Suddenly, the celebrations turn into tears of bitterness. Everyone, I mean literally everyone around me have red, red eyes. No one stops crying. My mother is so bitter that her tears just won't stop. I have never seen her so sad, so broken even in the worst days of our existence. My father is sobbing just like a baby. He sounds like he lost his own son.

The war isn't over, obviously.

On the other side, we can hear the fireworks. It's the partners' turn to celebrate now. The traitor is killed; their nightmare is over. I am incredibly pissed off at Muslims.

Angry and outraged, the Lebanese Forces, lead by Elie Hobeika—one of the closest men to Bashir—attack the Palestinian refugee camps of Sabra and Shatila, slaughtering hundreds of defenseless, innocent women and children in revenge. The attack has been facilitated by the Israeli Defense Forces, though, who surrounded the camp, let the Christian fighters in, and lighting the camps with illumination flares.

I remember Butcher and his *sugar* suddenly.

My mother thinks this is a horrible mistake—a sin. My father just doesn't want to believe that "our young Christian guys" did this. He thinks there's some conspiracy behind all those terrifying pictures of dead children... even the clear pictures of the massacres don't convince him. He refuses to believe that Christians can also be monsters.

Anyway, the barbaric massacre of Sabra and Shatila shocks the international community. As photographs of the dead circulate, Muslims throughout the Arab world are infuriated. Enormous demonstrations erupt in almost every major Arab city with demands for revenge against both Christians and Jews.

Fear, madness, violence, and terror—they're all knocking on the doors again!

All it took was one quick second, one quick explosion to wipe all those dreams away.

Obviously, we have lost. *They* win!

V
New Jersey

Following Bashir's assassination, his brother Amine Gemayel is quickly elected president. However, under pressure from outrage over the massacre—and possibly concern over meeting the same fate as Bashir—Amine claims reluctance to sign the peace treaty with Israel without approval from the Arab League and the Muslim Lebanese leaders. This is really just a way of saying "no," as the latter clearly isn't going to happen.

The new president is a huge disappointment to Israeli leaders. They decide Lebanon is turning into a quagmire that can sink anything. With the Lebanese government failing to keep its promises, and the scandal of the massacre having taken place under its watch, Israel withdraws its forces, leaving the Lebanese people to sort things out among themselves.

The night after the Israeli army leaves is one of the most horrific Lebanese Christians have ever suffered. Muslims, including those allied with the PLO, are furious about Arab towns receiving Israelis with flowers, rice, and champagne. Plus, the memory of what happened in Sabra and Shatila is all too fresh in their minds. As soon as the opportunity arises for revenge, they seize it.

The Christian militias are neither prepared to nor capable of defending all of our citizens simultaneously. As a result, entire cities are left defenseless.

The first Christian towns attacked are wiped out.

Other towns fall in quick succession, with thousands of innocent and mostly defenseless people killed.

Pictures of little children slaughtered in the laps of their mothers are beyond heartbreaking. My mother and I watch the news as mourners. It seems the days of Christians and Muslims residing peacefully has forever passed.

"Don't you think we should leave to some other country?" I ask her.

"Don't worry," she says, with familiar, bitter tears returned to her eyes, but she's never sounded so unconvincing. In the past, my mother has given speeches about how "no one can kick us out of our home." That sentiment has shifted to, "Where the hell can we go?" No country is eager to take in a poor family with zero special skills.

Christians are screaming for international protection. Once again, I ask the naive question, "Why doesn't America send the Marines?"

But this time, it actually does. President Ronald Reagan finally sends in U.S. ships and soldiers.

"New Jersey," one of the famous U.S. battleships is right on our shores to protect us. So, who's gonna dare to fuck with us now?" I assure my little brother, Dany, when I see the huge ship that was specifically sent to scare our enemies.

It is scary indeed, and neither Syria nor its allies would never dare to come near this giant that carries tons of explosives that could remove entire mountains maybe. I am thrilled and feel safe again. Dany is still nine years old, and it doesn't look like he fully gets what it means to have America on one's side. He will understand one day. I smile at him.

Just as I was struck by how much more capable Israeli soldiers were than our own, I'm impressed by the yet higher standard of the Marines, who have some of the best training and equipment in the world. I'm with my mother when I see them for the first time. "They look just like in the movies," I whisper into her ear. "Even better," she replies.

The Marines are friendly and respectful to us. And with them around, attacks against civilians plummet.

For a little while, Christians feel safe again. We have the protection of the strongest army in the world.

But this is not to last either.

On the Sunday morning of October 23, 1983, the Marine headquarters in Beirut is caught totally unprepared when a member of Hezbollah, a new party that we had never heard of before, drives a Mercedes-Benz truck filled with 12,000 pounds of dynamite directly into its building. The explosion is so enormous that it's heard throughout Beirut. It kills 241 Marines and injures 60 and is the single deadliest attack on Americans overseas since World War II.

President Reagan, already under political pressure to not get America involved in another Vietnam, decides to begin withdrawing all U.S. troops. The Marines pull out of Beirut on February 26, 1984.

Our Christian community is painfully shocked not only from the way the Marines were attacked, but from their quick retreat as well.

"How come this only happens when *we* are involved?" I complain to my mother, as if she could convince them to come back.

I feel so down from America's stand that I find

myself recording my second imaginary interview with an American president, Ronald Reagan this time.

I attack him with all sorts of questions until he is completely cornered: "Congratulations, Mr. President, you just let your best allies down," I end the interview, very satisfied from this last edgy line.

"Outspoken, but respectful," I congratulate myself when I hear it again.

Before the Marines exit, though, President Reagan extracts a promise from our Arab neighbors—especially Syria—that Muslims will stay out of the Christian zones. It's fine for Lebanese to kill each other near the borders and even to throw bombs at each other, but there'll be no repetition of the invasion and wholesale slaughter of Christian towns.

At times, there are ceasefires when we can let our nerves relax. But other times, the bombing of our town, which is close to a Muslim border, becomes so severe that my mother insists we have to get out for a while. When this occurs, my father takes us to Bouwar, a town located several miles away from the battles, where he, my mother, me, and my brother all reside in one cramped rented room. It's expensive, as we aren't the only family from a border town trying to stay alive.

We live this way, retreating and returning home based on the heat of local combat.

****

I am 16 now, and it isn't quite the life I have dreamed of, honestly. However, my mother still insists that she's so fortunate because we're all breathing in front of her eyes. That's all that really matters to her now. The country? She doesn't care too much about what is going to happen to the country.

"I don't pray for things to get better anymore," she turns at Jesus' picture. "I just ask him to stop them from going worse, that's all," she sighs. But it looks like *He* either can't or doesn't want to; I don't exactly know what His story is.

And once again, things manage to get worse.

In fact, the Lebanese Forces that Bashir had established has been divided into two big camps; one is lead by Elie Hobeika, the *designer* of Sabra and Shatila's massacre, and Samir Geagea, one of the fiercest fighters in the militia, directly controls the other.

The internal struggle for power enrages fast, and suddenly, Geagea and Hobeika clash in violent battles, causing hundreds of casualties and deaths among their best fighters.

Eventually, Geagea's men, known for being very ferocious in the battles, defeat Hobeika and kick him and what's left of his men outside East Beirut. With Hobeika gone, the struggle starts to surface between Geagea and President Gemayel.

After he was elected, Gemayel had to adopt a national speech to keep both Muslims and Christians happy. He clearly ended up pissing everybody off instead. Furthermore, his popularity ratings drop hugely, especially among Christians.

So, it is not only *them* that we're fighting now. It is us fighting us.

Even Dimitri, the man who fought next to Bashir for years, devoting his entire existence to protect Lebanon, as he always announced, has decided to quit the militia after the internal killings. He removed his uniform off his skin and is wearing suits now, hoping to find a civil job. "I am a fighter, Elie, a warrior," he says, smiling bitterly, "not a criminal who enjoys killing people," he answers me when I ask him about his decision to quit. "There is no cause anymore," he explains, "it's just a struggle between hyenas now... all over a dead body."

There are hundreds, if not thousands, of young men like Dimitri who couldn't find themselves aligned with either Geagea or Hobeika. For many, both men are very far from Bashir's values and principles; furthermore, they had quit, hoping to find a job away from rifles and killings. "It is gonna be impossible to find an employer as generous as the war to recruit them, though," my Uncle Joseph explains to me in one of our long discussions. "Unfortunately, war will find most of them once again." He's always pessimistic, my uncle, but what can I say? He's right every single time.

The Christian militia is no longer perceived as it was once before, during the days of Bashir Gemayel. After he died, the Lebanese Forces are no longer looked at as heroes but forces of de facto; people can't live with them, but they also can't live without their protection.

The bloody years of battles and combats transformed many of these fighters into wild beasts. Most of them were teenagers when the civil war started.

In West Beirut, our partners don't look like they are living a better life, as it shows in the news every night. They have more parties and armed groups than we have, though—Sunni militias, Shiite militias, Druze (a sect within Islam) militias, Palestinian militias—and it is really easy for the Syrian regime to manipulate all those differences and inflame sectarian clashes consistently, only to intervene and stop them later.

The Syrian president, Hafez al-Assad, is well aware that a stable, calm Beirut only means that he has to withdraw his thousands of troops from Lebanon, as Christian experts analyze.

The only justification for the presence of the Syrian Army is that the Lebanese people will slaughter each other again if there's no one to prevent them from doing so. Thus, al-Assad is a real maestro in igniting the fires and then putting them out according to the political necessities of each period.

Sometimes we hear about clashes between Palestinians and Sunni militias in which the Syrian Army interfered. Other times, it's the Shiite militias fighting each other, and again, the Syrian regime would intervene to halt the slaughter, always making sure that no one wins and no one loses.

Of course, many people know what al-Assad is plotting; however, few dare to speak it. In 1980, al-Assad had killed around 40,000 of his own people in *Hama* when they tried to remove him from power. Furthermore, he's not known for caring too much about human lives when it comes to his throne. Unfortunately, Lebanon is very crucial to his long-term plans for the Middle East; therefore, controlling it with an iron of fist is a must.

For this mission, al-Assad appoints one of the most infamous Syrian intelligence officers: Ghazi Kanaan.

Kanaan is very well known for making all those who disagree with the Syrian policies disappear quickly. He has this amazing talent of igniting clashes and then turning them off again. "He can be the fire and the water that puts it off at the same time," as one of my teachers in school describes him.

Politicians in the Muslim side of Beirut merely compete to please him. Unlike us, there's only one man who controls almost everything and politically decides on behalf of all Muslims.

In East Beirut, Kanaan's name is always connected with extreme brutality, torture, violence, and corruption. Sometimes, when I hear those horrible stories about him, I imagine Tony Montana (Al Pacino) in *Scarface*. That's how I exactly see him in my head, since there are no pictures of him in the news. It seems like he's one of those people who doesn't like you to remember his face.

Briefly, the entire country is divided into many tribes now, all fighting with each other. And there seems to be a couple of wars for every citizen. I can't really count how many we are surviving.

All I know is that we are trapped within 500 square miles. We literally live in a big cage; in denial, we call it home. Hundreds of thousands leave the country. Some escape to Europe and others to Canada and America. I sometimes have those emotional waves of envy, where I wish I were also stamping a new life on my passport. I don't declare it, though.

Like many, I still have hope that something will eventually change. I don't have a single clue what this might be, but I am waiting for it, nonetheless.

VI
Some Movies

My father thinks that we have already reached rock bottom. "It's good that we're finally here," he tells me. "It means things can only move forward from now on," he explains his interesting theory. He has always found ways and adapted theories to comfort himself. He simply believes that it can't get worse than the worst-case scenario.

From her side, my mother thinks he's naive, "extremely naïve." And unfortunately, two events will prove her right.

The first occurs in January 1986.

During a morning class, the principal interrupts to announce, "All those residing in Furn el Chebbak, please come with me to my office." I'm the only one to follow him into the hall. "Is my mother okay?" I ask. It's the first thing that comes to my mind.

"Yes, as far as I know," he says. "There has been a little explosion, though, and... Well, hopefully everyone is safe," he concludes awkwardly.

When we arrive at his office, there are over a dozen students from other classes, awaiting details. "A car bomb exploded in your town. That's all we know so far. Your parents will want you to be with them, so we're sending you home."

His announcement isn't a total shock. There have already been about dozen times when a car's been parked in a crowded residential area and left to blow up. It's the latest method our enemy has adopted to kill as many people as possible—without even the need for a suicide bomber.

While the school bus drives us home, I have a terrible feeling about my mother. *Something wrong has happened to her*, and I can't stop this feeling from attacking me. Some tears start to fall on my cheek, as if it is now certain that I have lost her.

The driver takes me close to my neighborhood, but he reaches a roadblock where Christian militias are allowing only residents in, so he has to drop me off there. I pass through the checkpoint and start walking the remaining blocks to home.

The sirens of many fire trucks and ambulances tell me the explosion is much bigger than our principle indicated. The closer I get, the more water and soap from the fire trucks run between my feet. I'm soon able to see that the explosion struck less than 50 yards from where I live.

My book bag grows heavy on my back. I throw it into the middle of the street and keep walking until I finally reach my building.

Shattered glass all over the stairs makes it hard to reach the second floor, but I manage.

Our apartment door is fully open. I start shouting hysterically for my mother.

There's no one inside.

I sit on the sofa. My bad feelings grow heavy on my chest, and I start to cry.

Then, I jump up from the sofa and run to the street. The explosion took place in the middle of a very crowded marketplace where my mother and our neighbors usually shop for groceries in the morning.

People are still shouting and screaming. More than a dozen corpses are still lying on the street covered in blood. Some young men are turning the bodies over to identify any survivors.

Terrified at what I might see, I sneak cautious peeks with one eye at the dead bodies.

I don't recognize anyone, which makes me less scared for a few minutes.

But then my legs shake every time the men turn up a new face.

It's too difficult to stand, so I sit on the pavement and watch people numb with shock aimlessly run back and forth. I want to believe it's just a movie, but no film I've ever seen contained so much ugliness.

A fireman eventually notices me. He helps me to get up on my feet after I tell him about my mother. "She's gonna be all right," he taps on my shoulder and kindly walks me back to my building.

As I climb the stairs this time, I hear the voice of my mother.

When she sees me, we both collapse with tears. She was helping a neighbor find her daughter when I came home. We'd missed each other by just 10 minutes.

"We can't go on living like this," my mother informs my father in the evening. "Find someone to buy our apartment. As soon as you do, we're moving." She sounds so determined that he even doesn't try to argue.

It's not easy to find someone who'll pay to live in a town next to a battle zone, though.

I'm also not sure my father is looking very hard, as

he's not eager to abandon his shop and lose his existing customers.

So, despite this awful event, we remain in our building for another half a year.

****

Throughout all this drama, I still have my same old crush. I continue to long for Carol.

The competition for Carol only becomes fiercer. She's a real beauty now—a princess. Older boys, with money and cars, are asking her out frequently. This makes me even shyer about approaching her. The thought of Carol saying no to me is devastating, and I just can't risk it. Sometimes, we exchange very quick conversations when we meet *accidentally* in the street. I mean very quick.

"Hi."

"Hello."

"It is freezing today, isn't it?"

"Yeah, it is really cold."

"Bye."

"Bye."

And that's as far as it goes.

Although I am starting to go out on dates, my true obsession is Carol. I even date one girl for a while just because she has the same name!

Spending time with girls and learning that they find my company pleasant emboldens me. I think, maybe I'm good enough after all.

So, after having carried a torch for Carol for many years, in the summer of 1986, I finally approach her. I stop her right in the middle of the street while she is walking back to her house. And after saying hello, I ask,

"Do you like movies? I mean, American movies?"

"No!" Carol replies almost immediately, looking very serious. "No! I hate movies, especially American movies."

I try to hide my surprise. Oh! I wish I could turn the conversation to the weather blah blah. Shit, this is totally not the answer I was expecting. I mean, who hates American movies?

"What do you like, then?" I ask, a bit petulantly.

"Why would you care what I like?" Carol asks.

"Because I want to ask you out on a date," I say, as smoothly as I can manage.

"Oh!"

What follows is a silence that lasts only two seconds but feels like days.

"Why don't you take me to church on Sunday? You can meet me here at 10:00 in the morning and we can attend Mass together. How about that?"

Well, if it were someone else, I would have left already. But this is Carol.

"Sure," I accept quickly. "That sounds great. I like Sunday Mass a lot."

"Really? Do you usually go to church?"

"Of course. Every Sunday. I never miss it."

"That's odd," Carol says, "because I've never spotted you in church."

"Oh! Well, I go to a different church than yours."

"I see."

I don't feel good about the direction the conversation has taken and choose a daring strategy: the truth.

"Okay, listen, I don't go to church. I find Mass

boring, and I don't even understand why people pray. If you'd like to go out with me, we'll be watching a movie. That's what we will be doing," I say with a determined tone. "Otherwise, I know there are 100 other boys waiting to ask you out, and you can go with one of them to church."

I'm prepared to give up and leave. Then Carol surprises me again—by shaking with delighted laughter.

"I knew you were going to have a breakdown when I mentioned Sunday Mass," she says between chuckles. "I just didn't realize it would take you that long to explode."

Carol imitates my voice mockingly, "Do you like American movies?" Then back in her own voice, she adds, "Of course, I do. That's like asking a girl if she likes chocolate."

I stand speechless. She's effortlessly outfoxed me.

Carol pauses thoughtfully and says, "But you know what? We should still go to church on our first date."

Seeing my look of horror, she continues sweetly, "Come on. It will be hilarious to make fun of the women wearing full makeup in the morning."

Carol then smiles. "If you take me to church this Sunday, I will go with you to the movies on our second date."

It takes less than a second to decide. "Yes! I love making fun of women in full makeup, especially in the morning."

"I will see you here on Sunday at 10:00."

On Sunday, I show up at eight. I waited years for this moment to happen, so two hours seem like nothing really.

There's probably no one else in the universe who could convince me to go to church. But for Carol, I put on a smiling face and walk with her to Sunday Mass. There's a shortcut that could get us to the church in just seven minutes, but I insist on our taking the long route so that everybody in the neighborhood knows Carol is with me.

As expected, the service is dreadfully boring. But luckily the church is loaded with women wearing full makeup.

When Mass ends, Carol insists we stay a while longer. She takes me by my hand to the very first row, right in front of Jesus' statue. She kneels down and gives me a look to do the same. "Kneel down, and let's pray," she whispers.

I don't object. I simply kneel next to Carol; while she's praying reverently, I look Jesus straight in the eyes, saying nothing.

Carol takes longer than I expect, though. After staring at Jesus with emptiness, a feeling comes upon me from having Carol by my side. I suddenly have a strong impression that I can talk to Jesus. I smile at Him and ask with my heart, "Did you fix this for me?"

It's a reasonable question. To have my fantasy of being with Carol actually come true is a kind of miracle. I mean, she's way out of my league.

"I'm still not going to eat your flesh and drink your blood, because that's disgusting," I say. "But, thank you. From the bottom of my heart, thank you."

We walk slowly back to Carol's home. When we reach her building, she kisses me very, very quickly on the edge of my cheek, but I strongly believe that our lips have touched. I can swear that they touched.

I had some previous *kissing adventures* with girls in my class, but nothing like this. Even though the kiss is extremely quick, it's deeply felt throughout my body. For the first time, my stomach experiences the mysterious cramps lovers often describe. Days later, I still get those cramps every time I think about the kiss.

I so look forward to our next date that I can barely think of anything else.

Before the scheduled second date, our little town is targeted by heavy artillery. Nothing extraordinary, just the usual.

However, what no civilians know is that Christian soldiers have turned the basement of Carol's building into a storage room for chemicals used to create weapons. I never find out whether the Muslims discover this secret kept even from the tenants or if it's mere chance, but one of the shells blasts the first floor of Carol's building. The resulting fire quickly spreads to the basement. And because of the chemicals, within minutes, the six-story building is engulfed in flames.

Somehow, Carol makes it to the roof. Firemen rescue her just as she's gathering the will to jump.

However, from head to toe, she's horrifically burned.

Carol is rushed to the critical care unit of our hospital. She's heavily medicated to ease what would otherwise be unendurable pain. It's only through sophisticated machines and skilled doctors that she's kept alive.

In fact, the extent of the burns makes it impossible to save her. But she is so beloved by everyone in our town that no one has the heart to unplug the machines and let her go.

Carol isn't allowed any visitors for the first couple of weeks. I try relentlessly to convince the nurses to let me see her for just a second. One of them finally explains they can't put anything on her body. "She is lying in a tub full of medicinal fluids, entirely naked."

A couple of weeks later, Carol's condition improves a little and they're able to cover her body with bandages. I and two of her friends, who also tried very hard to see her, are told we can enter her room for five minutes.

Before letting us in, a doctor explains that Carol isn't allowed to look in a mirror. "The psychological harm would be devastating," he says. "Almost every inch of her body has suffered third-degree burns. She might try to commit suicide if she sees herself."

The nurses help us put on hygienic uniforms. My heart is pounding rapidly when they open the door.

The room smells horrible. I'm very cautious about looking at the bed. While Carol's friends try hard to hide their shock and pretend everything is normal, I take a quick glance. Carol's angelic face has turned into something else... something inhuman. There is little flesh left. I can see her teeth even when her mouth is closed.

Unlike Carol's friends, who show real character in finding words to say to her, I'm completely speechless. Carol manages the strength to look at me and say in a very low voice, "Elie, I have been asking the nurses for a mirror but they won't bring one to me. If you bring me a mirror tomorrow, I will give you a real kiss next time, I promise."

I smile at her, hardly able to think of a reply. "I will," I lie, pretending that I hadn't heard the doctor's warning.

Then Carol asks me about her father. "I have a feeling Mother isn't telling me the full truth about his condition." Carol's instincts are correct; her father perished in the fire. But given Carol's extremely fragile health, the doctors are keeping this from her, as well.

"He's fine. I just went to see him before coming here," I once again lie.

Carol sighs. Even in her terribly weakened state, she's too sharp to believe my pathetic performance.

I leave Carol's room knowing deep inside that she won't survive.

Unfortunately, or perhaps fortunately, two days later, Carol is discovered dead in her bed. We all pretend to believe the official medical report that she died of infection. Obviously, Carol had finally convinced someone to bring her a mirror.

Who could have known that mirrors can be that dangerous?

Most of the town comes out to weep over Carol's white coffin. Rice and red roses are tossed from almost every balcony as the funeral procession passes by. The beautiful princess of Furn el Chebbak is gone forever. My princess!

The procession ends with bringing Carol's coffin into the church for eulogies. I will never watch a movie with Carol, I know, but she's managed to get us together in church one last time.

Almost everyone around me is crying. My mother sobs continuously. When the priest describes Carol's adorable character and playful spirit, the whole town sounds sobbing as well.

The only one who doesn't cry at any point during the services is me. I try to but simply can't. I can't really feel a thing. I am not even sad, and I seriously have no idea where the hell have I brought all this indifference.

Instead, I just stare at the statue of Jesus. I look Him straight in the eyes but have absolutely nothing to say.

Right before we leave, I look at him one final time. "You will never again see my face in Your house; not for a funeral, not for a wedding!" I tell him bluntly, right in His face. His peaceful looks on the cross do not intimidate me anymore. And I leave his church.

It turns out that Carol's death is the last straw for my mother, also. That night, she tells my father that we have to move out immediately, with no excuses. I never thought she'd finally admit that the war has beaten her, but somehow, this time she does.

My mother packs all our belongings. In August 1986, our family leaves Furn el Chebbak forever.

I have stories, tears, laughter, and lot of memories on every street of our little town. I know every building and almost every boy and girl in the neighborhood. In here, I built a million dreams, and it is all being taken away from me. Yet, it is Furn el Chebbak who basically taught me never to get attached to anyone or anything.

We stay in our tiny rented room in Bouwar, until my father manages to sell our apartment to make a down payment on a new home away from the combat.

Following Carol's funeral, my mother insists that I should let some tears out. She's afraid that if I keep the feelings inside, something severe will happen to me. What she doesn't realize is that something already has. War has already crawled so far under my skin that I actually feel myself aging.

For three weeks, I remind myself of Carol's face before I sleep… her smile… her cute gestures. But, it is getting harder now to bring her exact image to my mind.

I still can't bring any tears to my eyes, though. I hate indifferent, cold-hearted people, and I know I am not one. At first, I thought I couldn't grieve for Carol because it was too crowded to grieve. I find it extremely hard to cry in public, even in the presence of my mother. But here I am, even when completely alone... no tears.

It feels like my sadness is somehow trapped inside me, and I can't remove this load off my chest... I have no idea what it is, but I know it is intensely there, and it's damn heavy. One companion makes it a lot easier, though: music.

I listen to music for long hours. It just takes me places where no one could take anything away from me; Jazz especially.

Aline, a friend from school who knows my infatuation with Jazz, brings me an album one day.

"Have you heard of Ziad Rahbani?" she asks me. "Is there anyone in Lebanon, or in the Arab world even, who hasn't heard of him?" I answer. "I even memorized all his plays—"

"I am not talking about his plays," she interrupts. "Have you heard his music, his Jazz?" she asks with obvious enthusiasm.

"Not really," I reply.

"Here," she hands me the tape. "Listen to this; it's

a music called 'Abu Ali,' and it will be so hard to remove it out of your soul for as long as you live," she smiles. "Big words," I smile back. "Yeah, you'll understand once you hear it," she nods. "And by the way, he was only 16 when he composed this music."

At night, I lay down on my bed. I stick the earphones in my ears and push play... And that's it!

Five minutes later, I just can't stop my tears from falling. I cry for four consecutive hours.

Although very painful, they're finally out, those tears that I should have dropped. Finally, I grieve Carol, and I have no problem in remembering her face anymore; it's all back. But my heart is so deeply broken.

Exhausted, I sleep.

From that night on, Ziad Rahbani is my permanent companion. His music makes me cry at night, but he is just as powerful in making me laugh every time I hear one of his hilarious plays.

His mother is the great Fairuz, the singer whose angelic voice almost every Lebanese drinks coffee to in the morning.

Thanks to Dadou, Fairuz's voice has always been present in our house since we were born. "They should name the entire country after her," my mother always declares, "not a street or a boulevard; the whole country should be named Fairuz instead of Lebanon."

But it is not just my mother.

Almost every Lebanese, Christian or Muslim, has some kind of crazy crush on her. They call her the queen, the princess, the angel, you name it.

Also, Ziad's father, Assi, is one of the greatest playwrights and composers in the history of Arabs. He is perceived as one of the most influential artists of all time, perhaps. And with his brother, Mansour, they wrote some epic plays that still fill up millions of Arabs' eyes with tears.

But, regardless of whom his mother, his father, and his uncle are, Ziad is the obsession of almost every young man my age.

Ziad shouts out loud what people whisper behind their walls. He audaciously mocks what his father once called "a little piece of green paradise."

Unlike the epic plays of patriotism and heroism that permeate his father's art, Ziad is a harsh realist, who names the ugly truths as they are without compromising a single thought. Whereas his parents conclude all their plays with a shiny hope for the future, he predicts that the Lebanese people will turn the country into a hopeless jungle. His predictions are dark and pessimistic, and yet, somehow, I believe no one in the history of Arabs has ever made people laugh so hard about their tragedies.

He was acknowledged as a genius among his generation right after he wrote his first play when he was only 17. His music and catchy sentences spread widely throughout the country after his second play, *The Motel of Happiness*, in which he precisely predicted the entire Lebanese civil war.

He is my best ally for many long months. I can't wait until I get home from school to listen to his plays. My mother buys me my first professional pair of headphones because of my new obsession. She also loves Ziad but not enough to listen to him day and night.

It isn't just me, though. In school, dozens of my friends are infatuated with Ziad. Many try to speak like him, imitate his voice, his audacious wording, and his gestures. Ziad is not just an artist. To thousands of young people like me, he's more of a mindset.

For the elderly, Ziad is a special case. Although he's known for being a communist and, thus, an atheist, which is something very repulsive to most people in my country, they like everything he says. There is something in his character that makes everyone, Christians and Muslims, crazy about him. He crosses every line; he mocks all politicians and public figures. He makes fun of religion, culture, and social behavior. And they still accept him as he is.

My infatuation with Ziad is not a momentary crush. After I listen to all his tapes, I look in every record shop for anything new by him, but there is no more. He has not written or composed music for years. Rumors say he thinks it is too hopeless of a cause. "The problem is not the corrupted, ruthless leaders but the people themselves," he suggests in one of his last play *A Long American Movie*.

I am obsessed with every word he says. He is my rebel. He's blunt, sarcastic, and calls things as they are without compromise or hypocrisy.

In school, I focus more on the humanities than the sciences. I don't care if $e=mc^2$, and I would rather spend my time with the likes of Hemingway and Albert Camus than Einstein.

With Ziad Rahbani's plays and music, my books, my movies, my cigarettes, which I still smoke to this day, and legends like Bob Dylan, John Lennon, and Pink Floyd gathered in this small paradise of mine, and my room becomes the coolest place on earth. I don't mind staying home at all, especially when my parents are out and I can smoke freely.

Memorizing songs and watching dozens of American movies without subtitles help me learn English, which I find more charming than my native Arabic language. And although French is the mandatory second language that we learn in our schools, France and I do not really get along well. But I am head over heels in love with everything America represents, and I am not shy to declare it in front of everyone.

In fact, I have a secret plan to create my first connection with America: The American University of Beirut, or the AUB.

VII
Plan B, C, And D

The AUB is every student's dream, especially for those of us obsessed with America. It is, by far, my first choice, but it is located in West Beirut.

However, there is a truce now and the roads are open, so it doesn't feel like a hopeless dream to fantasize about.

It's my last year in high school, and applying to AUB includes lots of applications, forms, and tests. Telling my parents about my plans is out of the question. It's still very uncomfortable and unsafe for either Christians or Muslims to cross the borders unless there's something urgent. But I am so determined that I decide to steal my father's car and head toward the AUB for a visit, with only a hand-drawn map from a friend to guide me.

Could people there recognize that I am Christian by my face? Will they bully me if they know? Will they kidnap me? Will they kill me?

The paranoia matures in my head as I drive toward the other side of the city, until I reach the famous Raouché Street, a charming boardwalk overlooking the Mediterranean, where dozens of people normally hang out.

They look exactly like Christians; they are jogging, walking, holding hands, chatting, and smiling. I had assumed for a long time that Muslims do not laugh or smile, and I am truly surprised that the mood in West Beirut looks much more cheerful than what the news shows us. I am also surprised to see that even their buildings look exactly like our buildings; for some reason, I pictured their houses to be different.

The tense feelings I have vanish quickly, and I feel relaxed and am starting to enjoy the fact that I will likely make this journey every morning if I am admitted. I even become more optimistic that, perhaps, Christians and Muslims can live together after all.

All of this dissolves when I come upon a Syrian checkpoint. My friend has missed this important detail in the map. "The moron," I curse him as I wait in the line.

A rotten, despicable soldier asks me to approach. I slowly roll down my window. The soldier doesn't seem to be in any hurry, and he's looking somewhere else. I don't breathe. I am patiently waiting for him to wave his hand and let me pass.

"Where are you from?" he asks.

"Beirut," I say quickly. This seems to annoy him.

"Where in Beirut?"

"Furn el Chebbak."

The soldier suddenly bends his head down and sticks it into the car, looking toward the backseats, his gaze wandering all around. "Hum! You're Christian?"

I try to smile as I answer. "I am Lebanese."

Unimpressed, he asks again. "You're Christian?"

"Yes!"

"Give me your papers!" he demands. I hand them to him politely. He looks at them. "I have been told that you joke a lot about the Syrian Army in East Beirut. What is the latest joke about us?"

"I don't know any jokes about the Syrian Army."

"Come on. Tell me what they say about us in East Beirut?" Although his words sound friendly, he's not smiling and seems to be getting agitated. "What's the latest joke that you have heard?"

"I really don't know any," I say. "Look, I am just a student on my way to the American University—"

"Shut your mouth animal and just tell the joke."

"Don't call me animal, man. I told you I don't know any."

"Are you quarreling with me, dog?" Then he slaps me in the face. I am so fucking shocked.

"Why did you hit me, man? Why did you hit me?" I shout at him, outraged.

He slaps me again. "Get out of the car, you animal, get out!" He jerks open the door and violently pulls me out by my shirt.

Then, he drags me by my shirt down the middle of the road, walking toward a building across the street; it's obviously the Syrian intelligence headquarters. The car is still blocking the road, and the queue is extremely long now. I look at the people in the street, who have already gathered around. No one dares to open their mouths; they're watching the scene without interfering with the soldier in any way. He keeps pushing and cursing. "You animal, are you quarreling with me, you dog?"

I know he's praying that I will say something that will allow him to beat the hell out of me in the middle of the street. I walk with him inside the building like a lamb. I am scared and outraged at the same time. He finally gets me inside the smelly, filthy building, and we enter a room where another soldier sits on a broken desk, wearing a white sleeveless shirt with stains here and there. I am standing right in front of him, but he doesn't bother to look up.

"Keep this piece of shit here. I am coming right back," says the first soldier.

I am silent, and the room is foggy from the rampant smoking of the other soldier who has yet to look at me.

"So, you pissed off Abu Hassan?" he says suddenly. "Big mistake."

"I never said anything—"

"Shhhh! Shut it, shut it... I didn't ask you to tell me the story of your life." The soldier looks annoyed. Abu Hassan comes back into the room. This time, he grabs a newspaper and rolls it into a twist. He slaps it on his hand, walks over to me, and slaps me on the cheek. Then he slaps me to emphasize each word he says.

"Did-you-think-of-a-joke?"

The actual feeling of the slap doesn't hurt, but I am humiliated. The other soldier thinks it is funny and rolls up another newspaper. He starts asking me questions in the same way.

"The-man-asked-you-a-question-you-animal." The two soldiers are slapping me simultaneously now. All I can do is stand there and take it.

"You-need-education-in-the-A-U-B-?"

"We-will-educate-you-here," he stops suddenly. He looks at the second soldier. "Take him to the place where we educate our special guests."

"The education cell, you mean?" They both laugh.

"What? What are you talking about, man?" I say quickly.

"Stop saying man, you donkey; you say, Sir!" He shouts.

"Sir, my mother will literally die if I don't come

back home tonight. I am really sorry if I said something to offend you—"

"Don't worry about your mother," he says with a twisted grin.

"Can I at least call her, please? Just one phone call?"

"Our phones don't work. Walk!"

He walks me through a hallway, down the stairs, and into an extremely dirty cell with its door half-open. He pushes me inside and closes the door.

The cell is so small and disgusting, but this is the least of my worries now. The first two hours are the hardest; I can't stop thinking about my mother and what she would say if she knew the notorious Syrian Intelligence Service had detained me. I realize that I am more worried about my mother than I am about myself. I have to find a way to get out. Then a brilliant idea crosses my mind.

I remember hearing about citizens bribing the Syrian soldiers at the checkpoints. They are known for how cheaply they can be bribed. People always keep an extra pack of Marlboros, sandwiches, fruit, or vegetables in their cars; these soldiers will take anything, and they are not very hard to please.

I wish I had remembered this while Abu Hassan was harassing me; I could have avoided all of this with a packet of Marlboros, but perhaps it is not too late. I have something to offer Abu Hassan, so I knock on the door of my cell and call out.

A different soldier comes to the door. "What do you want?"

"Listen, Sir, I have a sick mother that I have to

check on. Please let me go, and I will give you my car, seriously! It is still parked out there, and I can give it to you right now." He bursts into hard laughter.

"You want to give me your car to let you out? Who are you anyway? Who put you here?"

I explain my story very briefly to the new soldier, who relatively understands compared with the other two. He tells me that Abu Hassan has already left to Damascus and that he won't be returning for two weeks.

"Take my car and let me go back home," I repeat, trying to make him laugh again. "It is a brand new car," I tempt him, as if he's waiting for me to give him permission to take it.

He walks me to his superior and explains to him that Abu Hassan must have forgotten me in that cell before he left for Syria. The officer doesn't even bother to listen to the end of the story.

"Send him home," he orders. The soldier walks me out of the building, and I see my father's car on the side of the road.

"Here's the car," I show him my father's new Renault. He walks with me, and we find out that the key and all my stuff are still inside.

"Take me for a ride downtown," he says. "I have a couple of things I need to pick up from the market. I am Ali, and you can keep your car."

I drive him to the market and to a clothing store. At each place, he gets what he wants and doesn't pay. I drive him for two hours before he gets tired and asks me to take him back. He unloads his stuff when we reach the barracks and finally releases me.

I drive faster than a Formula 1 racer back home. I

come up with a lie about a friend who had a terrible car accident and try to convince my parents that I was at the hospital with him the entire time, but they don't buy it. I insist, though, and they finally stop asking questions.

"Death feels much better than humiliation." I have heard this sentence from my father a hundred times before and never understood what he meant until today.

I just can't tell anyone what a coward I was. I should have punched the bastard in his face. I should have fought them. They would have shot me, perhaps, but "death is better than humiliation." I keep blaming myself for standing there and letting them insult me the way they did. It's so hard to stop boiling on the inside; the feelings of impotence are truly unbearable.

There are no courts or judges who dare to convict Syrians; they are the untouchables who can do anything that crosses their minds in the territory they occupy. In the eyes of the people who were watching me being dragged away, I saw they felt equally insulted and looked just as humiliated as I was. It's obvious they hate the Syrian Army much more than I do. Although I hate what the Christian militias have become, I now feel so grateful that they fought as hard as they did to keep the Syrian Army out of our areas.

It really kills me to delete the pictures of the AUB campus that I had imagined a dozen times from my mind. I believe that life on an American campus could be the best experience of one's lifetime, and graduating from the AUB is something I deeply want, but it's not worth it anymore. Nothing, absolutely nothing, is worth that kind of humiliation. Therefore, the AUB is another fantasy I have to let go of, and I must settle with what's available.

The fact that I am deprived of that experience feels so unfair. But nothing ever goes according to Plan A when you live in a war-zone. There are different rules in war, and the priority is to stay alive; this is the real Plan A we keep in mind all the time, and everything else falls under the category of luxury, even education.

Compared with the hundreds of incidents with the Syrian Intelligence Service I have heard, mine seems almost amusing. I got in trouble with Ghazi Kanaan's guys, and I am so lucky I was able to get back home. That building they took me to is where hundreds of innocent Lebanese people are beaten, tortured, killed, or deported to horrible prisons in Syria.

I still have six months before I graduate from high school, which gives me some time to think about the possible alternatives I am *allowed* to choose from.

I have lost the connection I wanted to build with America, but I have to accept it. It is not the first unfair reality, and I will do as so many others have done—Plan B, C, or perhaps D.

VIII
Two Americas

Amine Gemayel's presidential term is over; six years have passed since he was elected in 1983, and nothing has changed. On the contrary, our lives are heading backwards. Christians and Muslims, like usual, fail to agree on anything, especially when it comes to electing a new president.

The Americans, the Europeans, and the Arabs all try to intervene and sponsor a solution that can prevent the country from collapsing entirely. The partition of Lebanon into two states is not an acceptable solution for the international community, and so it is agreed that Beirut shall remain on ice until a final solution is found.

After 13 years of a terrorizing war, we are at the beginning of another nightmare. Words like "future," "hope," and "peace" are funny expressions that make us laugh every time we hear them. Future what? We don't even have faith in the next five minutes. And our story seems exactly like those never-ending TV series, like *Dallas* or *The Bold and the Beautiful*, with episodes that never seem to finish, and every time you think there might be an ending, a whole new set of conflicts float back up to the surface and launch the series all over again.

Amidst this chaos arises one of the most controversial Arab leaders of modern times: Michel Aoun. He's appointed by Amine Gemayel to be an interim President until our parliament can agree on an official one.

Aoun is a general in the official Lebanese Army,

which is a secular organization comprised equally of Christians and Muslims. For years Aoun has been harshly criticizing politicians on both sides for failing to solve Lebanon's problems, and has built a loyal following for saying out loud what most people are thinking.

Aoun decides the only thing that can save the country is the military. He quickly puts together a cabinet—that is, the country's primary executive body—consisting of six high-ranking generals: three Christian and three Muslim. As soon as the Muslim generals are announced, however, they resign—presumably under intense pressure from Syria.

Without hesitation, Aoun proclaims that his cabinet will run the country regardless.

The Muslims respond by announcing that they're forming their own government.

And Aoun responds by declaring a war of liberation against the Syrians!

Most Christians revere Aoun as another Bashir for trying to make Lebanon free again. But others view Aoun as a hothead with no qualms about sacrificing thousands of lives to a war that can't be won.

After six months of fierce battles, over 1,000 Christian civilians have been killed, and 4,000 injured, as a result of Ghazi Kanaan going beyond military targets and heartlessly pummeling our homes with bombs. Most Christians have entirely fled Beirut to avoid being the next casualties.

The international community decides to intervene by meeting in the city of Taef, Saudi Arabia to hammer out a plan to end the war. They ask all parties to recognize the new agreement—which ousts Aoun from power, and formalizes Syria's grip on the country. The reasoning is that Syria is a stabilizing force; but there's no date set for Syria ever leaving.

At first blush, the Taef Agreement might sound like a reasonable way to end massive bloodshed. But how would Americans feel if during their Civil War the international community decided that British troops should occupy the country until the US learned to behave itself?

Aoun flatly refuses the Taef Agreement. Tens of thousands of Christians gather around Aoun in his Presidential residence to declare their full support of his decision. Further, they donate their money, jewelry, and other belongings to support Aoun and his army. I am among them.

Aoun's uncompromising positions remind me of Ziad Rahbani. My family and me are among General Aoun's strongest supporters.

Then, for reasons I can't really understand, Aoun decides to disarm the unauthorized *Christian* militias—especially the Lebanese Forces led by Samir Geagea. Although Aoun's army is exhausted from its battles with the Syrians, he declares a war on his fellow Christian warriors!

Christians begin killing each other with unprecedented ferocity. Instead of victims, we become our own monsters. The next few months create more destruction to Christian cities than the Syrians did.

Once again, Aoun's battles lead to nothing of value and end in a standstill.

Aoun is so stubborn in his stand that everyone assumes he is secretly counting on a major international power to support him. However, his visitors always confirm that he is deeply convinced that the west could never ally with a brutal dictator like Hafez al-Assad against someone like him, who consistently calls for democracy, freedom, and peace. He counts, as many experts and journalists confirm, on the world's 'moral supremacy'.

And it looks like it is working so far.

****

Surprisingly, the Iraqi president, Saddam Hussein, invades the small, yet very rich in oil, Emirate of Kuwait. And this is obviously a game changer in the Middle East.

The Kuwaiti Forces collapse quickly, and the royal family runs away from the country in just a few hours.

The world denounces the aggression, and the United Nations asks Hussein to withdraw his forces immediately from Kuwait. The stubborn Iraqi president refuses to bow to the international resolution. On the contrary, he escalates his position into declaring Kuwait as a province of the Iraqi Republic.

At first, like many people around me, I couldn't understand how those unexpected events 2,000 miles away could affect us in any negative way.

However, there are serious concerns that Saddam might get tempted to occupy the wealthiest kingdom in oil, Saudi Arabia. The rumors escalate dangerously. It looks like Saddam Hussein has decided to turn the table on all the players.

Obviously, King Fahd of Saudi Arabia is ready to do anything to keep the nightmare away, even if it will involve breaking some very strict religious rules. He bluntly asks for the Americans' protection.

Luckily for the Saudis, the American president, George Bush Sr. is also hugely outraged by the invasion. He responds very fast and soon announces the formation of a wide international coalition to liberate Kuwait.

I am one of millions of Arabs who are merely astonished by the American president's quick and extremely decisive response to the invasion, as if New York or California were attacked.

Hundreds of thousands of troops head toward the Gulf from all over the world to kick the Iraqi forces out and restore Kuwait's sovereignty and independence. It took the entirety of Europe more than two years to persuade the Americans to get involved in World War II; however, for the tiny small Emirate of Kuwait (less than 7,000 square miles), they are prepared to send half a million troops in a couple of weeks.

It's really hard to persuade anyone that the American president has suddenly undergone some kind of awakening. There are more than 40 brutal dictators around the world that he has no issues dealing with. But for the sake of the Kuwaitis, the American president is prepared to shake the entire planet.

I am jealous of the Kuwaitis, and I wish the American president had the same affection and enthusiasm to restore our sovereignty, as well. But he's interested in something else obviously.

The decision to deploy half a million troops to Mecca, the holiest and most sacred city for all Muslims around the world, is something that my brain can never really comprehend.

There's nothing that could outrage the Muslim world more than sending American troops to that particular city.

Everyone knows that oil is a strategic interest that the United States has always protected; however, the big question is why deploy those troops to Mecca? Why not in Jordan, Turkey, The UAE, Bahrain, Qatar, or any other ally in the region, where the American Army would still be able to liberate Kuwait and defend the Saudi royal family at the same time if Hussein ever attacked the Kingdom. *Invading* Mecca is more than Muslims can swallow; millions are shocked, humiliated, and offended.

The mosques in every corner of the Middle East are inflamed by speeches of anger that warns the Americans from such a bold, audacious, and provocative move. Hundreds of American flags are burned in protest, and thousands of Muslims threaten to declare war on the U.S. if it ever sent the troops to Mecca.

Yet, the Marines land in the city of Mecca, disregarding all the warnings, infuriating thousands of young Arabs who vow to fight a sacred war against America until it withdraws its *impure* forces out of the holy land.

Osama bin Laden is merely one of them.

Saddam Hussein has always had ups and downs with the Americans. Yet, he quickly realizes that they're not seriously looking for a deal this time. So, he starts giving hot speeches about his plans to destroy Israel in the near future. This always succeeds to inflame the Arab masses, and Hussein knows well how to use it in times of crisis.

Most importantly, he suddenly turns into a

religious figure, with all of his speeches starting with "in the name of Allah," to get more sympathy from the public. The Iraqi dictator knows how to play on both religious and patriotic feelings, and despite his weak media, he succeeds significantly in promoting the idea that the war is all a Zionist conspiracy to destroy Islam and the Arab Nation.

Back in Beirut, no one knows what to expect from all that is happening around us.

At first, I think things might actually turn in our favor, especially with half a million American soldiers in the area. But as soon as we hear that Hafez al-Assad has agreed to send thousands of his troops to fight side by side with the American soldiers, we quickly realize that it can't end well for us.

Finally, the first attacks to liberate Kuwait are launched.

Thanks to CNN, we're able to watch the war as it happens, second by second.

Like millions around the world, I am mesmerized in front of my TV, watching the war live on air: the air strikes, the bombing, and the rockets.

The CNN unprecedented coverage is astonishing, somehow like watching a movie. The skies of the Gulf are on fire and the coalition, especially the Americans, overwhelm the Iraqi Army. The latter is defeated quickly.

The CNN and the American army win.

In the picture, thousands of Iraqi soldiers surrender in humiliation to the attackers. The myth of Saddam Hussein and his great army is soon broken, and the entirety of Kuwait is liberated in a couple of weeks.

Additionally, the American Army pushes the Iraqi

forces deep inside Iraq, up to the borders of the capital, Baghdad.

Millions of Iraqis revolt against the government forces when they see the Marines coming. The long-oppressed Iraqis thought that Hussein's moment had finally come; furthermore, more of them enthusiastically join the rebels, and Hussein loses control over more than 80% of the country. It looks like his days are really over. He's surrounded on every side, and Baghdad is his last resort.

But just when everyone predicts that the brutal, fierce, scary Hussein would end up like Hitler, killing himself in a shelter, the American troops withdraw from all Iraqi soil.

As soon as they're out, Hussein, who still has some of his best brigades defending him in Baghdad, launches a counter attack on all those who rebelled against his regime.
Unfortunately, CNN is not inside Iraq this time to cover the rest of that story.

Even though the Iraqi army was publicly humiliated and kicked out of Kuwait, Hussein declares victory. Why not? He's kept his throne, which is all that he actually cares about.

Back in my small country, people have various explanations for the emerging, very quick events. Some say it's a conspiracy against the Sunnis, whereas others confirm that the Shiites are targeted.

However, all agree that it's nothing but a Zionist conspiracy against Islam, supported and executed by the United States.

"Could someone be so stupid to anger a billion

Muslims just to please six royal families?" I ask Jamil, one of the journalists who usually hang out in my favorite coffee shop. "Perhaps you should count the oil barrels instead of counting how many Muslims are outraged. That's what counts the most for America, Nakouzi," he answers with sarcasm. He looks intelligent in his glasses, and he reads a lot of newspapers. "Come on," I argue, "what about the moral supremacy?" I say, taking a serious tone when pronouncing the expression, hoping to sound knowledgeable.

"Moral what?" He laughs. "Talk about oil supremacy, Nakouzi. Oil!" He returns to his newspapers.

I can feel that he thinks I am naive. But I am still not convinced at all that America, the greatest nation on earth, could forsake its values for a few billion oil barrels.

****

On October 13, 1990, at six o'clock in the morning, Syrian air jets, which had been previously internationally banned from flying over Lebanon's skies, launch the first attacks on the presidential palace where Aoun resides.

Meanwhile, the Syrian Army also launches a huge land assault from all the frontiers at the exact same time. Forty-five minutes later, Aoun -who declared five hours earlier that he will die fighting- knows he stands no chance against the attackers and he flees to the French Embassy in a tank, asking his troops through an official statement that the radio networks air "to stop the fighting in order to prevent the bloodshed."

Fearing for his life, Aoun is asked by the French ambassador to remain in the embassy, which provides him with political asylum. Most of Aoun's men refuse to surrender, though, and they keep fighting until the end of the day.

The Syrian Forces are in the presidential palace a couple of hours later, in the very heart of the Christian area, coming as a tremendous shock to our community, who never truly believed that the world would ever let Syria invade us. But, here they are, our worst nightmare, the filthiest, most disrespectful, corrupted soldiers in the Middle East—the most brutal regime who had killed thousands of its own people and tortured thousands of political prisoners in notorious jails—in the heart of our cities, and there's no one, absolutely no one, to fight them back.

Dozens of the best Christian officers are executed. They are shot in their fronts and buried in a mass graves. Hundreds of our best-trained soldiers are captured and sent to the dark, horrible cells in Syria.

We are broken and defeated, but most of all, we are scared as hell!

My mother removes all of Aoun's pictures from our house quickly. She's concerned that the occupiers might enter our house by surprise.

"We should not give them any alibis," she says with tears falling from her eyes, every time she removes a picture of her beloved general. As for my father, three days later, he's in front of his barbecue that he installed on the small balcony of our apartment, grilling his specially seasoned meat and chicken, as if nothing has happened.

"Seriously, Dad? Do you really think it is a good time for a barbecue?" I ask him.

"Yes it is," he replies decisively. "Sunday has

always been the barbecue day, and no one will ever change this, especially those Syrian dicks." He continues, getting a little angrier as he speaks. "Let them pass and smell our barbecue; that's how they will realize that we don't really give a fuck." Like always, my father has his own way to fight, and he *truly* believes that he can defeat the war with a barbecue. The Sunday barbecue, with a couple of glasses of Arak (the traditional Lebanese alcoholic beverage) and my mother's famous Tabbouleh are the best way he can find to beat his sadness.

For the entire war, his Sunday habit never stopped. Even when the country is entirely burning, my father insists on ignoring the drama and pretends that we are living normal lives. He is a fighter in his own way, and he always succeeds in smiling, despite all the disappointments and heartbreaks we have all experienced.

As for me, I am in a state of deep shock that causes weird, red stains to crop up all over my face and a 41°C fever for four days. My doctor assumes it's all psychological. Perhaps he's right.

My attachment to Aoun is not merely a political one. Of course, some Christians blame him for strategic mistakes, like fighting with the Lebanese Forces, for instance, but we have an emotional attachment to Aoun in that he somehow represents our pride and dignity.

For now, we don't know what to really expect, and for the first time since the war started, I feel that my people have lost their ability to fight. The war has completely worn us out, and this time, it is a knock out that sounds impossible to recover from.

We know al-Assad and his methods very well; he is a man who ruled every single inch of his country, which is almost 20 times the size of Lebanon, with fear, horror, and many, many secret service groups.

In more than 20 years, al-Assad was able to transform 20 million Syrians into scared citizens. People are tortured and executed for simply making silly remarks that dare to criticize al-Assad or his policies. It's enough to show just a little dissatisfaction from the political or social conditions in the country, even in a closed meeting, for someone to disappear forever.

It's often said that al-Assad terrorized his people so much that he became something like God. This is a man who didn't mind slaughtering his own people when they objected to his decisions, and we can't expect him to be any different with us.

So, Aoun is gone and America has let us down once again. "How could America do this to us? How could America leave us?" These are, perhaps, the questions that are on every Christian's mind.

What kept the Syrian jets away from our skies that whole time was not our own strength but the American veto on invading the Christian areas.

People quickly suspect that there's a suspicious deal behind this sudden approval for slaughtering us.

I feel terribly defeated, broken, and impotent, just like everyone else around me. It's so hard to believe that "We," the "pro-Americans of the Middle East," were left alone to face the cruelest, most brutal regime in the region, which was always perceived as an enemy to the United States.

"*How could this happen? We are exactly like the Americans: We share the same beliefs, the same values, and the same religion, as well. Doesn't all this count at all? What is wrong with the Americans*?" It just doesn't make any sense to me. I'm so angry, for the first time in my life, at America.

"What kind of policies are these? What kind of dark interests would make someone align with Hafez al-Assad, the strongest ally of the Soviet Union and the man who bluntly embraces communism, against Christians, who preach for democracy and peace for all our lives?" I complain to Jamil when we meet in the same coffee shop a few months later.

"Look, Nakouzi, it's really easy if you analyze it objectively," he answers, almost whispering. He explains.

"The United States needed as many Arab allies as it could join. The liberation of Kuwait was already perceived as an assault on Islam and Arabism, even before it started, and it was crucial to find strong Arab allies to embrace the military attack. Otherwise, it could have been easily pictured as a western war against Islam," he pauses, waiting to see if I am connecting the dots. Then, he lights a new cigarette and continues. "The Syrian president knew how crucial the need was for someone like him to get on board. So, he supported the war after he secured a silent deal with the Americans that granted him the full sponsorship and control over Lebanon. Got it?" He returns back to his newspaper.

"Hmm," I reply, admiring the way Jamil has put it.

He notices that I am still interested in the conversation. He adds, "al-Assad is one of the major key players to secure a minimum stability. And your friends, the Americans, have always melted in front of expressions like stability and security. The man is shrewd, and he simply knows how to politically take advantage of the western hunger for peace. He's a great manipulator—"

"He's a fucking ruthless dictator who deserves to be hanged from his balls," I comment in a low voice.

Jamil shakes his head. "Don't be an idiot," he chuckles. "There are too many complications that al-Assad could create in the Middle East if he wants to, and the western community recognizes now that without the help of some strong Arab leaders, like him, there would be no chance of achieving security in the region," he states his theory, squeezes his cigarette in the ashtray to put it out, and leaves.

Although Jamil's theory made sense to me, I am still dazed every time I try to analyze it.

After these dramatic events, it would be really hard to defend America anymore, even among Christians who were always perceived as loyal pro-Americans. Christians, and probably every other minority in the Middle East, are now directly warned that they can never count on the ethics of America to protect them. And thus, the expressions "moral supremacy" and "ethical force" are now funny slogans that people make jokes about in coffee shops.

I am quickly learning that politics has nothing to do with morals, ethics, or values necessarily. When interests are threatened, politics immediately become the opposite of all those virtues indeed. Before George Bush Sr., I assumed that this was an exclusive curse in the Middle East, but as it turns out, it's the same everywhere in the world, even in America.

Despite this fact, though, I can't hate America. Many like me feel the same. Or perhaps, there are two Americas: one that we have a magnificent relationship with—the one that represents freedom, laws, opportunities, and human rights—the America that we see in the movies, the America that builds dreams, and the other America—the one that kills them, the one George Bush Sr. and his foreign policy represent. I am pissed off at this one.

I am not the only one, I guess!

IX
Neutral, Objective, Bla Bla

The Syrians have won.

But life, as it tends to, goes on.

Michel Aoun survives. There's a rumor he cut a deal with the Syrians to keep his mouth shut in exchange for the lives of him and his family. He's exiled to France.

Samir Geagea accepts the Taef Agreement. He tells the soldiers in his Lebanese Forces to turn over their weapons, and he gives up his power to the Syrian-owned authorities.

Ghazi Kanaan, of course, already controls everything in the country. He makes it clear, from day one, that he is the same someone that no one messes with.

Politicians are scared to even disagree with him on the weather. His brutal reputation is the most efficient tool he has to keep everyone under strict control, and his powers are unlimited. He intimidates everyone equally, both Christians and Muslims, until he is regarded as a sultan or a king.

In no time, Beirut, which survived the scourges of wars, completely surrenders and succumbs to the secret intelligence services, just as the Syrians did before them, and people start to disappear.

The Syrians sponsor and form the first government. Unsurprisingly, it includes all the militia leaders who fought each other for years. In two words, almost every minister in this cabinet has killed at least 50 people with his own bare hands. A brilliant future is waiting for us, obviously.

It feels like the thickest, heaviest time we have ever endured. This time, we are completely defenseless, with no hope whatsoever. A bunch of gangsters, headed by a notorious Syrian officer, is defining our future, and we have to live with it.

The silence is unbearable, especially for those who fail to reprogram their brains according to the new lifestyle. I am one of those people, and the horrible silence, which prevails everywhere, is driving me insane.

I want to fight; however, fighting the Syrian regime with words and *branches of olives* sounds hilarious.

People are immensely tired from everything related to battles and fighting on both the eastern and western sides of Beirut. They seem ready to accept anything that quiets the cannons. Hypocrisy is at its peak.

I should have been in my second year of college by now had the conditions been normal. But my entire generation has lost two years of our lives because everything was paused.

I move on.

With AUB out of my reach, I decide to try Lebanese University, a public college in East Beirut. To be cautious, I attend as an auditor before officially applying.

My first journalism class is nothing like the calm, thoughtful, and scholarly atmosphere I expected. More than 600 students are gathered in an enormous and terribly noisy auditorium.

When the professor comes in, he heads straight for his desk, adjusts the microphone on it, and just starts talking. To my ear he sounds utterly bored, as if he doesn't give a damn about anything but collecting his paycheck.

He walks to the blackboard and writes "Neutrality" in big letters. Then he turns to us.

"Neutrality," he says. "That's what journalism is about. That's what you're here to learn—how to be neutral while covering a story. Neutrality is what you have to bring with you every morning in addition to your books, and also after you graduate, if you ever want to work as a journalist."

Students—including me—raise their hands. He anticipates our questions by continuing. "Of course, nobody is 100% neutral in life. When you're a journalist, however, you have to be as neutral as you can so your audience perceives you as credible."

All of the hands drop—except mine. He chooses to ignore me and writes on the board, "Credibility." When he turns around, my hand is still up.

"Yes?" he says, reluctantly calling on me.

"I don't think people should be neutral," I say. "If someone's country is occupied, you can't ask him to be objective—"

"Now you're giving a political speech," he interrupts. "That has nothing to do with journalism, Mister...?"

"Nakouzi."

"If any of you, like Mr. Nakouzi, feel you can't or shouldn't be neutral, there's no point in being here. And beyond this class, you should probably reconsider journalism as a career, to be honest."

"I think only walls are neutral, to be honest."

"Then journalism might not be the right path for you!" he replies sharply, ending the conversation. I pick up my books and leave.

I conclude this professor is an idiot.

But when I audit other journalist classes, I hear the same things: "be neutral," "be balanced," "be unbiased," "avoid opinions."

I'm the opposite of these things. I have opinions about everything! I fiercely refuse to be neutral!

I also don't understand how anyone can be "balanced" and "unbiased" while his country is occupied by thugs.

For the first time, I have serious doubts that journalism is my destiny. I have never felt this hesitant, even when I was 10 years younger. Maybe this whole journalism thing is a fantasy, I say to myself. And maybe I should start looking for a real major that can guarantee me a real job.

Two days later, I am at Notre Dame University, or the NDU.

One of the few lucky things that's happened recently is the establishment of Notre Dame University, an American-style college in East Beirut. It's not at the level of the AUB, but it offers a similar curriculum and all its courses are in English.

I take Notre Dame's English language and SAT tests. Two weeks later, I'm admitted.

My first visit is with a professor who meets all new students to discuss the career opportunities available to them. He strikes me as a polite, educated, and kind man with a consistent smile on his face.

I'm resolved to choose *something*, even if it's not

a perfect fit, just to take my mind off politics and get my life moving again.

"Economics?" the professor suggests.

"No way," I answer immediately. "There is nothing I hate more than numbers and budgets."

"Interior Design?" he offers.

"If you take one look at my room, you'll know that I'm in no position to design anything." I smile, hoping that he's not annoyed by my saying "no" to everything.

"What about Computer Science?" he asks with a large smile, as if he nailed it this time.

Before I can react, he adds, "Don't tell me you have issues with computers! Listen, the country is oversaturated with doctors, lawyers, and engineers. Computers are the future. This is a guaranteed career, son. Why don't you at least try it?"

"Computer Science," I say, nodding. *At least until I can find something else.*

As soon as I leave his office, a "what-the-fuck" feeling comes over me. *Computer Science?* I think. *You can't even stand a calculator!* But with Journalism off the table, I don't know what else to pursue.

Just as I feared, my first year of classes is dull torture. I barely manage CS.

To keep my sanity, the next year I include some elective courses that have nothing to do with career but that I'll at least find interesting. Among these is a theatre class taught by Raymond Gebara, one of the most respected playwrights in Lebanon. Gebara reminds me of Ziad: a cynical writer who portrays the dark side of human nature with a sharp sense of humor. Gebara stopped writing after he became partially paralyzed, but he's still strong enough to teach small classes.

From the first moment I see Gebara's battle-worn but always smiling face, I know that I'll love the old man.

There are only a dozen students in the course. Everyone else in the room wants to have a career in acting or directing. They consider the class as critical to their careers, because Gebara's connections can be invaluable for opening the right doors. I'm the only one there for the pure pleasure of hearing Gebara talk.

In our first session Gebara has us all sit around him in a half-circle discussing life, death, and love, and how they relate to theatre. He's famous for discovering great talents, and I assume this informal start helps him figure out the nature of his new students. Time flies by quickly. It's the first time I've seen students be disappointed when the bell rings.

As everyone prepares to leave, Gebara turns to me. "Nakouzi," he says gently, leaning all his weight on his walking stick, "will you help me to the parking lot?"

"Of course," I reply, running to aid him.

As we walk to the car, he asks, "Are you really here to learn acting, son?"

"No," I say, without even trying to lie. "I love writing, but I could never see myself acting. Honestly, I'm not taking this course because it'll lead to a job. I'm just here because I hate computers. I need to get away from cables and algorithms, and feel close to Hemingway and Shakespeare again."

"Well, I planned to make you all act different scenes from my plays in front of a live audience at the end of the three months." He pauses thoughtfully. "You know what? I have a better idea for you to get an A in this class."

"I definitely need an A," I say.

"You have a quality of voice that I've rarely heard in my long career. So while your colleagues act, you'll be narrating in the background. You can even stay behind the stage curtains if that makes you feel more comfortable," he says with a kind smile, just before his driver jumps out of the car to help him.

For three months we rehearse in the college's theatre. My colleagues have to memorize and act, while all I have to do is narrate from pages in front of me. For me it's easy and enjoyable, while my fellow students are sweating over the fact that Gebara has sent out hundreds of invitations to producers, casting directors, reviewers, and other top professionals in show business to attend the event and evaluate their work.

Finally the big day arrives. The sold-out theatre is packed with high-powered people in the arts.

The lights grow dimmer and dimmer until the room turns black. A breathtaking violin starts playing in the otherwise completely silent theatre.

Gebara is sitting with me behind the curtains. He gives me the signal to start.

My heart is pounding, even though I know it's impossible for anyone to see me. Every part of me is shaking: my hands, my knees, even my throat! Finally, I get myself together and start by announcing the title of the show.

Suddenly I undergo a transformation. The strong applause and warm feelings that come from every corner of the theatre fill me. I instantly relax and immerse myself in the natural rhythms of the production. After that I'm as comfortable as I would be reading poetry to a girl in my bedroom.

My fellow students do a great job, and the show is a rousing success. When we all take our bows, with Gebara in the middle, the audience applauds loud and long.

Afterwards Gebara makes sure to introduce the actors to every producer and director he knows, trying to create connections for future work. While we're all mingling, I suddenly hear someone asking, "And who is that voice we were hearing?"

Gebara replies quickly, as if he's been waiting for someone to ask. "That was Nakouzi!" He looks all over to find me until our eyes connect. "Nakouzi," he calls, "here's someone I think you'll be interested in meeting."

I walk over. "I'd like you to meet Mr. Moghames. He's the programming director of the radio network Voice of Lebanon."

Moghames shakes my hand warmly. "You have a great voice, son. I think you should come by for an audition."

"Anytime," I reply without hesitation.

He makes an appointment on the spot for next week.

"It's so funny," Gebara tells me later. "Of my dozen students, 11 stood on stage under bright lights. But who immediately gets chosen? The one who was hiding in the dark behind the curtains!" He chuckles. "It goes to show how predictable life can be sometimes."

"What? This is the opposite of predictable," I say, also laughing.

"You dreamed of being a journalist your whole life, right? So just when you give up on it, life throws you a reminder of who you're supposed to be. So predictable!" He insists.

The week after, I find myself in the audition hall in the radio building.

X
A Microphone With No Rebels

Around ten young men and women are waiting for their turn. They look very serious with all the notes and books they are holding. I have nothing in my hand or in my head.

I think about leaving. The youngest competitor in the room looks as old as my father. What am I doing here? I think before a man approaches me. “I am Selim,” he introduces himself.

Selim teaches Arabic and history, as he explains.

“I am a computer science student.” I smile after introducing myself.

Selim notices that I am overly relaxed, so, he reminds me that I should be nervous, “because it’s a big deal to have an audition at such a distinguished radio station.”

I don’t feel this way; I am comfortable as one could be. I am not taking this thing very seriously.

Someone from inside the studio comes out and calls my name. He walks me inside the studio.

I see a woman behind a large glass that separates the studio from a control room. She's in her forties and looks very elegant. Her features show the strain of hard times, and although she seems very professional, there is an air of toughness about her.

When she sees me, she gives me a nod and a gentle smile from behind the glass. I throw her a polite smile before the sound engineer shows me how to use the headphones and tells me to face the microphone. He leaves me alone in the room. I can't hear any noise with those headphones on.

The woman is busy talking to another gentleman, who appears to be almost the same age as she is. He is intently listening to what she is saying, and from the grin on both of their faces, they don't look very satisfied with the last candidate who finished before me.

I am taken in all of the beautiful aspects of the studio—the elegant leather chairs, the classy table, the professional headphones on my ears, and the high-tech microphone. This is the big time, and I can't help but be impressed. The very smooth voice of the woman in the other room interrupts my thoughts.

"Good morning, Elie. I am Wardeh (Rose in English)," she says gently.

"You're the Wardeh," I ask, a little surprised. She's one of the most familiar voices we grew up listening to.

Everyone knows Wardeh and her political needles that she jabs at politicians on her weekly radio show. I had no idea it was going to be Wardeh I was auditioning for. She's a celebrity, and I am a huge fan.

"Yes," she smiles back, "the Wardeh," she confirms. "I'd like you to simply tell us why you want to be a radio host," she says, getting back to the point. "There's a pen and paper if you want to write down some notes before you start. You have a couple of minutes to make yourself comfortable with the studio."

"Thank you," I say, "but I don't think I need them; I can start immediately."

"Will you repeat that again please?" she asks in the same lovely tone.

"I mean, my notes are in my head. I don't need to

write them down."

"Did you hear that?" she says to her assistant.

I've barely said one word, I think to myself. Have I screwed it because I said I have no notes?

"Please go on, Elie. Why do you want to be a radio host?"

"Well, I think your station is missing a young voice—someone who represents the youth in this country and who can talk about their problems, their ambitions, and their dreams without being loyal to this or that party—"

"Please go on," She interrupts me in the middle of my thesis, and she leaves the room.

"Go on, go on, please," the sound engineer repeats, when he notices my reluctance.

I continue, with a less excited tone, though. "I simply believe that all our politicians are hypocrites, and they should be held accountable for their actions. If young people like me don't have a voice in Lebanon, then—"

"Thank you," the sounds engineer interrupts again. "Mrs. Wardeh is waiting for you in her office. Could you please meet her up in the fourth floor?"

"Sure," I say. I was just describing her by being super rude in my head for leaving the room like this, but now I feel okay.

I am impressed by Wardeh's huge office. She invites me in and takes a seat behind a classic and stylish desk. I can easily tell she is a big shot in the network.

"Listen, I am interested in hearing more about your ideas. How old are you again?"

"I am twenty-seven."

"Really?"

"Actually, I'll be twenty-seven in a couple of months or so."

"Or so… Hmm! So, you're twenty-six. Anyway, tell me more about your plans. Do you have a particular show in mind that you want to host?"

"Yes," I say, and I shoot: "I will bring five or six brilliant college students every week: Muslims, Christians, Sunnis, Shiites, atheists… Students from different political parties and ideologies and from all over the country. I will put them in the same room with a politician to grill. We'll simply barbecue them—"

"I am starting to like the smell of your barbecue, especially that you included Muslims and Christians together in your studio." She seems intrigued by the idea. "Now, tell me, seriously, how old are you?" she insists on that point again. I can't tell her that I am only twenty-one there's no way she'll give me a chance if she knows.

"You want the truth?"

"Yes, please," she smiles behind her glasses.

"I am twenty-four." I lie.

The intrigue she was just showing on her face starts to vanish. "Okay! Let's forget about that now. Tell me, what kind of issues will you be talking about with your rebels in the studio?"

"We'll talk about everything: corruption, lack of freedom, education, economy… everything. Listen, hundreds of thousands of Lebanese people grew up listening to your radio station during the war. This station was the most credible source of news that people turned to when they wanted to know what was really happening. There was a kind of loyalty that people had toward this network, but now that the war is practically over, it is an opportunity for the 'Voice of Lebanon' to be the voice of the youth, also… the voice of the future."

"We'll call your show 'The Voice of the Youth'… No, no, no! We'll call it 'The Parliament of the Youth.' That's a better name. You're hired." She chuckles.

"I am twenty-three."

"Oh, come on!" she says. She sighs and looks at me over the large desk. She looks disappointed. "Elie, I can't put a twenty-three year-old on the air. Listen, your ideas are great, and you sound so full of energy and action, but you're too young for headaches. It is a minefield out there, you know."

"I love headaches," I say, trying to convince her. "Really, I truly love headaches. I am not just saying that to impress you, seriously!" I repeat it again.

"I believe you. I know someone who's exactly like you." She taps her pen on a stack of papers on her desk. "I will bet on you. You have three months to train and prepare a pilot," she says.

"You'll win the bet," I reply, with full confidence.

Wardeh is not officially the CEO of the radio station, but she acts as if she is. It's known that the head of the network never argues or objects to anything she says.

In no time, I am introduced to the whole staff, which mainly consists of voices that I grew up hearing my entire life. Suddenly, I have faces for all those voices, and they all look so different from how I had imagined them in my head.

It's all so exciting, and I love being part of it: the hosts running quickly in the hallways toward the studio to broadcast live-breaking news; the editors and reporters who come in and out, each with an obvious desire to catch a scoop here or there; the writers sitting in front of their blank pages, agonizing to come up with a new idea that hasn't been discussed on the radio yet.

Everything is so charming and irresistible; however, nothing is more orgasmic than sitting behind the microphone. I fell in love with that microphone from the first moment we met; it is such a magnificent tool that has the power to amplify my unheard, low voice. It’s exactly what I need!

After some time, we finally set up a date for the pilot. My first mission is to look for blunt, straightforward, and brave young graduates to confront a politician in a civilized, yet provocative manner. I have enough brilliant, educated Christian friends to fill five studios; however, I don't know even one Mohamed or Mahmoud to invite.

I contact the dean of students at one of the biggest universities in West Beirut, and he puts me in touch with some of his best students.

Finally, we're in the studio.

We have a politician that Wardeh has helped me contact. He agreed to take part in the show after I explained how important it is to listen to the voices of the youth.

For two consecutive hours, my guests grill him. He's completely unable to face the waves of criticism that are coming from every corner. He is bombarded, and the last minutes are so torturing, he can't stop looking at his watch, clearly regretting he accepted the invitation.

The pilot is a success. Wardeh is impressed. She says I have handled the explosive situations like a real expert. Truth is, I did nothing special, and the things that impressed her came up effortlessly, as if I was born in a studio.

For the first time in my life, I am asked to sign a contract. When I reveal my real age to Wardeh, she pretends she didn't hear me. "Just make sure you're not seventeen by the time you reach the lobby," she winks at me, "it would be illegal to employ a minor, you know." She closes the subject forever.

Years ago, the microphone was just a fantasy, but now, it has turned into a reality with a weekly show on the most popular radio station in the country. From my very first episode, I feel like I don't need notes like my other colleagues use. My introduction, my questions, and my points of discussion are all in my head; I can see them clearly, as if they are written on a screen or a prompter in front of me.

I felt so incapable and helpless before the show, but now, I feel that I have a voice. I have no clue where this will take me. But I find immense charm in unpredictable journeys. My life is now on the track I have always dreamed about.

I am finally on the air; however, Wardeh insists I stay away from super-sensitive issues, like religion, Israel, the Syrian occupation, and such taboos, which, in her opinion, risk blowing the entire show.

She is an expert, and she knows that the minute we start talking about those issues, Muslims and Christians will immediately take opposite sides, each in their sectarian or religious bubble. And this is an ugly truth that I don't think Wardeh wants to promote, especially having just come out of a long war.

According to her, the country is now supposed to

focus on what brings us together, not on what might break us apart again.

I am a newcomer to the industry, whereas she has years of experience, so I believe she might be right. Perhaps it is not a bad idea to focus on the things that link us together instead of complaining about our differences day and night. Maybe we need to put it all behind our backs so we can move forward.

Anyway, Wardeh has a big impact on how I am starting to see things; she is a positive person who simply believes that the country can still get over the war: that it is not a hopeless case, yet.

Her positive views reflect on my attitude, and for a while, I stop listening to Ziad Rahbani. His realities are dark and pessimistic, and I just need to breathe a different air.

Wardeh keeps a good distance from her employees, and she has a significant effect over everyone. But with me, things are completely different. I can call her anytime, knock on her office door with no appointment, and even take her out to lunch. We drink coffee together almost daily. I guess she enjoys my company and my enthusiastic theories.

Three months later, I accidently meet a redheaded, cute girl in the Radio building's elevator. Her name is Zeina, and she's no one but Wardeh's daughter. We immediately start dating.

Zeina is young, fresh, innocent, and very funny to be around. She and I have a joyful and cool relationship, despite all the tongues that never stop knitting stories about us.

As for Wardeh, she always pretends that she has

never heard anything from the blabbermouths, although she always knows who sneezes, at what time, and on which floor.

Once a week, Wardeh invites us, her daughter and me, to dinner. She picks one of the best restaurants in Beirut, where half of the ministers and the deputies of the country usually dine. Whenever she walks in, every politician stands up to salute her. She has an immense respect among them, and I admire her more and more as time passes.

She is a successful, powerful businesswoman in a world where most men believe that women are only "tools of reproduction and cleaning." I enjoy watching the various politicians come over to our table to chat with her, ask for some advice, and kiss her ass just to get a good comment in her show because her tongue can be very bitter when she wants to criticize someone. I am completely captivated by her strength, although she has no guns and militias behind backing her up. She only uses her words as weapons.

And although I disagree with her opinions often, it is always a great delight to debate with her. Her strong views are always backed up with facts, which makes her really hard to beat in an argument. But these debates help me strengthen my dialogue skills and evidence, and Wardeh's personality has a huge impact on my character and, thus, on my career.

When one of our sound engineers was insulted by the president's bodyguard while covering a press conference, Wardeh has taught every politician a lesson.

Amir, a 25-year-old sound engineer at the radio station, had noticed at the last second that the president's microphone was still off, so he ran quickly to turn it on before the latter started his speech.

One of the bodyguards got really pissed off by Amir's behavior. He pulled him violently by his jacket and slapped him in the face in front of all the reporters who were covering the event.

When Wardeh heard about the incident, she called the president and insisted that he and his bodyguard apologize to Amir; however, the president didn't call her back. The next morning, she announced the story in her show and declared that she would boycott all the presidential activities unless the president himself apologized.

Our president, Elias Hrawi, is known to be very stubborn. He ignores her for an entire week, hoping that she'd back off. Wardeh escalates and stops even mentioning him in the news bulletins, as if he didn't exist. She was even ready to escalate more when she received the call from the presidential palace informing her that the president had approved her request. She took Amir by the hand and accompanied him to see the president to make sure that his "honor" was completely restored. After the incident, my admiration for her quadrupled.

There is actually nothing to complain about in my first year in radio. I am happy, satisfied, and financially stable. The show becomes more popular, and I have more than a thousand phone numbers and addresses of young graduates from all over the country in my contact book.

However, the vast number of people with completely different political views and ideologies enlightens me to the fact that our country needs more than polite talk and fake smiles to really heal; there is still a huge, visible gap between Christians and Muslims.

Week after week, the social and cultural issues I usually discuss with my guests start to sound boring and inefficient.

I want to dig deeper into politics and break down the taboos about controversial issues networks usually avoid talking about. I want to break some taboos, some golden rules!

I know Wardeh will need convincing, so I decide to secretly tape a test show to prove there's merit to this bolder approach. I skip including a politician, and instead invite eight of the most thoughtful and responsible young people who've appeared on my show before to dig into an explosive topic: Israel. I want them to discuss whether Arabs should keep fighting Israel, or sign a peace treaty and accept the Israelis as neighbors.

It doesn't go as I'd hoped.

My introduction contains no personal opinions, just a series of provocative questions. It doesn't matter. Three of the Muslims interrupt me every time I mention Israel to scold me.

"You can't say *Israel,"* they object. "You must say *the enemy Israel*. Otherwise it's deeply offensive to our Arab nation."

When I'm done explaining the segment, all my Muslim guests refuse to participate in the show unless everyone in the room promises to consistently refer to Israel as *the enemy*. I refuse to give in to their nonsense. One of them replies, "Having anything to do with a show like this is treason." Then they all leave.

My Christian guests are as surprised as I am. We know Israel is a delicate subject for Muslims, but never imagined it is still forbidden to even discuss it.

If Christians and Muslims can't even talk about the issues that are at the heart of what divides us, what's the point of doing my show? I think to myself. I'm creating a sham in which Christians and Muslims get along; but just underneath the smiling surface, both sides are ready for the smallest excuse to kill each other.

XI
Vodka

It's been fun for this first year, but I suddenly have a discouraging feeling that tiptoeing around subjects won't solve anything. I feel down and gloomy, and the first thing I do when I return back home is bring up Ziad's tapes again.

"A Long American Movie" is my absolute favorite and, perhaps, his masterpiece.

Listening to Ziad ignites me all over again. Suddenly, all those positive views about turning a blind eye to the things that divide us seems like nonsense. Whose fool enough to believe that the ugly truths will disappear if we just stop looking at them?

Ziad's blunt realities make me feel like what I am doing on the radio is void, empty, and somehow futile if it doesn't tackle the sensitive issues that ignited the war in the first place.

I wish I could get him in for an interview; he's, perhaps, the only person who could shake things up and motivate all the youth, regardless of their religious beliefs. But it's almost impossible to even get his number, maybe harder than reaching the American president. I heard that Ziad was in complete isolation. He refuses to see anyone, and he made it clear a long time ago that he never does interviews.

I become more obsessed. I ask Wardeh if she knows of any number I could reach him on. She gives me an old number she has but warns me against getting my hopes up. She also is a great fan of Ziad, and she knows well about his moody character.

Anyway, I have his number now, and that is a good start.

As soon as I am back in my office, I dial the number three or four times before I finally muster the nerve to allow the call to ring through. Someone answers.

"Hello, may I speak with… Ziad Rahbani, please?" I stutter.

"I am Ziad Rahbani. Who is this?"

My heart leaps into my throat. It takes me a minute before I can regain speech. "I am sorry… but I have pictured an imaginary strict, uptight secretary who would answer the phone and start asking me questions. 'Who is this? How may I help you? What is the reason behind your call?'"

"Yeah! Fuck her. I hate her, too," he says and laughs.

I laugh, too. I become more relaxed. "Truth is, I have so many things to tell you, I don't even know where to start?"

"Start from the very end; I like the end," he answers quickly, in his special and unique tone.

"Okay, from the very end. Listen, I am one of those hundreds of thousands that grew up listening to your plays. I have memorized them word for word; I can recite them all by heart if you like. Your music: I don't have enough words to describe your music, except that… your music was in the background when I lost my virginity."

That makes him laugh now. "Which one is that?" he asks.

"'Abou Ali,'" I answer. "It is very successful with

women, trust me," I say. "It's like magic… Anyway, I think I have an interesting idea that I'd like to discuss with you but not on the phone. If you will allow me to see you for a half hour, then I will be able to explain more."

"If you will only tell me who this is?" he says.

"Of course, of course." I tell him my name. "I am a host for 'Voice of Lebanon.'"

"I am truly honored, but if this is about an interview, then don't bother because—"

"No, no, no. It is not. Look, forget about interviews, cameras, and microphones; I know you're not talking to the press. My idea is totally unconventional. Give me 30 minutes, and if you don't like it, you'll never hear from me again," I promise him. "Look, I have never dreamed of meeting anyone as much as I have dreamed of meeting you. I know that thousands like me worship you and you don't have the time for them all; however—"

"No wonder they hired you at a radio station. Your tongue definitely works from the bottom of its heart. Would you like to pass by my house tomorrow at seven in the evening?"

"What?" I am stunned. I can't believe it has actually worked. "Seriously? Or you're just shutting me up… because I will be at your door exactly at seven tomorrow."

"I am expecting you at seven tomorrow," he chuckles. He sounds serious.

It was unbelievably easy!

For me, Ziad is the equivalent of John Lennon, Roger Waters, or Woody Allen, or all of these combined maybe, and still, he picks up the phone himself and talks to me personally. Not only that, but I have an appointment with him. The prospect of meeting him twists my stomach in a way I haven't experienced since Carol agreed to go out with me.

The next day, at seven exactly, I knock on his door. It takes around thirty seconds for him to open. He looks very casual in blue jeans and a white sweatshirt. He is a little shorter than I am, and it is obvious he hasn't been to the gym for more than twenty years. I am utterly mesmerized standing in his doorway. It's actually Ziad Rahbani.

"Ahlen (Welcome)," he says. "Come in!" He stretches out his hand. "I am Ziad Rahbani!"

I laugh like a girl with a crush on a rock star. "You don't have to tell me who you are; I even know the size of your shoes."

"Really? What size?"

"Forty."

He explodes with laughter; it apparently sounds very funny to him that I know such a personal detail about him. He has a special kind of laughter that ends with a heavy snore, but still, it is funny and somehow cute. He takes me inside the apartment, and we sit in a very modest living room.

I spent all last night thinking of something brilliant to make Ziad laugh, but it only took a small, silly comment to please the man who makes millions of Arabs fall back on their backs from laughter.

His laughter breaks the ice, and I feel more comfortable. It doesn't take long before Ziad asks me to choose between vodka and coffee, the only available options he has.

"Vodka," I reply quickly. Coffee means the

session will only last for 30 minutes or so, but vodka? It will be at least an hour and a half kind of session, I assume. He brings a bottle of Stolichnaya and apologizes that it is not cold enough, as if I am really paying attention to the temperature of the bottle. He spends more than ten minutes explaining, in detail, that the freezer has stopped working.

"It's refusing to make ice now," he explains, "and I think it is doing it on purpose." He laughs. "Perhaps it is starting to confuse itself with a hair dryer or something. It just melts the ice now," he says, and we both chuckle. "It's a problem, because I can't tell whether the vodka is really from Russia or a local counterfeit," he explains.

"What exactly does your freezer have to do with that?"

"To find out how genuine vodka is, all you have to do is put it in the freezer and then pour a glass. If it has small chunks of ice in it, then it's been mixed with water."

"Hm," I say. "If this is really from Lebanon, we could be drinking vodka mixed with Benzene." I take a big gulp.

"Exactly," he says, taking a bigger one.

He is simple and easy to be with. We start drinking the stiff, heartburning vodka at approximately seven; ten minutes later, Ziad is already pouring us a second glass. He doesn't even ask me about the reason for my visit. Instead, the conversation leads us to his plays, his music, and the radio show he once hosted.

We sit for more than two hours drinking vodka, smoking cigarettes, and shooting bull like old friends.

I try to explain what a genius I think he is. It

electrifies him to even hear the word genius. “If you want us to be friends, never call me genius again,” he says seriously.

I suggest we name the country after his mother, “Fairuz instead of Lebanon”. He laughs.

“If you love Fairuz so much, then you'll love the album I am preparing for her.” He stands up and brings over a CD to show me. “It is a tribute to my father. To Assi I will call it. It's a re-arrangement of his most popular music and songs in a completely new distribution. I am putting them in one album. Would you like to listen to the unfinished—”

“Are you kidding me?” I ask before he can finish. He puts the CD in a hi-tech stereo, which is the only lavish thing in the apartment.

“Like I said, it is not complete yet,” he says. He’s known to be super perfectionist and only few people are privileged to listen to the unfinished “masterpiece”. I am one of them. *Oh, I am so fucking lucky.*

We listen to every song, growing more and more moved by the slow and sad melodies. I am in a different world. Every time a song ends, I beg him to play it again and again. We are on our second bottle of vodka by this point.

“Look, I still have no idea what you came here to talk about, but we're both too drunk to discuss anything serious tonight.”

“Absolutely… I can come some other time if you'd like me to.”

“Sure,” he says. We stand up and walk to the door.

It's a night to remember. I wouldn't have pictured myself getting drunk with Ziad, even in my wildest dreams. On my way home, I can't stop humming the breathtaking songs I am lucky to have heard before they are released; it is a privilege of its own. They're stuck in my head like a sweet, sweet dream.

Just the idea of seeing him again sounds unreal, but I am so concerned he might forget about me that I call him two days later. He recognizes me immediately and invites me to visit him on the weekend. This time, he introduces me to his girlfriend, Carmen. She looks like she doesn't trust her shadow, but it seems like she also likes my company. We don't talk about the reasons why I wanted to meet Ziad in the first place. We listen to music, we drink, we laugh, and Ziad plays the piano. And when he improvises, he can put the walls in tears.

On my second visit Ziad introduces me to his girlfriend Carmen. She looks like she doesn't trust her shadow, but she accepts me. I sense she welcomes someone who might reconnect Ziad with the outside world.

Once again we drink, laugh, and listen to music. At one point Ziad starts playing the piano. When he improvises music, he can set the walls to tears.

I come to realize how enormously isolated Ziad is. He's lost faith in his country and, worse, his people, so he lives very humbly with his lovely girlfriend and his compositions.

I want Ziad to see how incredibly influential he is to my generation. I wait until we're half-buzzed to finally bring it up.

"I have a suggestion," I begin. "You don't want to do interviews, and I respect your decision. But, how about meeting with young students without cameras or microphones—no media coverage at all, if you prefer. We can do it in a college auditorium: an invitation for graduates to come and chat with Ziad Rahbani. We can even take our vodka with us! I will hide it in soda cans; it will be just an informal conversation with young students. If you don't like what you see, we'll leave immediately. You can't say no to such a suggestion."

I rest my case.

"Come on, Ziad, you got nothing to lose," Carmen says. "If you don't like it, then leave immediately."

"No media coverage," he insists.

"No media coverage," says Carmen on my behalf.

"You will put Vodka in a soda can?" he asks.

"Stolichnaya… frozen," I assure him.

"Okay."

After convincing him, we set the date. My college, the NDU, is more than delighted to receive Ziad Rahbani after I offer to bring him in for an intimate exclusive chitchat with the students. It is still a young establishment and can definitely use this kind of publicity.

Meanwhile, I am still hosting my show, but all my excitement is now focused on Ziad's event. The debates, which once seemed so revolutionary, suddenly seem boring and nonsense.

The day has finally come.

In my car I drive Ziad to NDU. I borrowed my father's car especially for this occasion. It's early summer and it's getting really hot, especially in the traffic jams. My father's car has an air conditioner. I would do anything to make the ride comfortable. I don't want anything to bother him.

As I expected, we get caught in a traffic jam. I

close the windows and turn on the AC. But two minutes later, just when we start to cool down, Ziad asks me to shut it off.

"Are you kidding me, Nakouzi?" he says. "People are suffocating in their cars while we enjoy this cool breeze. This is so ugly, turn it off."

"Of course," I answer, not even trying to argue.

We finally arrive to our destination. As we enter the parking lot, we see it is packed with cars.

Inside the NDU campus, almost every student in the college is there to greet us. They welcome him warmly, surrounding both of us. Everyone is trying to talk to him.

Ziad looks at me, seriously shocked from the number of students that showed up. "Are all these people with us, or against us?" He asks me.

A very sexy girl succeeds in penetrating the crowd and hugs Ziad tightly. She kisses him hard on the cheek. With tears in her eyes, she looks straight into his and says, "You are my freedom." Ziad is speechless. Even him, the great Ziad Rahbani, can't find the right words. He looks so touched by the reception. I give him a triumphant 'I told you' look before we walk inside the big auditorium.

Finally, we take our seats at a long table with two soda cans and a microphone waiting for us. The crowd is cheering enthusiastically.

"Ziad! Ziad! Ziad!"

It calms down a little. Then a session of crazy questions and crazier answers begins. It lasts for more than 3 hours.

The event with Ziad becomes the talk of the college for weeks. He full trusts me now that he even accepts to write a song for me. I have been approached by many singers that offered Ziad Rahbani hundreds of thousands of dollars for an album. He turned them all down. However, it takes him 2 seconds to approve my request, completely for free. It's not that I ever wanted to be a singer in my life; however, putting my name next to Ziad's on anything is a great privilege that I won't miss.

In fact, Ziad also enjoyed the NDU event that he's convinced to take it to another level. I suggest a bigger hall, where we can invite graduates from all over the country.

This time, he agrees to invite the press after we were hugely criticized for not airing or taping the first event. "The Picadelli Theater," he recommends.

The Picadelli is actually one of the biggest theaters in Beirut, and I am sure it's gonna be packed, too.

Meanwhile, the flame I once felt for the radio is quickly fading. Ziad has awoken something in me again; I surround myself with books, and the old passion for writing suddenly bubbles to the surface. Ziad is so opinionated; he can provoke anyone to write.

Being around him has also given me a huge push of confidence. "If a genius like Ziad Rahbani finds me interesting enough to spend hours with, then I am certainly someone interesting enough," I flatter myself. I also have strong, controversial opinions about everything around me; however, my radio show just doesn't seem to be the platform to express them anymore.

The show has become too shallow, and many friends quickly notice my passion is fading. Above all this, Zeina and I break up after she finds out about my hidden adventures with many women, here and there.

I have a deep desire to resign. But I have a steady income at the radio station that I can't afford to lose. My lifestyle is getting a little more sophisticated and costly, especially with all the expensive bills from the fancy restaurants and clubs I have become accustomed to.

When Ziad is in a good mood, we—Roula, the hot journalist I am now dating, Carmen, and I—take him to new restaurants we never thought he'd go to. People embrace him every time they recognize him. They surround him with questions and autographs to sign. I invite Roula to host the Picadelli interview with me. She accepts without hesitation. She's also obsessed with Ziad as much as I am.

It is finally time for the Picadelli event. The theater is overflowing with young students, just like I imagined it would be. There isn't an empty inch in the room. Ziad, Roula, and I are sitting at a table in the middle of the theater, with three cans of "soda" on the table, of course.

Cameras and microphones are everywhere.

Many journalists and reporters sit in the front seats. Ziad and I look very casual for such a big event; however, from the dress she is wearing, it's obvious that Roula is taking it much more seriously.

After the introduction, Ziad starts answering the questions of the audience. Two hours of hilarious conversations ensue before a young woman reaches the microphone. She looks a little angry.

"My name is Katia, and I would like to ask an audacious question that I truly hope to get an honest answer for," she says with confidence. "A la Ziad Rahbani, if possible?"

"I will do my best to be audacious," he sincerely replies.

"Do you agree that your mother, Fairuz, the great icon of this country, sings in a concert that is organized and sponsored by Solidere, the company that is owned by Rafic Hariri, or excuse me…" she twists into a sarcastic tone, "Sheikh Rafic Hariri, the Saudi sultan."

The crowd loves what she has said; they applaud and whistle like crazy. "Solidere is a company that kicked thousands of citizens from their old homes just to build a tourist area for the Gulf princes to fornicate. Do you think it is appropriate for the great Fairuz to sing right in the center of that new, fake Beirut that they're building?" she asks.

The crowd is all heated up. They love the tough question that Katia just asked.

"No," Ziad replies simply, "I don't think Fairuz should sing there."

"If you don't think she should sing, then why don't you sign our petition," says Katia, who's still holding the microphone and refuses to hand it to anyone else. She holds up a petition that has Fairuz's picture on it with the words, "Fairuz, say no to the sultan."

"Definitely," he says. "Bring your petition, and I will certainly sign it."

Katia makes her way between the audiences. She can't believe he is agreeing to sign a petition against his mother's concert. The crowd cheers again.

"Ziad! Ziad! Ziad!"

Ziad signs the petition, and the hall explodes with applauds.

The next morning, we're on the headlines of all

three main newspapers. Our picture is on the front pages. One headline reads, "Ziad Rahbani to His Mother: Say No to the Sultan."

I check these newspapers twelve times. I just can't get enough after reading the same article again and again.

The interview was aired live on three local channels and the response is unbelievable; one TV appearance is enough to create the buzz of 300 episodes on the radio, perhaps more.

Amazing!

A few days later I receive a call from Walid Azzi, who recently became the General Manager of TV's ICN (International Communications Network).

"Congratulations, son. I've watched your interview with Ziad Rahbani. It was funny, dramatic, and controversial. That's the perfect recipe for television.

"Look, ICN is number eight in the ratings right now. I aim to turn it into number two within four years. Would you like to join my team?"

"You mean host a TV show?" I ask. I can barely contain my enthusiasm.

"A live primetime TV show, uncensored. I'll give you a studio with the latest equipment. Fill it with students and let them grill politicians. You've been doing this for a while on the radio, so know exactly what's involved."

"No censorship? Even on political issues?" I ask.

"No censorship, *especially* on political issues," he says. "The owner, Henry Sfeir, wants a controversy every week to break the fucking silence in this country. Can you do this?"

"You can definitely count on me to make some

noise."

"Fine, then. Bring your lucky pen, and come over to my office tomorrow at 9:00. I'll make you a good offer."

I'm amazed at how all this is turning out. *A live TV show*, I think to myself. *This is big*.

I call up Wardeh's assistant and tell her I need to see our boss urgently. She tells me to come right over.

When I enter her office, before we even make eye contact, Wardeh shoots at me, "Which network?"

"ICN," I say.

Wardeh smiles. "Television is a completely new journey. It's a much bigger audience, more fame, and more influence. You'll be a big star one day. Enjoy the ride."

XII
You Better Know When To Stop

I pack my stuff silently, and then I stare for a long moment at my name crafter on my locker. I feel nostalgic, and I already miss the place. I walk inside the studio and sit on the table. I stare at the microphone and apologize to it for the treason. I have to move forward.

My mother doesn't like the TV idea. She's very worried. She thinks I'm uncontrollable and that I will end up pissing someone off. "This is exactly why I want a TV show," I tease her, "to piss someone off." She begs me not to do it. She becomes more worried. "What happened to computer science?" she asks. "Why don't you go back to computers?"

"I shifted my major to management of international affairs and politics," I remind her again. She obviously forgets the stories she doesn't like. She doesn't even recognize that this is a factual major: international affairs and politics. "International what?" she laughs. "We can't even deal with our local crap," she reminds me.

She's not comfortable with the entire thing but knows there's not much she can do. I plant one of those long, sticky kisses on her cheek. She relaxes a little and ends up choosing the tie I will wear for the important meeting with Azzi.

Inside his office, Azzi receives me warmly and immediately suggests we take a little tour inside the building to show me around. The man doesn't waste time at all. I like it.

It is obviously a new operation. One can easily see that many of the cameras and sound equipment are still unpacked. Azzi shows me the newsroom, the control rooms, and the editing rooms: I guess he is showing off a little. But it's fine, I am liking it all. Finally, he stops at the floor with the studios; there are three of them of different sizes.

"I don't think this is big enough," he points at the first one. "You gotta choose one of these two," he says, as he enters one of them. "This can hold at least eight guests, in addition to you," he smiles. "And this," he continues, as we walk into the biggest one, "This is where you should play your game, son."

The studio can fit twenty or even twenty-five guests easily.

"Can you fill a studio like this with twenty brilliant, outspoken graduates to grill politicians weekly?" he asks me, with a challenging smile on his face.

"I can fill double this studio?" I say, challenging him back and throwing him approximately the same smile he still has on his face.

"Are these just words, or are you sure you can do this?" he turns a little serious.

"I have the phone numbers of a thousand graduates who would die to have the chance to explode on TV," I confirm.

"I can make that happen for them," he says. He walks me to the elevator and pushes the button down to the lobby. "Let me show you this." He walks toward a big door and asks the guard to open it.

It's a medium-sized auditorium with about

seventy-five chairs. The stage is huge, though, and Azzi takes no time to explain. “We can transform this auditorium into a studio,” he suggests. “We'll set up a fancy design on the stage for you and your initial guest,” he explains. “And your guests can fuck him up from the audience.” He points at the chairs.

He offers $1500 per episode; I would have settled for $300, quite honestly. I am so lucky that he didn’t ask me about my expectations before he made his generous offer; I would have even done it for $250.

“That's $6000 a month; $7500 when the months include five weeks.” I talk to myself like a fool as I jump into my car. Compared with the minimum wage in the country, which is about $200 dollars monthly, this is a salary of a rich man. Would a doctor make this much? I flatter myself when I tell my mother about her soon-to-be-wealthy son.

I am once again getting paid for something I would have done for free. I would have even paid a network to grant me such an uncensored platform.

Before I launch the show, Azzi introduces me to the network’s owner.

Henry is polite and classy, but he seldom smiles. His face looks permanently angry, even when he says something funny.

“Do you know who Roosevelt is, Mr. Nakouzi?” he asks in a half-arrogant tone, as he inhales his cigarette.

“Of course, I do.” I smile at him.

“We have nothing to fear…” he pauses, waiting for me to finish the quote.

“…Except fear itself,” I say to fill in the blank for him and to show him that I know a couple of things.

"Exactly," he says cheerfully, as if I made his day. "My friends and my financial advisors think I must be crazy to invest this kind of money on a TV network. It's just a waste of money they say."

I nod in agreement. I know that only a couple of TV channels make profits, and the rest all have to struggle for funding. "So, why did you open a TV network?" I ask. "Look. They have fucked the country, stolen it, and sold it for cheap," he says, shaking his head. "I just can't watch my country being raped like this. I am fighting them… everybody," he is becoming a little angry and patriotic at the same time. His face is all red. He sounds crazy but sincere. I like being around crazy, sincere people; I just admire them.

The meeting lasts for more than an hour, and Sfeir simply attacks everybody, starting with the Syrian regime, passing by the president, the prime minister, the militias, and every politician in the entire country.

At the end of the meeting, he confirms, again, that the network will broadcast my show live on air without implementing any kind of censorship.

"Bring all political parties," he recommends. "Invite Hezbollah also. Why not? Hezbollah is part of the Lebanese people, and we should start talking to each other," he continues, "after all, this is not a platform for Christians; ICN is a national network that represents everyone," he concludes in his usual presidential tone.

Henry is single, and his family is known to be one of the oldest families in the province of Kesrewan in Mount Lebanon. He clearly has some political ambitions to run for a parliamentary seat. The TV network is obviously not a financial investment for him; it's a political one.

He has progressive ideas, which call for true independence, democracy, and secularism. Thus, he's my ally by default.

A talented team has been assigned for my show, which has the same title as my radio program, "The Parliament Of the Youth".

From my very first episode, the buzz begins. The episode is about the Prime Minister Rafic Hariri and how the youth in the country perceive him.

Rafic Hariri appeared in Beirut a couple of years ago in 1992. Like many Lebanese at that time, we heard his name in the news, but we never really knew who he was except that he had left Lebanon when he was very young and somehow gotten close to King Fahd of Saudi Arabia and returned as a billionaire to Beirut.

The man is described as being a successful businessman who established a company that specializes in building and maintaining the extravagant palaces of the royal Saudi family. In fact, he is one of the closest people to the Saudi king, and with the latter's blessing, he decided to return back and "rebuild his home country."

His close status with King Fahd has opened the international doors wide for Hariri. He has big business deals and investments all over Europe and the United States, and he is now recognized as one of the wealthiest and most influential figures in the Middle East.

Before he arrived in Beirut, rumors said he had more than $20 billion in his account. It was actually a very smart campaign to imply that Hariri was not coming to government to steal, like most politicians are known to do, but to spend from his own pocket to rebuild the stricken country.

Part of his indirect campaign focused also on his vision to rebuild the capital as a new, modern city after removing all the traces of destruction and war. In essence, Hariri is a big tycoon who is perceived as a savior by 90 percent of the Sunnis in Lebanon.

As for the majority of the Shiites, who are mainly loyal to Hezbollah, Hariri is someone they will never trust. They accuse him, directly or indirectly, of secretly sponsoring and promoting peace with Israel, which is an unforgivable sin, especially when Israel is *still* occupying the south of Lebanon. To them, rebuilding the city only means that Hariri, as a Muslim, has abandoned the idea of war with Israel from his plans; furthermore, he always seems suspicious to them.

On the other hand, the Christians feel that Hariri deserves a chance, although they also have many doubts about his relationship with the Syrian regime. However, his moderate stances and public statements help to briefly calm down their concerns.

To me, Hariri is a Saudi Sheikh; I am not even sure he is Lebanese. I know nothing about him except he is rich and close to the royal families of the Gulf. And this is barely enough to solve any of the deep issues that have accumulated for years. Above all, I don't really trust his plans for rebuilding the country.

To begin with, he contracted a huge company to rebuild the old Beirut with the latest architectural techniques, which will make it look exactly like it was before all the destruction. The pictures of the future Beirut that Solidere, the contracted company, have published are breathtaking. The plan is magical, charming, and full of hope except that the company is owned by Hariri, himself, which raises a number of question in the heads of many people, including mine.

In a civilized country, this undoubtedly would be a scandal that inflames the press; however, the media in Beirut, or most of the media, to be fair, has gilded the issue, as if nothing is wrong with it.

In fact, the new prime minister also built a media empire that included a new TV network by the name of Future TV, a radio station, and a newspaper that promote him and his political agenda 24 hours a day. And not only that, but he also bought shares in almost all the major TV networks and newspapers, even the most respectful ones.

The wisdom in Saudi Arabia, where Hariri matured politically, is to always buy the problems instead of trying to resolve them. It is an approach that the Saudis have never hidden, and it is no secret that they pay big bucks for journalists, writers, authors, and politicians to praise them.

Hariri seems to be replicating that approach in Beirut. In just one year, he was able to buy many voices that polish his image day and night, no matter what he does. Newspapers, radio, TV networks, politicians, writers, intellectuals, and journalists all serve as part of his army of people and glorify him.

However, there are still some decent people that criticize Hariri no matter how hard he tries. There are only a few of them, but they attack him relentlessly and accuse him of bribing the entire community. Yet, their voices are too soft and inefficient to stand in his way.

Of course, the huge projects that Hariri purported could never have seen the light if Syria hadn't approved them; therefore, the stink of huge bribes to Syrian officers to keep them off his back started to surface. The expensive gifts that Hariri sends to the Syrians could probably build three Beirut's.

In his defense, some argue he has to bribe them or his projects will never be completed.

Hariri follows the path of keeping the Syrians happy instead of confronting them. He never says anything to piss them off. The man behaves like a tycoon or a great sultan in Beirut, but when he is in Damascus, he shrinks into just another small Lebanese politician who simply follows the instructions.

Although he looks kind, polite, elegant, and calm, there is something about him that I can't embrace or, perhaps, understand. His futuristic ideas are fascinating, but the way he runs things is suspicious, and I hate his charming smile whenever he takes pictures with Syrian officials. His good intentions and expensive suits are simply not enough to convince me. Moreover, the more he cajoles the Syrians, the more he drives me crazy.

"Neutrality"—the word crosses my mind again when I start writing the introduction for my first episode. "Fuck neutrality," I say to myself. I delete the word from my head.

"Rafic Hariri: Who is this Sheikh, and what is he buying here?" I start my intro. I go on with my questions about his companies, about the CEO's that he brought from his companies and appointed as ministers, his relationships with politicians who follow him around like little ducks, his suspicious relations with the myriad of journalists who polish his image day and night, and so on—questions I know will ignite very hot debates in the studio and will definitely make the buzz that Azzi and Sfeir want.

On the day of the show, 110 guests show up in the building; I invited more than 75 in case some couldn't make it. I definitely don't want my camera to catch any empty seats. This is a sign of weakness.

Surprisingly, all the guests I invited show up.

"You'd suspect some guests would not show up, even if you were throwing a party or a barbecue," Azzi says. He is thrilled and confused at the same time.

The place is fully packed; some stand, some sit on the floor, and others find a way to share one chair.

For a second, it looks like a sit-in or a protest more than a TV show. My guest on the stage is a deputy who was elected from Hariri's list in the last parliamentary elections.

The look on his face becomes more nervous as the room fills up; he can already tell that not all those young men and women are here to applaud him. I think he truly regrets agreeing to be part of the show the moment he sees the auditorium.

"Silence, please," the director shouts as politely as he can. "We're live in thirty seconds," he announces.

As always, I know I will overcome these heavy heart pounds after a minute or two; I try to calm down the quivering a little bit as the field producer counts, "three, two, one, and Top…."

I am shaking like a leaf for two seconds, and I have no notes in front of me to support me if I forgot my intro. But it only takes two horrible seconds, and then I feel like I am sitting in my living room.

Five minutes, and the episode is all fired up. Hariri

is being attacked from every side and corner. There are only few graduates present who try to defend him, but the absolute majority has fierce criticism against him and his cabinet.

My guest tries very hard to defend the prime minister, his boss, but he is booed like hell. And my audience, my rebels, are real experts at giving anyone a hard time if they show any sign of weakness. Yet, the attacks are all political, and I make sure the questions always stay away from insults and curses. I don't want the show to become a cheap platform for insults; there are many TV stations and tabloids that already claim that strategy to get his attention, hoping to get paid off.

Not me. The $6000 I earn monthly is a huge amount in my head, and most importantly, I am a journalist, not a pimp.

My first episode lasts for more than two hours, and it could have gone on for an extra hour if I wanted to prolong the excitement.

My phone doesn't stop ringing for an entire week. The show is a first, and every week, there's a new set of rules that I break. ICN news bulletins get big attention. There's a pulse of opposition that people actually like in our programs. We’re not number two yet, but we’re clearly making a good buzz.

The excitement drives me to escalate; four explosive, controversial episodes in four consecutive episodes. My boss is simply amazed. The Syrian occupation is my next episode. It is even more provocative than the previous ones. We promote the episode like hell; the announcement for this particular episode airs in every break.

"Nakouzi: this little criminal of war who trained in Israel; this small Mossad agent who was notorious for slaughtering Muslims on the Christian checkpoints in 1975…" This is what I read in a newspaper that Hariri directly finances and supports.

The article describes some crazy details about the training I received in some military camps in Israel and then describes how I killed Muslims, just because they were called Mohammad or Mahmoud, with my bare hands at a checkpoint for the Christian militias in 1975. The writer of the article explains—in boring details—about the leading role I had played in the refuge massacre of Sabra and Shatila, as well.

These stories usually make me laugh, but Henry insists I should reply to the bastard either on my show or through the same newspaper, which is legally obliged to refute the story, according to the laws.

I agree with him and promise to send an article to negate the story. I send one sentence: "I was five and a half years old in 1975," and I send my ID with it.

I am not looking for fans to take pictures with me on some red carpet; I hate red carpets, and I have never envied those who walk on them. Besides, ICN is definitely not the place for someone to establish stardom. The real stars of the country are the hosts and anchors of LBC (Lebanese Broadcasting Station), the oldest and most advanced TV network and is way out of our league. Furthermore, I am here to fight, not take pictures. I escalate the tone of my episodes, until people start to lose their minds.

"I am Colonel Sarkis from the Intelligence

Services," my caller introduces himself rudely, emphasizing the word intelligence.

"Sure," I answer indifferently. "How can I help you colonel?" I ask him politely.

"I don't need your help, Mr. Nakouzi," he says aggressively. "I want your cooperation. Listen to me well, because I never use words twice. The country is hanging on an imp's palm, and I won't let a little boy like you mess with civil peace and national unity just because he wants to have fun on TV."

"Mess with civil peace? Really?" I reply with a little sarcasm, which clearly unnerves him.

"Listen to me and do not interrupt," he shouts. "I don't know who your masters are: the Israelis, the Mossad, the Americans… And I don't really care. If you ever mention the word Syria from your mouth, negatively or positively, I will make sure you won't be able to pronounce your name in your next episode, got it?" he threatens, obviously, this time. "And if you don't know what this means, it means I am gonna remove your tongue from your throat so quickly that you won't have the time to even scream in pain," he finishes. "Clear?" he asks.

I remain silent for a moment, thinking of the right answer. "Got it?" he shouts again, higher this time.

"No," I answer, "I don't get it," I continue, pretending that I am calm.

"You mention the word, asshole. Just try me, and I will show you," he says calmly this time.

"Okay then," I reply with the same calm tone, "watch my next episode, colonel." He hangs up before I finish my sentence.

He sounded serious and very determined, but I

have to hide my fear; these military bullies are known to wipe you out if you show any sign of weakness. Nabil Loutfy, one of the advisors of the chairman who was present in the room, immediately informs Henry.

Five minutes later, I am in my boss' office trying to calm him down. He is outraged, as if I were his own son. He already tried to call the president; he then starts to write an official speech to the prime minister and the head of the army. He is taking it very personally. He wants me to feel protected, I guess.

"There's an entire network behind your back, son," he assures me. "What do you want to do?" he asks me gently. "Would you like to take a couple of weeks off and let things calm down a little bit?" he asks but really is suggesting.

"Watch my next episode," I answer with pride.

In my next episode, I invite some brave graduates that I know have the guts to tell things as they are.

The episode is about the Syrian presence in Lebanon, and will be right in the face of the colonel.

The episode explodes much more than I thought it would. My message is clear.

The colonel doesn't call. He got my message, I think, and flatter myself for standing up to him.

Yet, the next morning, I receive a phone call from one of my guest's mothers. She starts to shout, "If you don't have a mother to worry about you, my son has one who cares, and I want you to stop inviting him to your show, do you hear me?" she says, her voice escalating. She doesn't give me the chance to say one word. Her son, Edward, who is one of the regular guests of the show, pulls the phone from his mother and explains that after the episode, more than fifteen guests were arrested. The intelligence services wouldn't let them go before they all signed documents saying they would never be involved in any political activity or else they would be charged with accusations of inciting sectarian strife, harming the civil peace, and insulting a friendly and brotherly state.

I apologize deeply to him and his mother. She calms down after I promise her that I will never invite her son to my studio again. In the afternoon, I receive an official call from the National Security Office, ordering me to come immediately to their station; otherwise, they will have to bring me by force.

Sfeir goes on full alert; he loses his mind. He is ready to go all the way and make a scandal out of it in the main news bulletin; the entire network is behind my back, he reminds me.

Everyone recommends that I should go with a lawyer, but I go alone. A captain walks me to Colonel Joubran's office. He is cold, rude, and barely says hello before he asks me to sit down. He orders two coffees. "You got two options," he gets straight to the subject. "One, you act responsibly and watch your tongue; in this case, you can live as a respectful, decent human being," he says. I nod my head, waiting to hear the second option. The colonel doesn't continue. "And two?" I ask him, politely. "Oh," he chuckles, "you're waiting for two… I will show you option two next time you force me to bring you here… It won't be a cup of coffee, trust me."

He let me go.

The first thing I do when I get out the station is to call John, a talented editor who always comes up with great promotions for my episodes. He doesn't know anything about my encounter. "I need you to come out with an explosive promotion about Michel Aoun's exile," I say and pause for a second to check his reaction. He remains completely silent.

Of course, John refuses to do it before calling his superior. Minutes later, he calls me back. "Mr. Sfeir has given me a green light to go ahead," he informs me. "You're both crazy, I think," he whispers.

As a matter of fact, mentioning Aoun is very, very rare in the news and political programs. It is a name that could create a lot of trouble; however, "It is only in scary times that a man can prove what he is made of," I encourage myself.

They can kill me if they want to, but I will never allow them to see me scared. I resolve it in my head.

Anyway, as expected, the episode is explosive, exactly as I want it to be, even more. The next morning, no one is arrested, and all the calls I receive are to greet me. I jump nervously every time I receive a call from a private number, though, but fortunately, the colonel is never among them.

I feel extremely satisfied that I have won my first real battle against a colonel. Maybe I am naive, like Nabil, the CEO's advisor, always says. He has a long list of adjectives that he describes me with: reckless, shortsighted, and innocent is the last one he adds on the list. "I can fight mountains," I tell him. "No you can't," he chuckles. "And your confidence will kill you one day," as he concludes all our conversations. He's just a peaceful person who likes to stay away from trouble; however, underneath his words, I can feel that he admires my guts, even if he always says it is stupid to even think that one could win over this mafia. He just hates confrontations. Me? I like them.

The visits to the National Security Office are almost regular now. They invite me to come to the station for a "cup of coffee" regularly. "A cup of coffee" with the intelligence services means one of two things: You either cooperate and you'd be treated like a 'friend', or you play the stubborn guy and they'd become the constant pain in the ass. They shout and they warn. They have never laid a hand on me, though, I admit. Not even once. Furthermore, and since there's no physical harm, I listen politely, and the next week, I escalate more. It's a ritual now. They scare me sometimes, but not really. They have nothing on me; and every time an officer knows I am just twenty-three years old journalist, he becomes suddenly kind. I make some of them smile sometimes, even when they're warning me. I feel I can get away with anything.

My show on ICN is teaching me a lot about the country and how this farm is being managed, but most importantly, it is teaching me new things about myself. I am stubborn like a bull, and it's so hard to intimidate me. I kind of like this about myself. I am as peaceful as an ant; however, it takes much more than threats to scare me.

The weekly threats have now turned to almost daily. I don't give a damn; on the contrary, every time someone calls to warn me, I answer by escalating recklessly in the next episode.

Yet, a major event would turn things upside down.

On February 27, 1994, a bomb explodes in the Church of Our Lady of Deliverance in Jounieh, five miles away from my home, killing nine people and injuring many more attending Sunday Mass.

With the civil war over, such a tragedy is unusual. However, the government's reaction is entirely out of proportion—after an urgent meeting, the cabinet declares a state of emergency! "All news and political programs will be halted for an indefinite period, without exception," Minister of Information Michel Samaha announces. "It's strictly prohibited to broadcast any political news whatsoever until this sensitive crime is fully resolved." He further warns that any network violating the ban faces permanent closure.

Our Minister of Information ordering the media to *stop* providing information is a perfect metaphor for the insanity of Lebanon under Syrian rule.

Lebanon's more than 50 TV networks and 100 radio stations are outraged.

Henry calls in all senior staff the next morning, me included. He asks to hear everyone's opinion. Some recommend we simply accept the resolution and play things by ear. Others suggest we try to organize a unified stand among all media companies to denounce the government's unlawful resolution.

"What about you, Nakouzi?" Henry asks.

"Let's pretend we didn't hear anything," I suggest. "Give me permission to broadcast my episode, and I'll fill the studio in minutes." My colleagues shake their heads in disapproval.

"I think it's a brilliant idea," Henry says, his face lighting up. "That's what we'll do." He stands up, ending the meeting.

So many young men and women come to be part of my illegal broadcast that it looks like the scene of a sold-out rock concert. Dozens can't even fit into the studio and have to be turned away.

At 9:00 pm sharp, I begin my show.

Fifteen minutes later, there are over 100 soldiers and two tanks surrounding the building, ordering the crowd to leave immediately.

The door of the studio opens, and Walid jumps on stage and whispers in my ear. “We have to stop, son,” he says with great concern in his voice. “There’s a small army outside with weapons and very mean intentions.”

“Let’s keep our cameras rolling,” I whisper back. “Let the viewers see what they’re doing to us live.”

“Hey, *hey,* that’s *enough,* kid,” he says decisively, pulling my earpiece out. I want to argue, but there’s a “don’t mess with me” look in his eyes. I back off.

I inform the students that due to events beyond my control, the show has been canceled. “You better learn when to stop, son,” Walid says. “You really have to learn when to stop,” he repeats with some anger.

Henry is arguing with the Lebanese soldiers, accusing them of becoming puppets of Syria. They answer that they have strict orders to stop any political programs from airing.

I walk with Henry to his office, where the senior staff is already meeting to find a way out of this confrontation with the authorities. The majority concludes we should just calm down and wait things out.

That doesn’t satisfy Henry. “Why don’t we drop our pants and turn our ass so they can fuck us collectively?” he says, his face fully red again.

He turns to me. “Nakouzi, I haven’t heard your voice. What do you think?”

Before I can open my mouth, Walid shoots me a

look that says he's ready to punch me if I cross him on this.

"Well," I say, "I think we should do it again. Let them shut us down live in front of all our viewers. It's a scandal—"

Everyone else's voices drown me out. Except for Henry, they're all against me. One manager proclaims "I'm not wasting my time with juveniles," and walks out.

Henry decides to follow the wishes of everyone else and do nothing for a while.

Over the next two weeks the governmental TV network Tele Liban—which is conveniently excluded from the resolution—starts dropping hints that Samir Geagea is responsible for the bombing. There's no credible motive provided for why Geagea, an ardent Christian, would bomb a Church. However, it *is* credible that Ghazi Kanaan might choose to frame for murder the leader of the Lebanese Forces, which is the only remaining potential threat within Lebanon to absolute Syrian rule.

Within a month, the Lebanese Forces are dissolved and Geagea arrested. Around 1,200 of his supporters are arrested with him, and many sent to the horrific prisons of Syria.

Samir Geagea, who once had over 10,000 fiercely loyal soldiers under his direct command and vied for control of Lebanon, is eventually stripped of all power and imprisoned in a solitary underground cell in the Lebanese Ministry of Defense.

Ghazi Kanaan's message is clear: "No matter how big, strong, or invincible you think you are, I can easily destroy you and everyone you know."

During all these events, the media isn't allowed to cover political stories.

The silence is horrible.

But thugs adore such silence.

Six months later, the government decides to shut down around 50 TV networks and 90 radio stations, all at the same time, putting thousands of talented media professionals out of work—and extending the silence permanently for most media outlets.

Only five networks receive TV broadcast licenses going forward.

One is Prime Minister Hariri's Future TV—which surprises no one. The government's rationale is that Future TV represents the voice of the Sunnis.

The Speaker of the House has plans to launch a TV network called NBN to represent the Shiites, so he's granted a license for his non-existent channel.

Lebanon's President doesn't own a network, but he's a sponsor of LBC (Lebanese Broadcasting Corporation), which is the most popular network in the country...and was owned by the Lebanese Forces. With that group disbanded, the President appoints an entirely new Board of Directors who are thoroughly loyal to him.

The fourth license goes to popular entertainment network MTV (also known as Murr TV). MTV carries no news or political programs. But according to the government's spin, because MTV is owned by an orthodox Christian named Michel Murr—whose uncle is an influential Syrian-backed politician—MTV is another network that represents Christians.

Finally, Syrian ally Hezbollah gets a TV license to ensure there's a voice continually railing against

Israel...and that can serve as another mouthpiece for the Syrian agenda.

I suddenly have a new perspective on why I was never beaten up. There was no point to it.

The Syrians had a much grander plan in place that shut me up more effectively—along with most of my colleagues. And in the same stroke, the only Lebanese military threat to them has been neutered.

Ghazi Kanaan's scheme is utterly ruthless and shockingly efficient.

Two weeks later, the whole thing is over, and it looks like everyone has settled down and accepted what is written. To me, it is not just political this time; I am jobless.

For more than a year with ICN, I have been doing really well financially. I have rented my own luxurious apartment in Broumana, one of the best regions in Mount Lebanon. I have a nice Mercedes—not the latest model, but decent enough.

Yet, I start taking loan after loan just to be able to pay my rent, car installment, and some of my urgent expenses.

Four months later, I leave my apartment, shift from my Mercedes into a small Hyundai, stop going to my favorite exclusive restaurants and clubs, and temporarily return to my parent's house. My mother has kept my room exactly like it was while I was living here: clean, untouched, and ready. She always wanted me to get a secure, safe, and "real" job, as she calls it. She thinks that journalism in the Middle East is an irregular job, but I don't know exactly what she means by that.

I don't even bother to write my resume; there is

only one network that I can work for, and it is LBC, which is completely saturated with anchors and hosts already. But regardless, even if they have a vacant position, I know they won't choose a crazy host whose sole mission is to bring young people in to infuriate the authorities. It's probably because of similar shows that the government decided to shut networks down. The other network, Murr TV, has no political programs or news on its schedule, and of course, the other two channels are completely out of the question – they are strong allies to Syria.

Yet, I play indifferent the whole time, pretending that I am okay. But I am truly not. I feel like my journey has ended so quickly that it seems like it never happened.

So, I start dubbing Mexican soap operas, and I record some advertisements here and there that I refused to even consider before.

My latest masterpiece is an advertisement for cheese. It is running everywhere now, and it drives me crazy, especially when people recognize my voice. I have honestly never imagined a shinier future than this. I just can’t believe how my life shifted quickly from a troublemaker and a journalist to someone who persuades people to buy cheese. It is killing me, especially that I can't think of any happy ending for this crisis.

However, I have no choice but to change the direction of my life and find something stable and safe, which means boring, of course.

I look at the newspaper ads, hoping to find someone who wants to hire a previous TV host to help him.

“Help him what?” I ask myself. “What could a TV

host do if there are no TV stations?"

I close the newspaper.

XIII
Deeply Shallow

My phone rings, and it is the last person I would have ever expected it to be.

"Good evening, I am Pierre Daher," the voice says.

"You mean... *Pierre Daher*?" I ask, just to make sure it is the same Pierre Daher who runs LBC.

"Yes," he chuckles softly. "George Ghanem has encouraged me to call you. What are you doing nowadays, Nakouzi?" he asks without introductions.

What the hell, I think to myself. George Ghanem is the most popular news anchor in Lebanon. His brother, Marcel, is the host of the most popular political show in the country: "The Talk of the People." I am so surprised that George recommended me to Daher.

"What am I doing?" I chuckle. "Well, it looks like you haven't heard the cheese advertisement, my latest revolution," I joke with him, just to ease my nervousness a little bit.

Daher is the man who is behind all of LBC's success. He was able, in no time, to make LBC a very successful network, even compared with the western channels. He is a direct person, known to go straight to the subject with no introductions whatsoever.

Some people don't like his undiplomatic way of saying things, but somehow, he is respected for that at the same time, as I hear consistently. I have only met him once before when I hosted him in an episode about the role of media, and I have much respect for him. He never wastes one second outside the main subject.

"So, you're available?" he asks.

"I am so, so available. I have no offers whatsoever. I am broke, and I am bored to death," I answer frankly, in a modest attempt to level up with him.

"I am introducing a new morning show with three main women anchors. Would you like to be the male anchor of the show? It is something similar to "Good Morning America." Have you ever watched it?"

"No, I've never seen it," I say, a little turned down by the idea of a morning show. "What would I do on a morning show, anyway?"

"You tell me... How would you fill 30 minutes live daily?" he asks.

"Can I have a daily guest?" I ask, a little hesitant.

"Yeah, sure," he replies quickly. "I don't see why not. What exactly do you have in mind?"

"For example, I can read the newspaper headlines and analyze them with different journalists, analysts, or even politicians every morning," I suggest. "People are used to watching the news at eight in the evening. What's wrong with telling them what is going on at eight in the morning?" I try to impress him with my new creative approach.

"I like it," he says immediately. "Why don't you pass by my office tomorrow at 11? Let's talk about this with the director." He hangs up the phone while a thousand ideas start to struggle in my head.

Passing from primetime to a morning show feels like a demotion, but my options are so limited. It is not a dream come true, but perhaps I can impress Daher with my talents. Perhaps I can jump from 9 am to 9 pm again. After all, it is just a 12-hour difference.

The next morning, I am at Daher's office. He introduces me to Simon Asmar, or the "star maker," as people call him.

Professionally, Simon is recognized to be the master in the TV entertainment industry.

LBC is already on satellite, and it airs to the entire Middle East, trying to compete with another giant, MEB. It is a network owned by a Saudi tycoon and has an unlimited budget compared with LBC. Yet, Daher thinks he can really compete, even with the small budget he has.

Simon is described as being tough, arrogant, rude, and blunt. It is also said that he can be a real asshole sometimes and that he usually insults those who work with him.

However, I realize quickly that he is the opposite of everything that he was described as being. In reality, he is a very kind and polite and a real professional. He's not an asshole; he just can't stand stupid people. Stupid people make him mean, and he hurts them with his harsh remarks.

He won't shout, he won't get angry, and he won't curse. On the contrary, he remains very calm; he'll smile as he delivers a tough comment that will make you bleed.

I am actually impressed by his accuracy and devotion to small details. Nothing can get passed him, absolutely nothing.

He is a school that one must pass by if they want to become a star, whether a singer, an actor, a musician, or an anchor.

I take every remark he gives me very seriously except one. I never keep notes in front of me like I am supposed to. He doesn't argue much, but he warns me: “first time you stumble on the air, you will have to put notes in front of you.”

“It will never happen,” I challenge him.

It only takes me one month on LBC on a morning show before almost everyone recognizes me on the street.

During my days at ICN, few people recognized me, and I was never looked at as a celebrity, but with LBC, it is an entirely different experience.

I don't have to introduce myself anymore; most people know my name and who I am. I am also getting special attention at clubs, restaurants, stores, and everywhere else I go.

I was never a fan of fans, and it starts to disturb me a little, especially when someone asks to take a photograph with me or insists that I sign an autograph.

Simon quickly realizes that the more people flatter and complement me, the grumpier I become.

The Arts' River, the resort Simon has recently launched, quickly becomes a huge tourist attraction, and people from all over come to see their favorite stars and hear them singing live.

The place is always packed. Simon's table is consistently crammed with new stars, celebrities, and VIP every night. This particular table is the main attraction for hundreds of fans that come to take pictures with their idols. I am a regular guest at his table, and it really upsets him if I don't show up.

"Fame is an asset that you're hugely underestimating, Nakouzi," Simon says when he sees me struggling to smile for a 12-year-old boy, who insists that I take pictures with all the members of his family.

It drives me crazy when someone makes a comment about my tie, shirt, or suit, even if it is positive. For me, this career is not about being handsome, wearing nice suits, and "taking pictures with people who have the IQ of half a chicken". I always complain.

"If all people were smart, then TV networks would be bankrupt," he chuckles. "So, you better get used to 'idiots'," he says, and laughs out loud.

I am not asking to be surrounded by rocket scientists, but there is a minimum.

Yet, there are much bigger stars than me who are literally stalked and surrounded by thousands of fans all the time, so I didn't have it that bad.

In my category of political hosts, Marcel Ghanem is definitely the most famous of us all, but he is someone who's rarely seen in public places. Politicians are his friends mainly, and they hold their dinners and parties in private. He is known to be very close to the most influential politicians in the country, starting with the president and the prime minister. George and Marcel, as it's said, form a very powerful duo that influences the daily political life in the country; George writes the nightly news bulletin and Marcel hosts the most powerful weekly talk show without any doubt.

I envy him for his powerful platform, but I don't like how close he is to politicians; these are the faces that I want to fight, not to befriend.

"I want hot debates and political controversies; I want to piss off some politicians," I confide to Simon, hoping that he can throw a word to Pierre to grant me my own primetime show.

"You have to be grateful that you have this opportunity while more than a thousand of your colleagues are still looking desperately for a job," he answers me when I complain too much.

So, I am grateful for my little morning corner, and I start hosting authors and writers in addition to political journalists. The feedback is really good, so I include some politicians.

The response is positive to my segment, and as it turns out, the viewers seem to enjoy listening to politics in the morning.

Months after the show has begun, Pierre announces that LBC is also launching its satellite service to Europe and the two Americas. LBC is now called LBC International. "Great," I say. "I feel international now."

On another level, I am becoming more successful with women who I thought were way out of my league before. I am dating models, actresses, dancers, and so many beautiful women that I can't keep their names straight anymore. My life is crowded with beautiful women. Most of them are stupid and deeply shallow, but I don't mind a shallow woman if she's stunning.

I jump from one nightclub to another, always accompanied by a woman that turns heads. At my table, one can usually find at least one or two big celebrities. In restaurants, I am treated like a VIP and taken to the best and most exclusive table in the house.

I am now a regular customer of Aishti, the most expensive store in Lebanon, and my skin can't bear anything less than $5000 Zegna suits anymore. My debts are growing even bigger.

I have an entire new set of friends, a new apartment, a new car, and even my physical appearance is different.

There's nothing to break the routine, until in April 1996, when some dangerous altercations between Hezbollah and the Israeli army, which still occupies South Lebanon, escalate into a full military operation that the Israeli government calls: "The Grapes Of Wrath."

The fierce fighters of Hezbollah have grown into a serious nightmare for the Israeli soldiers. With the huge support the Organization is receiving from Iran, it often succeeds in killing or injuring many Israeli soldiers almost daily.

Israel has clearly decided to put an end to the permanent threat on the borders.

As soon as the military operation launches, many predict that Hezbollah's fate will be similar to that of the Palestinian fighters' in 1982. Except that Hezbollah fighters are Lebanese and they can't be possibly deported out of their country. Besides, Hezbollah is immensely respected and popular among 1 million Shiites in Lebanon. So, we have no idea what to expect.

After weeks of intense fighting, Hezbollah surprises all experts and defends all its positions, causing embarrassing damages to the attackers.

Even the latest hi-tech weapons that the Israelis possess appear pointless against the suicide attacks and the new tactics that Hezbollah is now using in battles.

On April 18th, the Israeli forces bombard a United Nation's shelter, in the very small town of Qana, where more than 800 families have taken refuge. As a result, 106 civilians die, and hundreds of wounded fill the hospitals.

The absolute majority are women and young children. The scenes are beyond painful.

The pictures outrage the international community, and for the first time in its modern History, Israel is hugely criticized, even in the western world. The images of those innocent children reminded Muslims of Sabra and Shatila's massacre once again, but it is solely committed by Israel this time.

The Israeli government immediately expresses regret for the loss of innocent lives, saying that "Hezbollah's position was the intended target of the shelling, and not the UN compound that was hit due to incorrect targeting based on erroneous data."

No matter how hard Israel tries to justify what happened, the cruel scenes of Qana's victims are unforgettable. And eventually, "the Grapes of Wrath" halts under huge international pressure, leaving Hezbollah triumphant, over what was always perceived as the strongest army in the Middle East.

Muslims all over the Arab world embrace Hezbollah. And the latter not only survives the war, but also comes out more powerful.

It is especially during big events that I miss the journalist I used to be. *It's safer, calmer, and much easier now with my new life, so, why screw it up with something stupid?* I remind myself daily.

But no matter how hard I try to deny it, I long for those old fights.

****

Anyway, the days pass by slowly, there's no action, until Simon informs me that I'll be interviewing a poet named Samia. I'm asked to greet her well because she's a cultural attaché of Dubai, and will be evaluating a project LBC wants to sell Dubai's ruler Mohammed bin Rashid al-Maktoum.

Samia arrives Monday morning...and she's stunning. Right before my segment begins, I smile at her and say, "I'm confused. Are you the poet or the poem?"

"Which is more interesting to you? Because I can be both," she replies with a wink and one of those smiles that can mean eight different things at the same time.

The interview goes well. I then ask her to lunch at City Café, which is a favorite spot for writers, journalists, and politicians.

She's smart and sexy. I start telling her how much I love poetry.

"Before sex, a man will pretend he adores knitting, if the prey knits," she observes. "After she fucks him, he won't read her book if she writes one."

"I have a brilliant solution for this, but women feel offended every time I suggest it," I reply, taking a large sip of vodka to boost my creativity.

"I'm not easily offended. Please share it with me," she says, taking a sip of red wine.

"A woman should sleep with a man immediately, before their first date. First fuck, and then date. That's the best way to spare yourself from hearing a pack of lies."

"Hm," she says, taking another sip. "Interesting thought."

"You can always try it," I suggest.

"I won't fuck you, Nakouzi," she says, getting so close our faces almost touch. "I'm sure you'll find a 20-year-old model to take care of you tonight, so stop trying," she adds, giggling.

I'm now counting on the wine to change her mind.

But before I can pursue my plan, the waiter comes over. "Mr. Nakouzi, I am sorry to interrupt you. The Prime Minister has just arrived, and he's asking if he can join your table."

"The Prime Minister?" I ask, confused. "Prime Minister of what?"

Before the waiter can answer, Lebanon's Prime Minister Rafic Hariri appears with two ministers in his cabinet. Samia and I immediately stand up.

"Prime Minister! I thought the waiter was joking with me," I say. "It's nice to meet you."

"It's nice to meet you." He looks over at my companion.

"This is Samia. She's a cultural attaché of Dubai. She's also a talented poet, with several published books."

"It's a rare pleasure to meet a poet after a cabinet meeting," Hariri says.

"I'm honored," Samia responds.

"Well, are you going to invite us to sit with you, Mr. Nakouzi?" Hariri asks.

"Oh, of course! Please, sit down."

XIV
Off Record

And just like that, one of the richest and most influential men in the world is sitting at my lunch table. A consummate politician, he waves and sends humble smiles to the other diners in the restaurant. The two ministers with him clearly aren't happy about this turn of events. However, it's also clear they'll do whatever they're told.

"Tell me, Mr. Nakouzi," Hariri says politely, "why do you attack me on all your shows?"

We're all surprised by his blunt honesty.

"I never attack you, Prime Minister," I reply immediately, careful to show respect. "I attack your policies."

"That's fair," he says, nodding. "Okay then, what is it about my policies you don't like?"

"Well..." I hesitate. "I'm not sure you're going to like the answer, and I really don't want to ruin your good mood."

"Not at all," Hariri says. "I invited myself to your table specifically for this. Please, be as frank as you can."

"All right. First of all, the Syrians are occupiers. But for you, they're friends. I can't understand the Prime Minister of my country befriending a brutal dictatorship."

"I understand," he says gently. "So you want to treat Syria as an enemy. Should I declare war on Syria?"

"We fight them until they leave. We don't bow to killers and pretend they're our allies."

Samia quietly gasps at *killers*. We're in a public

restaurant, which might have Syrian Intelligence agents secretly listening to every word. People have disappeared for saying a lot less. But the Prime Minister asked for the truth, so I'm going to give it to him.

"Hasn't your friend Michel Aoun already tried this?" Hariri replies, putting his finger on the open wound. "Do you remember what happened next? Or more precisely, could anyone forget what happened next?" He smiles at his ministers, who both approve of every word he says even before he says it.

"No one can forget. However, let's also recall that the entire planet abandoned him. That's why he lost the war."

"And what makes you think the world has changed since then?"

"It has not," I admit. "But—"

"There are no 'buts,' son," he interrupts for the first time in the conversation. "As a wise man said, it's insane to keep doing the same thing over and over and expect different results."

"So if your country is occupied, it's insane to liberate it?"

"I never said that. But there are different ways to deal with the problem—diplomacy, for example."

"Oh, really? Then why don't you convince Hezbollah to use only diplomacy? Why don't you order Hezbollah to stop all military actions against Israel?" I got him with that. "According to you, Michel Aoun was crazy to try to oust Syria, which has perhaps the 97th strongest army in the world. But when Hezbollah tries to defeat the 5th strongest army in the world by force, this is patriotic?"

"You can't compare Syria to Israel," Hariri objects. "Israel will always be the enemy. Syria will always be an Arab country, a neighbor, and a friend."

"I'm sorry, but I don't look at it that way. As a Lebanese citizen, I've been hurt much more by Syrians than Israelis. I believe many people feel this way. They just don't say it out loud. And they don't discuss it on the news... because you know what happens to people who speak their minds on the news," I shoot at him, referencing the notorious media shutdown of a year ago.

"I'm sorry people feel this way—"

"It's not a matter of what we feel, Your Excellency. It's a matter of losing our beloved relatives, friends, and colleagues. It's about all the families the Syrians have destroyed since they arrived here."

"Well, don't blame *me* for bringing them here. I never invited them to come."

I realize that Hariri doesn't like the Syrians, and he flatters them only because he has to. No one expects Hariri to openly criticize the Syrians. However, it sounds like he just did. He looks uncomfortable about that, and I feel a bit sorry for him, so decide to back off. I've made my point, and there's no need to keep pushing.

But the Prime Minister hasn't had enough. "So, what's the second of all?" he asks, showing he's a good listener.

"I don't like your Saudi way of running the country."

The two ministers look very unhappy. Even Samia turns red and gives me a look. The Prime Minister is the only one who remains cool.

"What do you mean by 'Saudi way?'" he asks.

"The Saudi strategy of paying to eliminate problems. The Saudi way of buying newspapers, buying TV stations—"

"Hey, hey," one of the ministers interrupts, "what kind of talk is this, Nakouzi? You're sitting with the Prime Minister, for God's sake."

"—and sometimes buying people," I complete my sentence without even looking at the minister. I'm talking to the big boss, not his entourage.

My words come out harshly, but Hariri takes it. He calms the minister, who's now standing over me, and asks him to sit back down.

"Do you truly think that I buy people, Mr. Nakouzi?"

"Perhaps you hire them, or rent them. I don't know exactly what the right term is."

"Well, you're someone who finds guests to criticize me on his show almost daily. Have I ever tried to contact you before? Have I ever tried to 'rent' or 'hire' you to say good things about me?"

"No. I'm just a small anchor on a morning show." Part of me hopes he'll respond, "You're not a small anchor, you're a great journalist." But that doesn't happen.

"Then who are you talking about?" Hariri asks.

"I am talking about big journalists, politicians—"

"Stop talking in abstractions. Name names," he demands, again surprising me.

"I can't tell you the names of the people on your payroll. Only you know that, and you're famous for your discretion. I can name the people you *can't* buy, though."

"Oh, really? Please do—besides Michel Aoun."

I rattle off the names of journalists who consistently attack him. When I mention certain reporters, he looks at his ministers and chuckles, as if to say, “Look how naïve and stupid this guy is.”

I pause, then mention some politicians I know give him headaches. There aren’t many of them.

“Enough,” Hariri says. “It always breaks my heart to see intelligent young people getting manipulated. Listen, I’ve been Prime Minister for four years now, and I learned a valuable lesson that I’d like to share with you, off the record.

“Almost everyone has a price. Some get paid from here; others get paid from there. With some, you have to stick your wrist in their mouth before they feel it is enough. With others, you have to stick it up to your elbow until they’re full. And others might take it up to your shoulder before they’re satisfied.” He stands up at this. “But it has never reached my shoulder so far.” He looks at his ministers and at my guest, who’s currently barely breathing from the tension, and stretches his hand out before he leaves.

Samia and I stand up respectfully and shake his hand warmly. He looks triumphant as he walks between the tables, as if he won the debate.

Thirty minutes later, I’m with Samia in her hotel room. She’s apparently the kind of poet who’s more turned on by bluntness than romantic lines and wine. Even if I lost the argument with Hariri, the night with her is worth it.

The second morning, I go through my usual routine with the newspaper headlines. Then during a commercial break I have an idea. I grab my cell phone and call Pierre Daher.

“Yes, Nakouzi,” he answers.

“I have two minutes before we go back on air. Here’s what happened to me yesterday at the City Café.” I give him a condensed version and ask for permission to share it with viewers, exactly as it happened.

“Just promise to not add salt and pepper to your tale,” he replies. I’m surprised he agrees so easily.

“I’ll be as accurate than a tape recorder.”

“Go ahead, then,” he says, and hangs up.

Ten seconds later, I’m telling the story precisely as it occurred. I put special emphasis on the Prime Minister’s comments about the Syrians; and about his wrist and elbow, and the shoulder he hasn’t had to resort to yet.

As soon as my segment ends, my phone rings off the hook. The calls are nonstop for hours.

Some are friends applauding me for my bravery. Some are reporters—the story makes the front page of six newspapers the next day.

And some are colleagues who tell me I was out of line—especially in revealing anything said off the record, which is normally as sacred a trust for a journalist as the sacramental seal for a priest who’s heard confession.

But the most notable call is from Nouhad Machnouk, a former journalist who’s now the Prime Minister’s senior advisor. Nouhad’s thick voice gives an air of seriousness and wisdom to whatever he says.

“Do you mind if I tell you something sincerely as a colleague—I mean, not as an advisor to the Prime Minister?” he asks gently.

“Please do.”

"I think you did well as a journalist today. I can understand your feeling good about this scoop. But on a personal level, I think you blew an opportunity to have a serious, respectful relationship with one of the most important figures of our time."

"I understand your point," I say a bit too impatiently, wanting to end the lecture.

Nouhad feels my attitude, so cuts to the chase. "As one journalist to another, I'd expect you to have a better understanding of what to reveal and what to keep to yourself. You're going to have a lot of trouble finding any politician to tell you anything ever again. And a good journalist doesn't want this to happen to him."

"We look at this differently," I reply. "I don't believe anything a high-level politician says should be off the record."

"Good luck, then," he says, and hangs up.

While I wouldn't admit it to him, Nouhad made good points. Why should officials give me inside stories if they expect I'll instantly go on TV to announce every intimate detail?

The next morning brings more buzz. Six of the 10 newspapers I read from every morning attack Hariri like never before. On the front page of one, an editorial, written by the president of the Editors Syndicate, grills the prime minister and wishes that he would have cut out his tongue before making such scandalous, humiliating, and degrading statements at his private dinners. Even the newspapers that usually defend him attack him in different editorials inside their pages.

I am also in the headlines. And his office hasn't denied a single word. I was so damn accurate that he couldn't negate. Besides, he knows it will make it even worse.

Daher is thrilled. "Great catch, Nakouzi," he greets me. "Keep going out with poets to dinners," he says.

A week later, my poet goes back to Dubai; however, she suggests we try a long-distance relationship. I am not even able to maintain my short-distance relationships, but I quickly agree. She calls me after she shows her boss, Al Maktoum, the presentation. I even know before my boss that LBC has won the pitch to promote Dubai's most important festival.

Whoever said one shouldn't mix business with pleasure is deeply mistaken.

A couple of months later, I find myself in Dubai, hosting the morning show from one of its big malls for the entire Shopping Festival month.

My girlfriend turns out to be very close to the ruler, and thus, for one month, the parties never stop. Al Maktoum has a remarkable energy that keeps him awake, active, and fully functional. He loves poetry, and understandably, his advisors think he's another Tolstoy. He's friendly, modest, and his people worship him, as I hear every day.

For me, the man is a mystery; I just don't know how he finds the energy and the time to build all these towers and malls while partying that much. He must be a real genius. I can't wait until I'm back in Beirut, though. This city is nothing like Beirut.

I fully realize that outside Beirut, I am like a fish out of water; I suffocate.

On a professional level, I know that my encounter with Hariri will be the best that will happen to me on a morning show.

Suddenly, I feel that LBC, women, fame, and all this lifestyle don’t suit me anymore.

I want politics. I want to create that buzz every week. Yet, the LBC grid is full; there's no place for anyone else in the primetime slot, as Daher keeps telling every anchor that pitches him a new idea. I don't even pitch him. It's not even worth trying. But I am boiling and I am bored like hell from this morning show.

Besides, Daher's political agenda is too complicated to understand; sometimes he's with the Syrians, and sometimes he's against them. Sometimes he attacks the prime minister, and other times he caresses him. People don't blame him, though; he's got a network and 1000 employees he has to protect.

But I am no longer satisfied with this job, promoting Dubai and shopping festivals.

Fuck this, I decide one day. I am not doing this any longer.

XV
Rings

It doesn't take too long before I am invited to a private dinner at a friend's house: David Issa.

He's someone incredibly active in setting up events where he invites many journalists, reporters, and anchors from various media. I usually never attend such dinners, but with David, it is impossible to say no. The man will surround you from every corner until you agree.

I arrive to his dinner two hours late, hoping to skip the biggest part of the evening.

I have never felt that I belong to the media body, and little by little, I am realizing that PM Hariri was not perhaps totally mistaken when he said almost everyone has a price.

These days, payrolls are at their peak, and I kind of prefer to stay away from the circles of journalists who smell bad.

There is already a hot conversation going on when I arrive.

A young man in his early thirties looks like he is arguing with everyone at the table. The discussion is so explosive, no one notices me sit at the table.

“I don't blame the Syrians,” the young gentleman says. “I blame us; we decided to humiliate ourselves and behave like cockroaches,” he continues. “We placed our heads under their boots, and instead of fighting, we invited them to stick their…” he nods his head and pulls the word back, after his very charming companion, his wife obviously, gives him a severe look to keep it in his stomach, "in our ass," he finishes, and the voices grow louder.

"Who is this guy?" I whisper in the ear of my host. "Oh, you don't know Michel?" David replies, astonished that I haven't met him yet. He grabs me by the hand, and we walk right toward the young man.

"Michel El Murr," David says, "I want to introduce you to—"

"It's a pleasure to meet you," Michel interrupts, showing me clearly that he knows who I am.

"So… You're the famous Michel El Murr," I say, and shake his hand. He's no one but the CEO of Murr TV.

"I like what you do in the morning," he smiles.

"Thanks. And I like what you just said at the table," I answer with the same tone.

"I know," he laughs. He has clear blue eyes, and his hair is struggling to stay on his head. It looks like he's going bald very soon.

"It is a shame you're on LBC, though," he says bluntly, as I take my first sip of vodka. "You should come work with me."

"Are you serious?" I ask him, not quite sure if he is just throwing around words.

"I am on Pepsi," he smiles and shows me that he is only drinking soda. "I'll double your salary, and you'll have a team of five people to help you, a fully equipped personal office, and a primetime show," he states his offer. "But," he continues without giving me a moment to answer, "this offer stands for 24 hours only."

"I'm in," I answer.

I admire passionate people who fearlessly speak their mind, and Michel is obviously one of them. He has the ideals of Henry Sfeir, but is focused on making his TV network a success as opposed to using it as a springboard for a political career.

From his undiplomatic way of naming things as they are, one can quickly see this guy would never make a successful politician.

He is perhaps four or five years older than me, and it feels like we have very common feelings about the Syrians. We both hate them equally.

The next morning, I am at his office. I sign my contract.

Pierre Daher is with Lebanon's President on a trip to Brazil, so there's no opportunity to check for a counteroffer. Besides, this isn't about money; it's about working with someone who shares my fighting attitude about getting Syria out of our country.

Michel El Murr is obsessed with little, small details and a *sick, sick* perfectionist. If the ashtray were not perfectly aligned with the pen on his desk for example, he wouldn't be able to focus on anything. A slightly displaced carpet or a curtain that's not perfectly straight could ruin an entire meeting for him. He has to fix these first, and only then, he would give his full attention. Perhaps this is why he's so successful in TV.

He's an elegant, warm gentleman with a friendly face, and he is also someone who can't keep his lips zipped if he sees something he doesn't like.

Michel's network is immensely popular, but it's devoted to entertainment. That's probably why it survived the media shutdown; it's never posed a threat to them.

Now Michel's decided he wants MTV to be taken more seriously, and that means adding news to his programming.

After weeks of extensive meetings, we come up with the concept of the show: Two teams consisting of students mixed with journalists, authors, politicians, and other celebrities debate each other on controversial topics normally taboo for Arab television, such as premarital sex, abortion, and separation of religion and state.

The show's title is *Take a Stand.*

Thanks to its uniqueness, the show does well. However, Michel insists that topics be socio-political—for example, the first episode is about civil marriage. My real passion is politics.

Another barrier for me is that MTV already has a political anchor named Maguy Farah. I'm not supposed to step on her toes.

However, eight months later, I become impatient. I'm struck with an idea and rush into Michel's office. "What if I could get Rafic Hariri, the prime minister, on my show?" I throw my words quickly.

"Maguy has already invited him many times, and he still refuses to appear on her show," he tells me.

"Exactly," I reply, "If I get Hariri, Maguy can't complain that I stole one of her guests."

"And you think you can convince him to appear on your show?" he asks, with a doubtful smile on the face.

"Let me try. I open up to him. "I have an idea that I think he might like."

"I will be grateful if you do," he laughs.

If I was able to convince Ziad Rahbani once, I can

convince ten Hariri's, I encourage myself. Besides, a new president is elected, or appointed by the Syrians to be more accurate: Emile Lahoud.

Emile Lahoud was the officer that Michel Aoun asked his forces to surrender to, when he was removed from the presidential palace by the Syrians. It turned our that he's a pro-Syrian to the bones.

Lahoud headed the army and got very close to Ghazi Kanaan and the other high ranked Syrian officials, until Hafez el Assad embraced him.

It is very known that Lahoud hates the guts of el Hariri, even though they spread warm smiles at each other's in the news.

Hariri needs to regain some popularity that he lost in the last couple of years to prepare himself for a power struggle that's obviously coming soon between the two.

Still, I need something really exclusive and big to convince him to make an appearance with me. I am not one of his favorite journalists. But I have an idea that could tempt him; a plan that could remove that old cloud between us, as long as Hariri is smart enough not to hold a grudge.

I dial Nouhad el Machnouk, the advisor who recommended earlier that I should apologize to the prime minister. He answers with the same respectful tone, even though he sounds a little surprised to hear my voice.

"I have an idea that I think could be more efficient than apologizing to the prime minister," I say after the salutations. "Don't you think it is a little late for 'efficiency'?" he chuckles.

"No," I answer quickly. "Here's the idea. How about bringing fifty brilliant young graduates, representing every political and religious party in the country, in a live discussion with Rafic Hariri on MTV?" I continue, "He would be the first Arab prime minister, confident enough to do it in our nation's history," I say.

If anything is going to catch the attention of Machnouk, it is definitely this last sentence. And I can feel it from his long pause on the phone. "Interesting," he replies. "However, I truly don't know what he will think about it, so, I can ask him if you'd like me to," he proposes.

Thirty minutes later, Machnouk calls back. "His Excellency would like you to explain the idea more," he says in a serious tone. "Can you come right away?" he says, surprising me.

I get to Hariri's office with lightning speed.

"Mr. Prime Minister, I thank you for replying so fast," I smile.

"Welcome." He smiles, then pulls his smile back, as if someone reminded him that he should be a little upset. He is a good-hearted person, and it is really hard for him to hide it, no matter how much he tries to look tough. He somehow reminds me of my father—one of those people who can't hold a grudge even if they want to.

"So, you want me to debate with fifty young graduates, live on the air?" He gets to the point right away. "Yes," I answer with confidence. "I can't think any other Arab president or PM who has ever done this before?" I explain.

He thinks about it, trying to remember if it was done before. "Jamal Abdul Nasser, maybe?"

"I am not sure," I answer quickly, "but if he did, it could be one of the reasons why he's still the most popular leader in modern Arab history," I tempt him.

I am not a great fan of Abdul Nasser myself. I personally think he's an idiot; however, I know that the PM loves him.

"Hum," he thinks about it. "And all political parties will be represented, right?" he asks. "Definitely. Everyone will be represented; those who agree with you and the others who don't."

"Of course," he nods. "And how can you guarantee that things won't get out of control?" he asks and continues, "I mean, I encourage young people to express themselves; however, there's a minimum standard for the conversation."

"I have been doing this for a very long time and you can trust me to take care of this. I will be choosing the best of the best; they might criticize your policies very harshly, but they will never be disrespectful," I assure him. "Let's do this," he says and shakes my hand.

It is a big scoop to have someone like Hariri 'live on air', likely being grilled by all sorts of questions. Yet, Machnouk informs me that the PM has no objection to anyone I want to invite and says, "We don't want to know anything about the questions in advance. His Excellency wants it as spontaneous as it can be."

Everything goes as planned. The episode is a huge success, and for two weeks, it's the talk of town.

Not long after, Maguy decides to resign. With no colleague's toes to worry about, *Take a Stand* turns into a purely political show.

I am back, I am in the middle of the ring again, and I am ready to fight. Who? It's simple and easy: The Syrian occupation and everything that resulted from their presence. At least, this is my plan.

As MTV develops a reputation for being more than just an entertainment network and its news audience grows, Michel starts getting the kind of headaches I've been used to for years—politicians and other government officials call daily to complain about various aspects of MTV's coverage. Michel's blunt style works well for him in entertainment. But politicians are immersed in lies and hypocrisy, and the last thing they want to hear is unvarnished truth. Michel needs someone diplomatic to deal with them.

As luck would have it, around this time a childhood friend of his reappears. Walking by Michel's office one afternoon, I'm shocked to smell cigar smoke. No one is allowed to smoke anywhere near Michel.

"This is Khalil El Khazen," Michel introduces the man in the elegant suit sitting in his office.

"Khalil and I grew up together," he says. "I trust him more than I trust my brothers," he adds, while Khalil smiles gently.

"It's a pleasure to meet you," I look at him and smile politely. "If you're a 'Khazen,' then you must be a Sheikh," I say.

"Of course, he's a Sheikh," Michel says.

"Call me Khalil, please," he says politely and inhales his cigar very professionally. He looks to be in his mid-thirties, but he smokes as if he is sixty-three.

"Khalil started this TV network with me from the very beginning," Michel says. "However, he left for London three years ago; he helped in launching an Arab satellite channel and now he's back," he briefs me. I nod my head, waiting for what all this has to do with me.

Michel continues. "I just appointed him to supervise all the political content on the network: the news, the current affairs, and the political talk shows. Khalil is the most trustworthy person for the job; I would like you to coordinate everything with him from now on," he says friendly.

Khalil is his childhood friend and comes from a distinguished political family. Therefore, he is perhaps, the right man for the job; however, for me, this Sheikh represents everything I hate.

First of all, I am not a big fan of people who are born with titles. He looks rich and sophisticated; bourgeois enough to put a scarf around his neck. My first impression about this guy is not really encouraging.

"Mr. Nakouzi," Khalil says. "Would you like us to have dinner anytime soon?" he asks. "I function better at night when there's vodka on the table," he chuckles. "Let's do it tonight if it includes vodka," I answer without hesitation, "and don't call me 'Mr.,' Sheikh," I say gently. "Perfect," he says, "then don't call me Sheikh," he replies quickly. We exchange numbers.

My perception of Khalil when I leave Michel's office is a little better now that I know he is a vodka-drinking night owl. But still, I am not sure if he's gonna be a help or a pain in the ass.

Two hours later, we're having dinner at the exclusive Cercle D'Or restaurant in the Casino Du Liban, one of the classiest, most sophisticated, and expensive restaurants in the country.

It takes a couple of glasses of vodka, and after that, we become inseparable. He turns out to be the exact opposite of what I thought he was.

He is still classy, sophisticated, generous, and educated. But what makes him so special is an unbelievable sense of humor and sarcasm; he's witty and very quick in coming up with a smart joke out of nowhere.

He carries three phones, though. Most of them are used to deliver different favors for people who never stop calling him.

In brief, he is an energetic, adorable individual that every one falls in love with.

Now, we have a daily ritual that starts at noon and ends at five in the morning. We start our day with a regular meeting in the office for two hours, go out for lunch in one of the popular restaurants, and leave the network at 7 pm.

We meet again at nine and start our regular tour of restaurants and clubs—a tour that always ends at Sydney's, one of the most exclusive bars in Beirut and open 24 hours a day.

We call it our second office, and we usually invite all our guests after the episodes are over. At our regular table, there are deputies, ministers, journalists, and activists every night.

To my surprise, I discover Khalil isn't as rich as he appears to be. On the contrary, my friend is in debt, just like I am, but we never complain about it.

"We live a life of champagne with a beer pocket," as some friends say.

Politically, Khalil is not really far from where I stand; however, he worries too much and never agrees with my wild suggestions to fire it all up.

He strongly believes that aggressiveness toward

the authorities will only provoke them to react foolishly and dangerously. He embraces the theory of playing it smartly without inciting them directly, especially the Syrian and Lebanese intelligence services, who practically run the entire show. "These are the hardest to fight," he says, "not only because they're violent, but because they're stupid. It is insane to be brave in the face of someone who's too mentally retarded to understand bravery." This is his wisdom.

"I am appointed to improve the ratings, Nakouzi," He reminds me all the time. "And if MTV wanted a hero they would have hired Batman, not me!."

The last thing Khalil wants is for MTV to end up like ICN: shut down and forgotten. He makes it clear from the very beginning of our relationship.

Khalil is overly cautious when it comes to sensitive political issues; however, sometimes I get away with a sentence here or an unconventional, outspoken guest there. It's not exactly how I want things to be, but at least I am on primetime and my show accumulates loyal viewers week after week.

Anyway, nothing threatens to disturb our stability. But then one night, Khalil insists on taking me to a karaoke night "for a change of mood," he says.

My friend decides to sing "My Way."

The clubbers in the Equinox applaud him warmly for his choice. He starts and goes out of tune a dozen times, but everybody still cheers him on.

I am somewhere else, though. My focus is all headed toward a table in the center of the club where two women sit alone.

The brunette among them is the woman I usually

fantasize about in my dreams. She is stunning with a sexy body, long black hair, and a stylish, arrogant look. I stare at her for ten minutes without even blinking, and I know that she notices me. She tries to act indifferently, but I can tell she's making an effort to ignore me.

"A new love, Nakouzi?" Khalil chuckles, as he looks toward her table. He's still in Sinatra mode. "Ouff!" he says when he sees her, and agrees with me that the woman is breathtaking. "This is a woman that I could love for 24 hours easily… maybe 48," I say. "You mean 24 consecutive hours?" he jokes. "Consecutive," I insist.

I am someone with a terrible paranoia from being rejected, and I have never done this before, no matter how buzzed I was. But I walk toward her table, and with no introductions, I whisper in her ear, "You look sad; what's wrong?" I ask in very intimate way, as if I've known her for years. "I am *dangerously* pissed off," she answers bluntly. "Give me your phone number," I say, looking at her to show that this is a statement, not a question. "I am very famous for taking care of *dangerously-pissed-off* people."

The next day, I call her. I invite her to dinner, pretending that I have an episode about modeling. "I want you to be a guest on my show," I lie.

We have dinner at L'Entrecote.

Chantal has no idea whatsoever about politics. She is someone who unintentionally detached herself from war, and it is as though she has built a bubble around herself. She can't tell me the name of our prime minister; she can't name one political journalist, one deputy, or even one politician.

For her, Syria controls everything in the country,

and she refuses to waste her time following the news of "puppets that can't move a muscle without the permission of the Big Boss," she says. Although she is politically uninformed, she has a point about politicians being puppets.

She's a model and has recently joined a musical band, "The Four Cats", something very similar to the Spice Girls. Her extreme passion is the gym, and the rest of her time is mostly spent with American movies and TV series, American comic books, or, most importantly, American music. Arabic for her is only a means of communication. she is not a fan of Arabic culture. In two words, she is just like me, a "pro-American" by default, and she isn't shy about admitting it.

Disney had a great impact on her life when she was a little kid. "But it has a greater impact on me as a woman," she jokes. The world of Disney was her escape from all the ugliness that surrounded her during the war, as she confides to me. She simply wishes the world was really cartoonish, like Disney. Behind the arrogant look, there is a little child that she perhaps has succeeded in hiding before. She is not as tough as she pretends to be, though.

In just one week, 98 percent of the women's phone numbers I have in my contact list are all deleted. And ten days later, I take her to my parent's house. I introduce her to my parents and announce that we're getting engaged in two weeks.

I have seen more than fifty different looks on my mother's face: angry, happy, sad, heartbroken, and excited, to name a few. However, the face she makes when I drop my news is completely new; it is a mixture of all the other looks happening at the same time.

On the coattails of that news, we also inform her that we have decided to live together for a couple of years before we get married. She thinks this is a very, very bad idea, especially for Chantal. “People are gonna rip you with their tongues,” she warns her. “I really don't give a damn what people think or say,” Chantal answers almost immediately. “We are not in America,” my mother insists. “Says who?” Chantal chuckles.

My mother realizes that no matter what she says, she won't be able to sway us. Gentle and sweet as she always is, she smiles politely and wishes us luck.

Truth is, I totally understand her concerns. She is mostly worried about Chantal. After all, many of my ex-girlfriends ended up crying on her shoulder when I decided to break up with them… or disappear. She fears it is just another crazy passion that will end soon. She simply can't believe that I dramatically changed from the ultimate womanizer to the respectable, lawful man in just ten days.

But, isn't this what love does for a living? Turning people upside down. Isn't that why it is called “falling” in love? If everything stays the same, and if your entire world doesn’t fall totally apart, then it’s something else that happened to you.

Seventeen days later, Chantal and I are on a ship in the middle of the sea, with just a couple of close friends, getting engaged.

It takes a couple of months before my mother and my fiancée get close, unbelievably close.

XVI
True, True Believers

We wake up on some crazy, thrilling news. The Israeli Government has surprisingly withdrawn its troops from South Lebanon. It all happened in 24 hours. The Lebanese people are simply shocked; it's too good to be true.

After more than 25 years of occupation, the Israeli State has apparently found out that it is becoming unbearably costly to keep soldiers on the Lebanese soil. Hezbollah has succeeded to turn the occupied area into a living hell and it is said that Israel can't afford to stay anymore.

The once unknown Shiite group was able to achieve alone what the entire Arab nation and all its armies combined had failed to accomplish. It's now more powerful than ever.

The celebrations all over Lebanon hit the streets. Even Christians, who were never actually threatened by Israel directly, celebrate the 'liberation'. For many, this means there are no more alibis for Hezbollah to keep its weapons and for Syria to keep its soldiers in Lebanon.

On the first episode after the liberation, I invite one of the high ranked deputies in Hezbollah, Nawaf al Moussawy.

"When will the organization dissolve itself and hand its arms to the Lebanese army?" I ask him before anything else. He doesn't look happy with the question.

"It's too early, brother Elie," he answers calmly, "why are you in such a hurry, we have our brothers in Palestine, who are still living under the Israeli occupation. How can you forget?" He reminds me.

"But this could take like 60 years or so?" I follow up. "Even if it takes 100 years," he replies immediately.

From his answer, I realize immediately that our story is far from over. Lebanon's welfare will be always connected to an external agenda. This time, it's Iran who decides our fate. That's a whole new fight, but are there any fighters left?

****

"I don't care where you are; just drive to 'Chez Sami' immediately. There's someone you *have* to meet, trust me," Khalil calls in a hurry.

"I'm not moving," I say drowsily. I have a terrible hang over from last night's drinking and I plan on not moving, especially if Khalil called. He's 24 hours open and he never rests.

"Yes, you are," he says, chuckling. "I'm sitting next to the future. And we're both waiting for you."

"I'm not budging unless you tell me who it is."

"Pierre Gemayel."

Thirty minutes later I'm at one of our most popular seafood restaurants to meet the member of a legendary family—Lebanon's equivalent of America's Kennedys.

Pierre Gemayel is the nephew of Bashir Gemayel, the legend who the Syrians assassinated in 1982, and the son of Amine Gemayel, who took over the Presidency from his slain brother. Pierre was only 16 when the Syrians exiled his family to Paris after his father Amine's term as President ended. Always working to avoid even a possibility of challenge to their rule, the Syrians accused Amine of stealing hundreds of millions of dollars, and warned him that he'd be arrested, and then killed, if he ever came back to Lebanon.

For over 10 years Pierre's kept a low profile, rarely making any statements. But last month, at age 27, Pierre surprised everyone by returning to Beirut. He's practically daring the authorities to arrest him for the crime of having the last name *Gemayel.*

The truth is there's reason for them to be concerned. Pierre brings more than his last name; his looks and manner of speaking are actually similar to Bashir, and so likely to bring many memories flooding back to Lebanon's Christians.

"Why are you here?" I ask him.

"To fight," he says. "I won't stop until the last Syrian soldier is out of Lebanon, Hezbollah is disarmed as a political party, and Christians are back on their feet again."

"That's a lot of battles for one dinner," I reply.

"Those are just for starters," he says, laughing.

Pierre has strong opinions about ending the exile of Michel Aoun and freeing Samir Geagea. He also wants all political prisoners held in Lebanon and Syria released.

He's trouble. And he knows it.

"The Syrians can fabricate a thousand reasons to put you in jail," Khalil warns.

"Yeah, I know," he says, chuckling. "But they'll have to kill me to shut me up."

"Actually, nothing will stop them from killing you if you became a real threat," I tell him bluntly.

"Call me crazy," he responds, "but I come from a family that still believes this country is worth dying for."

From others that might be just a patriotic line; but I feel deeply that he means it.

"I'm going to run in the upcoming elections," he continues. "For our voices to be heard, we need to shout inside our institutions. Even if I lose, people will remember the noise I made. And that's how anything starts—with some noise. Right?"

"Definitely," I say. "I think you should be a guest on my show."

A mere week later, he is.

Pierre comes across as brave, smart, and spontaneous. The more I ask him tough questions, the more he thrives. I love having someone on the show who's not afraid to say what should've been said a long time ago. He's happy to shock people...and to shatter the silence.

Sometimes Pierre sounds like a crazy dreamer. But so did his uncle.

For Michel, it's the first time he's ever watched a political show all the way through. As soon as it's over, he jumps out of bed and heads to the studio just to shake hands with Pierre.

MTV's phone operators are bombarded by hundreds of calls. Almost all of them are thanking us for airing such a gutsy interview.

The next day the entire country is talking about the episode. My mother tells me she never stopped crying the whole time, and that her neighbors had the same experience.

But it's not all good news. Khalil asks me to join

him in Michel's office in the afternoon for an urgent meeting.

As soon as we're together, Khalil starts rattling off the outraged phone calls he's received from numerous officials. "They've all warned me that MTV is playing with fire, and they won't hesitate to 'punish all those who might expose the civil peace to danger.'"

"*Civil peace*, my ass. They can't do anything to us," I say. I look at Michel and see that he agrees with me.

"It's serious," Khalil insists. "They'll let it pass this time. But we have to promise this is going to be the *last* time."

This outrages Michel. He looks at me. "Let's bring them a nightmare every week. What do you say, Nakouzi?"

I've been waiting for him to say those magical words since he hired me. "Of course. If you back down once to these assholes, they'll own you."

"And what happens when you confront them?" Khalil asks. "Do you remember last time?"

"It's different now," I say.

"Really? Just what is different?"

"Come on, Khalil," Michel interrupts. "They can't shut down networks anymore."

"Oh? Why not?" Khalil persists.

"Because the country will explode in their faces if they try to shut MTV down," I say. "The people will—"

"Are you joking? What country and which people are you talking about?" Khalil interrupts, his tone getting angry.

"I say we confront them," Michel states decisively, ending the debate. "But this doesn't mean that we should be reckless and stupid," he adds, looking at me. "We do it carefully."

Khalil is silent. He obviously doesn't agree. But he knows that nothing can sway Michel once he's made up his mind.

"What do you suggest, Nakouzi?" Michel asks.

"Exactly what you said. Let's give them a nightmare every week."

"Do you have someone in mind?"

"Gebran Tueni. He'll make them crazy."

Gebran Tueni is the publisher and owner of *An-Nahar,* the most distinguished newspaper in Lebanon. He's continually writing articles criticizing both Syrian and Lebanese officials. The Syrians don't bother him because they don't feel threatened by newspapers, which are read by less than 10,000 people in Lebanon.

But Gebran appearing on TV is something else again. I invite him along with one of the deputies most loyal to the Syrians and Hezbollah. Gebran wipes the floor with him. The episode is another talk of the town.

At this point activists who've been banned by all the other networks get in touch. I no longer have to search for guests, because they're coming to me.

This only escalates as we approach the next parliamentary elections—both my and Khalil's phones are ringing off the hook.

I propose that we start a daily show about the elections, giving all serious candidates a fair chance to present their views. Michel takes four minutes to approve it. He has only one condition: "Let's give *everyone* a fair chance, pro-Syrian as well as anti-Syrian."

We name the show "Parliament 2000." I'm on the

air for three hours every night, including Saturdays and Sundays, and couldn't be happier. MTV is now seen as the primary platform of the opposition, giving a voice to those who've had to be silent for years. I'm full of optimism that something will change.

Suddenly the possibility of getting anti-Syrian deputies in the parliament doesn't sound as impossible as it did four years ago. Besides, Syria's dictator Hafez al-Assad passed away a few months ago. He's been replaced by his son, Bashar al-Assad, who is trying to project the image of a young reformer to the Western world. We don't know how long the charade will last, but decide to use it to our advantage.

I bring on 4-6 candidates every night. To my delight, they start competing with each other in criticizing Syria and the way it rules Lebanon. Viewers love it, and MTV's ratings soar. More importantly, polls show the popularity of these candidates to be soaring too.

However, amidst all the chaos, I escape with my fiancée for a day to Cyprus. I have a date that I can't miss—our civil marriage.

In Beirut, civil marriages are not acknowledged. You have to belong to a religion in order to get married. You must be a Sunni, Shiite, Maronite, or Druz to start a family. If you're not, then you haven't earned the right.

We fly to Cyprus and get married in our jeans in front of a civil judge.

"Do you, Elie Nakouzi, take Chantal Kaissar to be your beloved wife… for better and for worse?' the judge asks me in the automatic tone that they usually throw this sentence with.

With all the uncertainty of the world, I answer

quickly: “Of course I do,” I smile at my stunning wife.

The judge smiles and he asks the same question to Chantal, who answers shyly: “I do.”

Who knows? I think to myself, perhaps she’s even more uncertain than I am.

“I now announce you husband and wife; you may kiss the bride,” the judge concludes. “I already kissed her a million times,” I say, giving him the smiley who-needs-your-permission look. He gets it. And I kiss my beautiful bride…“

We come back to Beirut the next morning, and by 8 pm, I am ready in my studio for my first episode as a married man. I start the show by announcing my civil marriage in a challenging tone, urging the new candidates to support laws that allow young Lebanese to have a choice about the way they want to get married.

“…And now the church: who else do you want to fuck with my friend, who else?” Khalil whispers in my earpiece.

A day before the elections we stop bringing on candidates, as required by Lebanon’s election laws. We then shift from promoting the elections to covering them. In fact, we spread our cameras all over Lebanon to help prevent fraud.

No one expects the opposition to win a majority in parliament; the Syrians would never allow it. But even if just one or two anti-Syrian candidates are elected, we’ll have voices to “shout inside our institutions,” as Pierre put it.

As expected, there are hundreds of violations during the elections: bribery, intimidation, threats, and even some violent incidents. Despite this, the opposition manages to win seats for *eight* candidates.

Most of these winners were banned from appearing on the other networks and had almost no funds for political campaigns. The only appearances they made were on my show, leaving no doubt how powerful MTV has become in influencing public opinion and breaking the cycle of fear. In fact, the candidates say publically that they stood no chance if it hadn't have been for MTV, and me personally.

I feel proud when I watch an interview with Mosbah al-Ahdab, one of the young Sunni candidates who impressed me so much with his progressive ideas that I invited him on three times. "Elie Nakouzi made me," he says. "If it weren't for him, no one would have heard me."

Such statements are heard beyond Beirut. The March 8, 2001 edition of France's *L'Express International*, which is the equivalent of America's *Time Magazine*, names me as one of the 100 most influential people in Lebanon. According to the article, "In just a few months, Nakouzi's status has changed from talk show host to television star. On his daily show during the election campaign, this soft-spoken, chic, and dapper young man with a pleasant smile succeeded in expanding the boundaries of free expression in Lebanon.

"All of the candidates—and God knows there were many—appeared before his camera without any political or religious distinction, and all were able to express themselves freely. In Lebanon, where most television networks show a pronounced political or religious allegiance, this was a true first, a lesson in democracy given by this likable host.

"Though a celebrity, Nakouzi does not have a big head. His marriage in Cyprus to a singer was carried out with the utmost discretion. Cyprus was also chosen in order to celebrate a civil wedding, and not a religious one as is the law in Beirut."

I greatly appreciate the recognition. And I have a lot of plans to create more buzz.

The *Domino Effect* is the basis for my little conspiracy. And if I have learned anything about freedom from all those books I've read in my life, it is how contagious freedom can be.

Once the virus hits you, there's no medicine on earth that can pluck it out from your system. Just like religion, once you catch it, you can never stop the urgency to preach about it. I have nothing hidden in my agenda; freedom is the only item on my bucket list.

Every September for the past 18 years the loyal citizens of Ashrafieh, the hometown of Bashir Gemayel, holds a memorial service in his memory. The media has always virtually ignored it.

But not this year.

MTV heavily promotes and covers the entire ceremony. It's an emotional day that makes many cry. I struggle hard to keep my own tears hidden.

Right afterwards, during prime time, I conduct an exclusive interview with Bashir's wife Solanje and son Nadim, who haven't spoken on television since Bashir's assassination. Nadim looks a lot like Bashir in his 20s. Because the family has lived in France, Nadim isn't fluent in Arabic; but his resemblance to his father is enough to bring him all the popularity he needs.

After the show, Chantal and I are invited to dinner

at the home of the Gemayel's. We're sitting at the table with Pierre, Nadim, and their younger brother Sami. I whisper in Chantal's ear, "One of these guys might be elected President one day."

"Yes," she whispers back. "And then the Syrians will kill him."

It's really harsh of her to say that. But I know she's probably right.

XVII
The Black Stain

My career couldn't be going better—my name is in the news and my show's ratings keep rising.

Financially, I'm a wreck. My habit of spending much more than I can afford on restaurants, clothing, and cars was bad enough when I was single.

But now that I have a family I've also made a down payment on an apartment with a monthly mortgage, and that I've furnished in a manner keeping with my image. This has created debt beyond anything I've dreamed of before.

To make matters worse, I've been borrowing from loan sharks, so am paying outrageous interest charges.

My paycheck each month vanishes almost the moment I receive it. I'm now at a point of taking out loans from new loan sharks just to cover the interest payments to my old loan sharks. I have no idea how I'll ever get back in the black.

I swallow Xanax pills every night just to keep the specter of my creditors away.

I once planned to own a boat and a villa in the mountains. Now my greatest ambition is to get to zero in my accounts.

Unfortunately, I'm $300,000 short of reaching zero.

I feel optimistic that I'll eventually be able to monetize my fame beyond my salary. But I have no idea when or how that will happen.

One Sunday morning at 11:00 my cell phone rings

from a private caller. I assume it's one of the loan sharks reminding me of a payment due Monday. But that guess isn't even remotely correct.

"This is Rafic Hariri," the voice says after I answer. "Can you pass for a cup of coffee in the afternoon?" he asks gently. "Even if I have commitments, I'll cancel them, prime minister," I say.

Hariri doesn't normally have meetings on Sundays. His weekends are reserved for family and close friends...and I'm neither. I can't imagine what this is about.

At 2:00 pm I'm sitting on a plush chair across from the Prime Minister, who's on a coach in his residential office. He has on blue jeans and a blue sweatshirt, which make him look much younger than his usual suit. He seems cheerful, so I'm guessing this isn't bad news.

He starts with typical political chit-chat, which reveals nothing I didn't already know. He'll be head of the cabinet again, because his block of candidates succeeded in winning an overwhelming majority in parliament. The subtext he doesn't mention is that the newly elected president, Emile Lahoud, is a puppet for the Syrians. Lahoud would love to throw the Prime Minister in jail, but after Hariri's overwhelming victory the only way to get rid of him would be to kill him. And assassinating a leader with Hariri's international influence would be a dangerous move, even for Syria.

We have a light political conversation about his future cabinet plans for an hour, but it's obvious that's not the reason I'm here.

"Enough politics," he says abruptly. "Tell me

something. I heard from a friend that you have serious financial troubles. Is this true?"

"I have financial *difficulties*, not troubles," I reply a bit too quickly.

"Hum, difficulties," he chuckles. "I used to use this word a lot: difficulties," he nods his head and continues, giving me a look that says he knows a lot about life, money, and debts. "Would you like me to help?" he asks in a fatherly tone, looking me right in the eyes as he says it.

He doesn't sound like a politician anymore; he sounds like family.

"Why would you help me, prime minister?" I ask him gently. I don't want to give a quick answer. I feel that a yes might be as regrettable as a no, and I need some time to process this surprising situation.

"I don't need specific reasons to help everyone I help, Do I?" he asks. He stands up and walks toward his desk. It is a rhetorical question, but I still respond. "Yeah, I always wanted to ask you," I say, "why do you help all these people? Does it give you a sense of satisfaction to—"

"It is a sense of gratitude… to God Almighty, who made all this possible," he interrupts.

He sits at his desk, and I can hear him opening the drawer. He pulls out a big brown envelope and he places it in front of him. "Do you gamble, Elie?"

"No," I answer quickly,

"Why are you in debt, then? How do you spend your money?" he asks with curiosity. "Women, luxurious restaurants and hotels, clothes," I state my weaknesses. "Honestly, I don't even know how I spend all this money." I smile, without trying to hide my little 'misdemeanors'.

"What is the size of your debts," He asks, chuckling. "You mean all my debts?" I feel hugely embarrassed to drop the amount. "Yes, all of them," he insists. "Well, something around 350 or 400 thousand," I sigh, "however, most of these are long term loans and installed on payments," I ramble.

"And how big are your short term loans?" he asks, "the ones that you have issues in dealing with now."

"Something around eighty-five thousand," I reply quickly. I just want this conversation to end.

The prime minister opens a drawer in his desk, and I can hear him counting: "10, 20, 30, 40, 50, 60, 70, 80." I take a quick glance to find out that he's sticking ten thousand dollars pack in the envelope. Then, he takes a last pack, removes five thousand dollars from it, and adds it to the envelope, which he brings with him and places on the table in from of me. He sits.

"Take this," he points at the envelope. "It's $85,000," he says. "It will help you start paying your loans," he says.

"And how can I return this favor back?" I ask in an embarrassed voice, incapable of hiding the redness I can feel rushing to my face.

"I will tell you how," he answers without hesitation. "There's someone I'd like you to meet. He's arriving in about five minutes. His name is Bassel Fleihan."

"I'm not familiar with him."

"He's one of the most brilliant economic experts in the country. He works at the International Monetary

Fund in *Washington*," he says, stressing the last word.

"Hm." I pretend that I'm impressed. The truth is I'm not able to focus on anything else but the envelope. If I take it, I will literally become a whore. And if I refuse, it will be extremely difficult to keep the loan sharks off my back. It's virtually impossible to get this much money in one shot. I'm struggling mightily to turn his offer down.

"Speak with him," the Prime Minister continues. "Then invite him to lunch, as my treat. Listen to his plans and ideas. If you like what you hear, just give him a chance, like you gave Pierre Gemayel and hundreds of other guests, by putting him on your show. Grill him with any question you like. Bring on any economic expert you want, no matter who it is, and let them debate. That's all I'm asking—give him a fair chance."

"That's it?" I ask. "Why not simply put him on your own network, Future TV?"

"No. If he debuts on Future TV, he'll be perceived of as 'Hariri's man.' I don't want him introduced to the public this way. Some will start attacking him before they even hear his plans."

He's right. Everything he's saying makes sense.

The phone rings. Bassel Fleihan has arrived. We move to another room, where Hariri introduces us.

Fleihan is a true gentleman with a kind face and a permanent polite smile that can't be faked.

We chat for 10 minutes and agree to have lunch soon. The Prime Minister walks me back to where we began. The envelope is still sitting on his desk. He takes it from the table and hands it to me.

I don't know what to say. I've never been in a situation like this in my life.

I end up rambling some words of gratitude, and walk out.

As I drive home, a thousand thoughts are competing in my head: *What if someone finds out about this? What if Hariri is setting me up? What if it was all recorded? What if Michel and Khalil find out?*

The more what-ifs cross my mind, the more the money seems not worth the potential consequences. There's enough in the envelope to give me a break from loan sharks for a long time, but I can't feel good about it.

I don't tell Chantal. It's bad enough for me to bear this burden without imposing it on her too.

Too much money in your account can cause the same anxiety that a lack of it causes. Having $85,000 in my room keeps me up all night. Maybe that's what happens to people when they don't earn their money. Maybe one gets used to it at the end. I have no idea.

Anyway, the secret tortures me even worse the next morning. I feel I will explode if I don't talk with someone about it. I have no idea how Khalil will take it, but I have to tell him.

"Yesterday, I was bribed," I reveal to him after the fourth vodka. "Bribed?" he laughs. "Who bribed you?" "Hariri," I answer. "He gave me $85,000 for a small favor."

There is a deadly silence for only ten seconds, perhaps, but ten seconds can be very, very long and slow in this kind of situation.

"Are you fucking with me?" he asks, becoming very serious. "No." I tell him the full story.

He listens to the entire story. "Look," he says, "let me take care of Michel. If this is what you're worried about, I will explain the situation to him in my own words," he offers. "He'll probably give you a lecture about never doing it again, but it will pass eventually," he says.

"So," he returns to his regular, humorous tone, "it takes two or three Bassel's to resolve all your financial issues." He laughs, clinks his glass with mine and swallows a huge sip that empties it.

The next morning, I am at Michel's office. "Fuck you, Nakouzi, why did you do this?" He asks without introduction. "Why didn't you tell me?" he blames me with a serious tone. "I fucked up," I answer him, "I really did."

Michel sighs. "Look, I don't like this but I know that you're in deep debts, so, I will make an exception that I have never done for anyone in my life. Get Bassel Fleihan and coordinate with Hariri on 3 or four episodes, until you resolve all your financial issues. I wish I were able to pay your debts, but I can't honestly… so, go ahead, do it, but next time, let me know," he finishes.

I can't believe what I have heard from Michel. I thank him 36 times perhaps, without finding any other words to say. "Thank you, thank you… really, thank you," I leave his office.

Two weeks later, after struggling about it almost day and night, I call Bassel Fleihan and apologize to him about not having the lunch or him on my episode.

The problem is I have already spent the money that I took from Hariri and covered the most urgent loans; thus, returning it is not an option anymore.

I know it will screw my relationship with Hariri forever. I send him an apology through his advisor, promising that I will return every penny I took as soon as possible. "It's a debt," I explain.

"He doesn't want to hear from you," his advisor says when he calls back after five minutes.

To wipe away my mistake as a journalist, it's not enough that I turn down Bassel Fleihan. So I invite one of Hariri's worst nightmares, Jean Louis Kordahi.

Kordahi is President Emile Lahoud's protégé, and perhaps the only one close to Lahoud who people respect. Kordahi is perceived as a credible, transparent, hard working, and efficient technocrat. He's a brilliant communications' engineer, and since being appointed as the Minister of Communications has saved millions of dollars by closing many loopholes.

Having Kordahi on my show will outrage Hariri. But this is the only way I know to keep myself from falling into a dark hole I might never climb out of again. If I cave once, I might end up doing it 100 more times, perhaps spending the rest of my life accepting money to promote one politician or another. "I'm more financially fucked up than anyone suspects," I tell Khalil. "But I'm still a journalist, not a whore;"

The episode with Kordahi is even fiercer than expected. Kordahi never attacks the Prime Minister personally, but he dissects his entourage, especially those who previously worked in the Ministry of Communications. By the end of the episode, Kordahi has the vast majority of viewers supporting him in his battle for government reform.

I could've retained, even enhanced, Hariri's respect if I'd simply turned down his money.

But I didn't, and the damage is done.

All I can do is make a solemn vow to myself that I'll return every penny as soon as possible. It's the only way I can sleep again.

XVIII
What's Next?

"Do you want to know who's on my mind next?" I call Michel to ask him. "Who?"

"Michel Aoun." I drop the name.

Michel doesn't bat an eye. He calls MTV's lawyer and asks if there's anything illegal about Aoun appearing on MTV.

"According to the deal he made, Michel Aoun is banned from making any statements for five years—"

"And those five years have passed," Michel interrupts him.

"Um...yes," the lawyer stutters.

"Is it legal or illegal? Could they sue the network for it?" Michel presses him.

"Not legally, no. But politically, it's—"

"That's all I need to know. Thank you," Michel concludes, and hangs up.

"Go ahead," he tells me. "Contact Aoun in France. If he says yes, I'll fly out with you."

Two days later, Michel, Khalil, and I are on a flight to Paris. We keep the reason a secret to ensure the authorities don't stop us from traveling.

As soon as we land, Michel calls MTV and orders his staff to start broadcasting an incendiary teaser for my next episode. We expect everyone in Beirut will be glued to their screens for this one.

As soon as the promotion starts airing, Khalil's phone is pummeled with calls. Everyone is losing their minds, either warning him or threatening him.

The same essential message comes from the President's office, the cabinet, Homeland Security, Army Intelligence, and Syrian Intelligence: "Stop the promotion and cancel the show."

For all of them, Michel has one answer: "The show is on. Watch it."

Many turn to Michel's father Gabriel, who's considered "the voice of reason" at the network. But Gabriel is even more stubborn about this than Michel.

Aoun himself starts worrying that we'll cancel. Michel tells him, "There's no warning on earth that can stop this interview, no matter where it comes from."

The supporters of Michel Aoun set up giant screens in almost every town, as if they're preparing to watch the World Cup. Although his actions during the last year of his rule were highly questionable, and it's been 12 years since his exile, Aoun is still an inspiration for many as a stubborn voice against corruption and injustice.

The situation gets really tense and the authorities threaten to take some legal action if the show is broadcasted.

Khalil comes up with an idea to reduce their anger a little. "What if we bring someone to counter Aoun? Someone who disagrees with him? This way, we can defend ourselves by saying that both point of views are represented, the anti- and the pro-Syrian," he suggests.

"It will be hard to convince Aoun," Michel answers, after thinking about it for a moment. "We promised him that he'll have the full time to express all his views—"

"We can extend our episode for half an hour or

even 45 minutes. He can talk about everything he wants, as long as there is someone on the other side to respond," Khalil quickly answers.

"What do you think, Nakouzi?" Michel asks me. "I can play the devil's advocate if this would back them off a little. That's what I initially intended to do anyway," I answer my boss.

"They're smarter than this," Khalil interferes again.

Finally, we all agree that we shall at least give it a try. We have to think of someone that Aoun doesn't find unacceptable, though.

Khalil comes up with the name. "Charles Ayoub," he breaks the silence. "That's it, Charles Ayoub," he repeats the name again. "First, he's a journalist and the publisher of one of the most distributed newspapers in Beirut," Khalil explains while we consider the guest. He continues, "Second, and although he supports Syria fully, he's the only one who fought against the decision to exile Aoun out of his homeland... He always disagreed with Aoun respectfully but never insulted him," he reminds us. "Third, he's a very close friend of the president and the heads of all security and intelligence agencies in Syria and Lebanon," he says, with a winner's tone.

Both Michel and I agree.

Despite his pro-Syrian stands, Charles Ayoub is a decent journalist who always fought for his colleagues' rights to disagree. For him, Israel is the real enemy, not Syria; however, he doesn't just say this to gain a parliamentary seat or a high position. He's someone who still believes strongly in the Arabism of Lebanon.

I call Aoun and drop the suggestion immediately.

"I respect Charles," Aoun answers quickly. "At least he's not a hypocrite. I don't mind," he says.

When I call Charles to invite him, he doesn't take a second to approve. "You know how bad it could affect the distribution of my newspaper in the Christian side of Beirut if I attack General Aoun; however, I am definitely willing to do it. The truth is the truth, and people should hear it, even if they don't like it," he concludes.

And the show is on.

Expectedly, Aoun fires on everyone and everything; he attacks Syria by calling it a terrorist state run by criminals and corrupt dictators. He attacks Hezbollah and calls them gangsters and terrorists who abuse religion and Islam to implement an Iranian agenda. "Drug smugglers," he calls them. He attacks the president, the cabinet, the security services, the speaker of the house, and of course, Ghazi Kanaan. The General doesn't forget anyone.

Of course, Charles presents a completely different point of view, focusing on Israel as the sole enemy of Arabs, describing the Syrian occupation as being a “needed presence to assure stability”.

Somehow, I also manage to play devil's advocate for the entire episode, trying to represent the authority's point of view.

Our *symphony* hits the crescendo, and the more outspoken my questions, the fiercer Aoun becomes. Each time he calls Hezbollah a terrorist organization, Charles interferes to call it “resistance.” And this ignites the exiled general more and more, until we finally wrap after three hours.

We leave the studio and go out for a calm evening

along the Champs-Élyseés. It was a tremendously nerve-wracking day. But now that it's ended, we want to relax and celebrate our success in luxury.

Jamil al-Sayyed, the head of General Security in Beirut, has other ideas. He calls Khalil and says, "Nakouzi has to apologize on MTV's prime time daily news broadcast, or I will have him arrested at the airport."

"Apologize for what, General Sayyed?" Khalil asks politely.

"For offending the President and a friendly state, for inciting sectarian sentiments, and for disturbing the civil peace," Sayyed responds.

"Hold on, General," Khalil says. "It was just an interview, and—"

"Let him apologize, for the sake of everyone," he interrupts, and hangs up.

"Apologize?" I ask when Khalil shares the conversation. "We don't even have to discuss it. Let him arrest me."

"No one will apologize," Michel says. "We will travel together, and they'll have to handcuff us together."

Ten minutes later, Michel's father Gabriel calls to make me a better offer. "Son, if you don't feel like you want to come back now, stay in Paris for a couple of months or so. We'll take care of your family and your expenses, so you don't have to worry about anything. We can send your wife over if you like."

"It's a very tempting offer, and my wife would love it," I answer. "But I've already packed."

On the plane, a million thoughts cross my mind. *Can I handle prison?* I ask myself.

No, I decide. *I can't stand solitude and*

imprisonment. I'll collapse. I just have to hope it doesn't come to that. I close my eyes and try to not think anymore.

In an attempt at bravado, I'm the first one to get up when the plane lands at Beirut's airport. The truth is I'm immensely nervous and just working hard to hide it.

We agree that we'll behave normally, and simply smile if Security Forces arrest any of us. They'll be eager for a reason to humiliate us, so we'll act calm and give them no excuse.

We walk side by side until we reach the passport area. "If it is going to happen, it's going to happen here," I whisper.

Michel goes first. The guard takes his passport, looks into his eyes, fills out some papers, stamps his passport, and gives it back to him. He doesn't seem to even be aware of who Michel is.

Khalil is up next. It takes Khalil 12 seconds to turn someone into a friend, so he chats up the guard until they're talking like family.

Finally, it's my turn. The guard motions for me to approach. He takes my passport while Khalil is still standing next to him on the other side.

The guard stamps my passport normally. Then he says quietly enough for only me to hear, "Send the man a big hello from me next time you're in Paris," and shoots me a smile.

"I will," I say, and give him a thumb up.

It's weird. After all those warnings and threats, nothing happens. It looks like we've gotten away with doing an interview that inflamed the entire country.

For me, it's a sign the old fist of iron is starting to

loosen. “They just don’t know what to do with us. We’re beating them,” I tell Khalil. “We’re beating them.”

After Aoun, it's hard for me to back off.

"What's next” is Michel's favorite question nowadays, after each big scoop. I like the question, too, and I always have an answer he likes to hear.

Besides, people are now describing MTV as “the true voice of the opposition.” We have a reputation to maintain.

But this time I go out on a limb. “Samir Kassir,” I answer, with a wicked smile.

Even Michel has to pause when faced with this guest.

Khalil remains silent, pretending he didn’t hear anything. “What do you think?” Michel asks him.

“Why not announce MTV is forming its own militia? That’s the only step left after this.”

“Come on, don’t exaggerate,” Michel says.

I nod in agreement. “Bashar el Assad would never screw up the image he’s building for the West by shutting down a TV network.”

Khalil shakes his head. “You’re crossing all boundaries because you think the new guy in Damascus is different from his father. A smile and a nice suit don’t change the killer underneath. I’m afraid you’ll both soon discover how wrong you are.”

Khalil has reason for concern. Samir Kassir’s column for the newspaper *An-Nahar* has been described as “the weekly bomb.” He’s not just fearless in his writing—he’s sharp, deep, and venomous.

Samir is insanely brave enough to call for not only the liberation of Lebanon but also the overthrow of al-

Assad's own regime in Syria. That's what banned him from all TV networks initially. One could cross the local red lines sometimes and gets away with it, but to come anywhere near the Syrian regime is a different story. If there's anyone who doesn't know when to stop, it's him.

I'm one of his greatest fans, and we've spoken many times. However, I've never invited him on my show because I know that whatever he'll say on air will cross a line with the authorities they'll never forget or forgive.

When I call to invite Samir to my episode, he just doesn't take it seriously. "Come on, Elie," he answers, "you know they won't allow you to put me on air. You'll end up calling me a few hours before the show to apologize."

"This will never happen on my show," I assure him quickly.

"You know that I won't miss the opportunity to be on your show; however, I really don't want to put you in trouble. Do you really want to do this?" he asks, giving me one last chance to change my mind. "More than anything else," I reply, with the same challenging air.

Like always, and since it has been working perfectly fine recently, I also invite a pro-Syrian figure to create the balance.

This time, it's Marwan Fares, a deputy who owes his status and parliamentary seat to Ghazi Kanaan personally. He's devoted to defend the Syrians' actions. And it looks like he'll make it to the cabinet soon as a minister of information or culture, perhaps.

Marwan is reluctant at first, especially when he hears the name Samir Kassir. "I have to think about it. Give me a couple of hours."

A few hours later, Marwan calls to accept the invitation.

In minutes, the promotion is on air. I simply expect the ratings to soar. However, in addition to the usual warning calls that Khalil and Michel receive in these circumstances, this time, there are different kind of calls: Samir's friends and colleagues are putting on a huge pressure to cancel the show. Many think that Samir could get himself killed if he's allowed to speak uncensored.

My phone doesn't stop ringing either. Even Gebran Tueni, the fierce rebel, wants me to call Samir and cancel the show. He's worried about him like hell.

Samir works as a freelancer in Gebran's newspaper. Apparently, when the authorities couldn't sway MTV to cancel the show, they turned to Gebran. The latter, worried about the safety of Samir, has tried very hard to convince him to apologize and withdraw from the show. He simply can't, so he's turned to me, hoping to convince me to call Samir and back out of airing the episode.

"Listen Elie. Sometimes you gotta protect your boxer from hurting himself in the ring," Gebran explains to me on the phone. "Please pull him out. There are very bad intentions to fuck Samir up, I'm telling you," he says seriously. "I am receiving dozens of calls, and I am seriously worried about the consequences."

For 15 minutes, Gebran explains how serious the situation is. So, I promise to have lunch with Samir and try to sway him back.

"Look," Gebran emphasizes one more time, "Ghazi Kanaan is personally outraged about Samir. He's waiting for a little mistake to... maybe kill him, I don't know," he concludes, succeeding to shift me to an alert mode.

I call Samir immediately and invite him to lunch. "“Yeah, hit me with it. You’re going to have a headache. You’re going to have a stomachache. Don’t hesitate, I’ve heard every one there is,” he says, chuckling. “You don't have to invite me to lunch, you can cancel on the phone,” he says.

"I am not canceling anything," I reply with pride. "Let's have a quick bite and talk."

Samir orders two espressos. "Make them triple shot," he asks the waiter, "my friend and I will need some extra caffeine, obviously." He smiles at me. "Yes, Nakouzi, tell me, why do you want to cancel the episode? I guess you're here to apologize, right?" he says, very calmly.

“Samir, buddy—"

"Don't Samir buddy me, Nakouzi. Just drop it with no introductions. You know me!" he interrupts me, keeping the same smile on his charming face. "It's not only our enemies who don't want you on the show, Samir. It's also our friends," I say, cutting the crap.

"What do you mean?" he asks, surprised.

"I mean, everyone is so worried about you. There are rumors that Ghazi Kanaan wants to fuck you up, and everyone thinks that we should not give him more reasons to—" He doesn't let me finish.

"Do you think I am scared from Ghazi Kanaan, Nakouzi? Do you think a corrupted, low criminal could scare me?" He looks at me, right in the eyes, as if he's blaming me for even thinking about it. "Come on, Nakouzi," he challenges me. "Don't fear this bastard.

That's exactly what makes him thrive—"

"Let's just avoid getting in trouble with him personally, that's all I am saying."

"No, no, no, no, no," he almost jumps off his chair, "we should do exactly the opposite. This is the man we should be fighting, Nakouzi, not his puppets," he goes on.

"This man kills people for breakfast, Samir—"

"Are you afraid of him?" he asks in a friendly tone.

"Yes, very much, to tell you the truth."

"Me, too," he laughs, "but let's not show him... And remember, there are no scary people; there are only some people who get scared.

I shake my head. “What are you talking about?”

“Imagine that we all show Ghazi Kanaan we aren’t scared of him. At that point he stops being scary. "I get you," I smile.

“Let’s make that happen, Nakouzi, don’t retreat. "Where are your balls, install them again, and let’s do this show.” He bats on my shoulder.

"Shit; we're gonna get in trouble, aren't we?"

"Of course, we are," he laughs. "But this is what we do for living; this is what you signed up for, right?"

"Let's not mention Ghazi Kanaan or Bashar al-Assad by name, though!"

"I will only mention them if I need to," he avoids the promise. "*You* don't mention him if you don't want to, but I walk uncensored my friend… uncensored."

Again, he hits me with his irresistible smile, the son of a bitch. He's brave, so brave, and it sounds like there's no one on earth who could possibly intimidate him.

After all, if Ghazi Kanaan couldn't, then no one would.

"See you on Tuesday, then," I say.

As soon as I am out, Khalil calls.

"So? What did he say?" he asks quickly.

"He said there are no scary people; there are only some people who get scared," I quote Samir.

"Hmm," Khalil chuckles. "Then, let's get ready for next week's headaches."

"You better," I reply immediately, without even trying to make it easier on my friend.

Samir is trouble. But he's lovely trouble!

The episode is one of the most explosive I've ever hosted. Samir exceeds even my expectations. In just the first few minutes, he turns to the pro-Syrian deputy who's my other guest for the evening and asks him, "How was your dinner last night?"

"What do you mean?" asks the deputy, looking at Samir like he's lost his mind.

"I'm talking about your dinner with Ghazi Kanaan last night, when he taught you, like a little student, how to defend the Syrian occupation and its many crimes. Aren't you ashamed of yourself?"

Samir has said on national television the name that no one dares utter even in private conversations.

Kanaan works criminally hard to run the country from behind the scenes. He hates when anyone uses his name, even if it's to flatter him. Like Harry Potter's *Voldemort*, he prefers dark places to the light of day. When people mention *Ghazi Kanaan*, people disappear.

I know how much trouble Samir has just put us all in. But I play it cool and go along with his dangerous game. “Why don’t you answer?” I ask the deputy in an innocent tone. “Is it true that you had dinner with General Kanaan yesterday? What exactly did you discuss at that dinner? Just answer the man. There’s no need for tension.”

Khalil is shouting in my earpiece, “Pull the name from the table! Change the subject immediately!!!”

But I’m so happy that someone’s finally had the guts to say *his name*, I can’t bring myself to follow Khalil’s order. I pursue Samir’s inquiry about Kanaan.

After the show, Khalil and I have our first official fight. We don’t speak to each other for two weeks. It’s only resolved when Michel invites us both to dinner to patch things up over vodka.

Meanwhile, since the night of the episode Samir is continually harassed. Two cars full of armed men from Syrian Intelligence follow him everywhere. They sit next to him in coffee shops and restaurants, doing their best to intimidate him.

When that doesn’t work, Ghazi Kanaan and his puppets devise rumors linking Samir to a made-up conspiracy supposedly created by the Mossad and CIA. If charged and found guilty, Samir would face prison, and even execution for treason. But Samir won’t shut up. He continues his fierce attacks through his weekly column, using his poisonous ink to hit the Syrian regime at its core. He’s unbelievably stubborn and courageous.

Things aren’t great for me either. Almost daily I hear threats, or am told about some scheme to destroy me. Some warn me Syrian Intelligence is fabricating evidence to ruin my reputation, and that it involves prostitution or drugs.

"If they can find one woman on this planet I paid to fuck, let them put me in jail forever," I reply. "As for drugs, if there are machines that can detect traces of drugs in one's body from the day he's born, let them test me with them. If they find even one microgram of hash, I'll accept a death sentence."

They have nothing on me. My background is clean, and it makes me feel strong and confident.

A few weeks later, I call Gebran Tueni, who's still upset that both Samir and I have disregarded his advice, and invite him to lunch. He refuses at first, taking a stand, but two minutes later he agrees. "I can't get upset at you two," he says.

"We are all one gang, Elie. And we must be cautious that they don't fuck anyone of us. We need Samir as much as we need people like you; however, these are sensitive times. We better be smart and wise," he recommends.

Despite Gebran's concerns, I have an inner feeling that we completely got away with it.

A month after Samir's interview, the Syrian and Lebanese secret services attack a peaceful protest organized by the Lawyers' Union. Ghazi Kanaan isn't done, obviously. The protesters are savagely beaten, and dozens are arrested. They include Habib Younès and Antoine Sfeir, two journalist colleagues and good friends of mine.

The same day the Security forces break into the home of Toufic Hindi, a frequent guest on my show, and arrest him as well.

I call Michel. "Have you heard? And will we do something about it?"

"I'm already at MTV," he replies. "Meet me at the studio," he says, as if MTV is now the revolution's headquarters.

An hour later I'm live on air. I criticize every official in the country, and invite opposition figures to come to MTV right away to condemn the security state we're becoming. Soon after politicians, journalists, and activists fill our building. Even Khalil doesn't argue this time.

For three days, we talk about nothing but the assaults and arrests, pressuring for the release of the activists.

The Intelligence Services counter by claiming Habib, Antoine, and Toufic have admitted to working with Mossad agents.

While we're certain our friends have nothing to do with the Israelis, we aren't sure whether their captors scared them into incriminating themselves or simply fabricated evidence. They're highly skilled experts at both tactics.

Syrian Intelligence starts leaking tapes that are hard to defend. Our three friends appear calm and unforced while making confessions of treason.

But it doesn't stop there. Some newspapers that are mouthpieces for Ghazi Kanaan claim that MTV, and me specifically, are involved in providing the traitors with a platform to promote their conspiracies.

A couple of days later two cars are assigned to follow me everywhere, echoing what happened to Samir Kassir. They follow me from my home to my office, into the restaurants, coffee shops, and even nightclubs — everywhere. I see them every time I turn around.

They never speak to me, though, even when I try to provoke them with a friendly "hello" in the morning. They're obviously following strict orders to never interact with me in any way. Once I'm clear about this, they're no more intimidating than stray dogs.

After about a month I mention them on my show, telling my audience that the authorities are spending resources on the odd and silly behavior of watching journalists while the country is filled with more than 1 million guns in the hands of sectarian militia members.

The cars and men disappear a few hours after that.

The number of people supposedly involved grows bigger every day, including popular deputies who aren't on board with Kanaan's agenda. It's psychological warfare, as well as a patient plan for laying the seeds for mass arrests.

This goes on for over a month, and it's looking serious. But then a massive event beyond Kanaan's control interrupts everything.

XIX
9/11

It's a Tuesday, and I have an episode lined up that I expect will be extra fun for me. It's a debate between two great friends: Samir Franjieh, one of the brilliant minds of the opposition, and Charles Ayoub, a frequent host in my show after Aoun's episode. I disagree with Charles in every political discussion probably, but I respect him and deeply value his friendship.

I'm in Khalil's office finalizing show details when his phone rings. "Turn on CNN right now," the caller tells him. Khalil does. A plane has crashed into the World Trade Center.

It's chaos. No one knows what's going on. Was the crash an accident? Or was it malicious?

And then many questions are answered in the most horrible way with the appearance of the second plane.

It's hard to describe our feelings in the seconds that follow. For a brief time we think this might be a movie. It's just too shocking and surreal to be truly happening.

We flip channels. The second plane hitting the towers is now being replayed on every network in the world with a news division.

Khalil and I look at each other. We can't find the words.

And then the climax comes: the collapse of the towers. "This is real. This is fucking real!" I shout as it all falls down. We both jump out of our chairs and stand in the middle of the office, looking at the screen with eyes and mouths wide open. The images of the towers falling, and of the people falling or jumping from them, are burned into my mind together with my horrible memories of the war.

Regularly scheduled programming is canceled on all the TV networks. My show becomes a nightly discussion of 9/11. When MTV doesn't have political programs of its own to air, it broadcasts CNN's live coverage.

The death toll is 3,000. It's a large number, even in Lebanon where we lost 250,000 civilians during our civil war. No battle in Beirut ever snuffed out 3,000 innocent lives in a few minutes.

Everyone's wondering how the United States will retaliate. I, among many, guess the first target will be the Saudi regime, which is the primary home of religious extremists. The Jihadist doctrine comes in large part from Saudi religious Sheikhs who release crazy pronouncements daily in mosques throughout the Kingdom.

In addition, it's well known the Royal Family was the main source of funding for bin Laden during his war with the Soviets in Afghanistan. He turned against them after American troops landed in Mecca during the first Gulf war. The Royal Family responded by trying to portray bin Laden as a criminal and terrorist; but by then it was too late.

Bin Laden's *Robin Hoodian* style appeals not only to Saudis, but also to Muslims everywhere, actually. In the eyes of most Arabs, bin Laden is morally superior to the Royal Family because he gave up the comforts and luxuries of wealth to fight for the entire nation. Further, he’s considered a hero who with very limited resources managed to fight the two biggest powers on earth, the USSR and the US, in the name of Islam.

There are rumors the Royal Family is terrified of what America might do next. However, America decides to attack Afghanistan.

I am no expert in international politics, but I find it extremely weird to go after the Taliban, even if it is embracing or hiding bin Laden. Al Qaeda is an idea more than an organization, and Al Jihad has no exclusive location or demographics.

Afghanistan? I just don't understand it, but America is still my ally, no matter where they decide to strike, I resolve in my head.

Suddenly, the Taliban, who have never been seen before, are more famous than Britney Spears. They are all over the news, but no one has pictures of them except some old footage that the media replicates whenever they mention them.

It is like declaring war on ghosts, but it takes less than one month to remove the Taliban from power; however, even I, the greatest fan of America, am not really overwhelmed. No one predicted the Taliban would defeat the international coalition that was lead by the United States. Thus, their fall was inevitable, and sane people knew it.

Nevertheless, locally, we have reason to believe that the winds of change are coming. The American presence in the area, even if it's in Afghanistan, is always comforting for people like me and for all minorities in the Middle East, I believe.

The US surely won’t stop there.

XX
God Bless America

It is probably useless to count how many times I have dreamed of visiting America; however, I have never tried to apply for a visa before. It includes lots of forms and applications. And even before 9/11, the percentage of those who succeed in attaining the stamp on their passports is really low.

After 9/11, I imagine it would take years before the United States let any Arab enter its territory.

Yet, An unexpected consequence of 9/11 is that it gets me an invitation to the land of my dreams.

A group of Lebanese Christians who fled the civil war, called the Maronite Christians' Diaspora, are organizing a conference in Los Angeles. The goal is to loudly proclaim not all Arabs are terrorists; and that Christian Arabs have always been, and continue to be, strong allies of the United States. Guests include such luminaries as US Senator Joe Lieberman.

The organizers invite eight Lebanese journalists to cover the event. I'm lucky enough to be one of them.

I can hardly wait until the day we fly to America. I wish I could take Chantal with me. But she's pregnant in her eighth month. She can't hide her jealousy when I show her the American visa, stamped for five years on my passport. I promise to take her on a trip to the United States after she gives birth to our first child.

Chantal has already named him before he's born—Gio, she has chosen for the world to call him. She's unbelievably in love with him even before he's out. She has even purchased a personal computer for him and created an email address in his name. He's everything she can think of now, which makes her react less crazy toward my usual flirting with women. It's been like heaven for a while.

When we arrive in LA, I use my senses to try to absorb every part of it into me.

The city looks just the way I remember it from the movies. LA is so different from Lebanon: no military checkpoints, no soldiers in the streets, no pictures of warlords and politicians on the walls—and most importantly, no Syrian soldiers to worry about.

I can smell freedom in the air. And I can observe freedom in the eyes and smiles of every American I see—even if they aren't consciously aware of it themselves.

In the evening our hosts hold a dinner to welcome us. Each of them tells stories about how they ended up in the US. It's an emotional meal, with many tears. They miss Beirut terribly, but won't return while our country is occupied.

After dinner I hang out with Marcel Ghanem, who's a news anchor at LBC. He's the brother of George Ghanem, the journalist who recommended me for my job at *Have a Good Day*. We go to a fancy bar and order two bourbons. I've never had bourbon before but like the sound of the word; and it seems fitting to try new things in the US.

The Asian waitress who's taking my order suddenly gets a closer look at me and, to my shock, is mesmerized. "Are you Antonio Banderas?" she asks. "Oh my God, you're Antonio Banderas!"

"No, I am not Banderas," I say.

"Oh, all you stars do that. You don't want people to recognize you in restaurants," she whispers, giggling.

"No, no, seriously. I'm not Antonio Banderas."

She finally leaves with our orders. But five minutes later she returns with two other Asian waitresses. They both agree she's right about my being Banderas.

"Okay," Marcel says. "We can't lie to the beautiful ladies anymore, Antonio."

"I knew it," the waitress says, jumping with excitement. One of the other waitresses pulls out her camera and starts taking pictures.

I end up signing autographs for all three of the ladies: "With Love, A.B." After that they leave us alone.

Ten minutes later Marcel goes up to his room, exhausted from the flight.

I'm still too excited to sleep, though, so stay and order more bourbon.

Two young men who observed the picture-taking approach me. "Are you a star or something?" one of them asks politely as he extends his hand. "I'm Bob, and this is Dan."

"I'm Elie," I say, shaking his hand, and explain the confusion.

"Oh, you don't look like Banderas at all," Dan agrees.

"I tried to convince her that I'm George Clooney, but I failed," I explain, and they both chuckle.

They are decently dressed and they sound funny, polite, and smart. It turns out Abraham and Daniel are Israeli Jews who've just arrived to LA for a vacation.

When I tell them I'm Lebanese, there's some initial

tension. “You don’t look Arab,” Bob says. Of course, they would have never thought to join me if they knew I was Arab, I guess.

There's a little tension in the air at first, but after a few drinks, we’re all relaxed.

I saw Israeli soldiers from a distance when I was a boy, but this is the first time I’ve ever sat and chatted with Israelis civilians. They don’t look like fierce enemies, as they’re always described in the news. They’re polite and calm, and appear to hate violence and war as much as I do. They both feel much more relaxed when they know I was born Christian. First, they confused my name Elie with Ali, one of the most popular Shiite first names. Hezbollah has perhaps more than 5000 Ali's in his ranks.

"They'd grant you an immigrant visa in two minutes in the United States, right?" I ask them. "Not that easy," Dan explained, "but yeah, it is very possible, though," he admits.

"Then what makes you return back there?" I say. "Scientifically, You’ll never have peace of mind as long as you live in Israel. You’re surrounded and incredibly outnumbered by hundreds of millions of Arabs who literally pray five times a day for your deaths. I’ve often wondered why anyone would choose to live like that if he doesn’t have to,” I spit it all out.

"It's home," Daniel answers, and his buddy agrees strongly.

The argument goes friendly but blunt.

Before we part Bob suggests taking some pictures of us together, but I decline. “Contact with any Israeli is illegal in Lebanon. Such photos could put me directly in jail, or worse.”

"Oh, right," he says. "We're the enemy."

We all laugh.

The next two days I focus on covering the conference. Most of the discussions revolve around the Syrian occupation and Hezbollah. There are no limits on what can be said, of course, so many describe Syrian officials as criminals and Hezbollah members as terrorists. Further, the organizers write a petition asking for immediate American intervention to remove both Syria and Hezbollah from Lebanon.

As a result, LBC decides to tape the conference, and broadcast only the discussions that won't enrage the authorities.

In contrast, MTV broadcasts the conference live. Michel insists from Beirut that I make sure there are no time delays or editing.

Marcel senses danger, and makes only a couple of brief appearances on panel discussions. "I don't want to be part of this insanity," he tells me. "These people are staying here. We have to go back to Beirut."

I don't care. I chase down US Senators and Congressmen, and ask them questions that I'm hoping will provoke them into action against Syria.

To my surprise, Khalil informs me he hasn't received a single phone call from the authorities. "No threats, no warnings, nothing. All is good here. Simply enjoy the rest of your trip."

After the conference ends, we have three days to enjoy ourselves before we need to leave. To our great fortune, Lebanese-American billionaire Ramon De Sage (originally Raymond Abi-Rached) has heard about us journalists, and he sends his private jet to fly us all from

LA to Las Vegas. He books suites for each of us in The Venetian, a hotel more luxurious than anything I've ever encountered.

Ramon misses Lebanon and can't stop talking about his days there. Very kind and extremely generous, he takes us to the best restaurants, bars, casinos, and extravagant nightclubs.

The evening starts with a dinner at the Paris Hotel in the famous Tour Eiffel restaurant that overlooks the extraordinary, charming Bellagio Hotel and its illuminated water fountains: a view that you'd easily confuse with a computer wallpaper—just unreal! The Eiffel tower in Vegas has the same exact size and height of that in Paris, and still, the water flowing out of the fountains can reach the highest floor in a breathtaking, splendid scene.

From the Paris Hotel, we pass by the Bellagio and the MGM, and at four in the morning, Marcel and I are in the Venetian hotel-which has replicated the river of Venice in Italy- inside one of those little Venetian canal boats (Gondolas), singing in a very loud, opera voice: "God bless America, God Bless America, God Bless America."

"If Vegas has impressed you this much, wait until you see New York," the concierge who's helping me in setting up my luggage says, after I confide to him how painful it is to pack. "I fell in love, head over heels, with this country," I open up as we take the elevator down to the lobby. "New York," I sigh.

In the plane, a strange thought angers me for the entire flight back. I miss Beirut a lot, but at the same time, I don't want to return. Suddenly, I wish if I could bring my family and move to America.

I remember Dave and Dan and the lecture about how irrational it is to come back to a place where insanity and anger surround you from each side and corner. And here I am, on a flight back to insanity, anger, oppression, humiliation, and occupation.

At least the Israelis have a government that defends their sovereignty. What have we?

Somehow, Beirut starts to sound unworthy.

XXI
Freedoms?

When my flight from America lands in Beirut, it's midnight. I'm exhausted, and I hugely miss my pregnant wife.

After the guard scans my passport, though, he looks at his computer screen and gets a strange expression on his face.

"Let me recheck this," he says. He runs the passport through a second time...and shakes his head. "Mr. Nakouzi, someone's issued a warrant for your arrest."

"Excuse me?" I reply, not taking it seriously. "For what possible reason?"

"I'm sorry, but I'm not allowed to disclose this information. Please come with me."

I'm taken to the security office, where an officer in his mid-30s is at his desk.

"What's going on, Captain?" I ask nervously.

"We received a warrant this afternoon from the Ministry of Internal Affairs. I have to arrest you and take you to the General Security building."

"Are you joking? What am I being charged with?"

"I can't tell you that. A car is coming for you in 30 minutes. You can wait here until then." In a lower voice, he adds, "I'm not supposed to have you in my office, but I'm a fan of your show."

"Come on, man," I say, "tell me what the charge is. I promise I won't let a soul know you did."

"Sorry. I have strict orders to not even talk to you."

I sit and try to figure it out. *Was it something I said while covering the conference? Was it something one of my interview subjects said?*

Then another thought occurs to me. *Oh, shit. What if someone took pictures of me at the bar with David and Daniel? Intelligence could make up a story about them being Mossad agents!*

I glance at the captain. "I'm fucked, aren't I?" I ask him

He looks at his watch, refusing to make eye contact.

I light a cigarette without asking permission. He clearly doesn't like it, but says nothing.

"You've got to reveal what this is about, Captain. Even a criminal has the right to know why he's being arrested. Treat me like a dangerous criminal and tell me."

The young officer retrieves the warrant, stares at it, and finally spits it out, "It's a bounced check."

"What?! Are you kidding me?"

He's not kidding.

I start to relax. A bounced check is almost a joke compared to my other scenario.

Still, it makes no sense. I'm on excellent terms with all my loan sharks. Besides, what they do is illegal, so why would any of them get the police involved?

"Captain, there's something wrong here. I really need more information."

After several minutes of my insisting, the captain reveals two more details. "The name of the complainant is Vincent K. And the check was for $70,000."

That's crazy, I think. I *did* give Vincent a $70,000 check—but only as security against his loans. I've been making my payments regularly, so he has no reason to cash in the deposit—especially not without talking to me first.

Without asking for permission, I take out my cell phone to call Vincent.

"You can't do that!" The captain objects.

"Let me talk to the guy, Captain. Trust me, this is just a misunderstanding."

He's irritated, but gives in.

Vincent picks up. Before I can utter a word, he says rudely, "Listen, Nakouzi, I don't want to have anything to do with you! Don't call me, don't talk to me. Just give me my money and then throw away my number!"

"What the fuck is wrong with you, you bastard?" I shout angrily.

"What's wrong?" he shouts back. "They came to my house, they threatened my mother, and they threatened me!" He calms down a little and adds, "Please understand."

"Okay, fine. You'll have your money within 24 hours—"

"It doesn't matter," he interrupts. "I can't take the money until at least Wednesday." Before I can point out today is Thursday, he hangs up.

I call him again and again. He won't answer.

The only person who can drop the charges is refusing to accept his money.

It dawns on me that someone in authority has decided to keep me in jail for a week, or longer, for a large bounced check to a loan shark. This situation can be used to undermine my credibility as a journalist. It might even destroy my career.

"You've got to let me make one last call," I ask the captain.

"I shouldn't have even let you make the first one."

"It'll be just 30 seconds, I promise. After that you can take my phone."

He grudgingly agrees.

I need someone who's both rich enough to sign for the amount I owe and heavily connected to the authorities. It's 12:30 am, and there are very few people with enough pull to wake up a government official.

Fortunately, I know one man who can turn things upside down in the middle of the night: newspaper publisher Charles Ayoub. I strongly disagree with Charles about his pro-Syrian positions. But he's a great journalist, and a fierce defender of his fellow journalists regardless of their political beliefs, which is why he's universally respected.

When I call, Charles quickly answers. "Nakouzi! Are you okay, my friend?"

"I'm *not* okay, Charles. I'm in deep trouble and need your help." I start telling him what happened.

He doesn't even let me finish. "I'm getting dressed and heading for the airport immediately. But first put the Captain on the phone."

"Charles Ayoub wants to speak with you." Charles is close friends with Jamil al-Sayyed, the head of General Security, so the captain becomes very alert when I drop Charles' name. He takes my phone and walks out of his office to speak privately.

A few minutes later he comes back. "You picked the right man to call. I'll be taking you to the General Security building myself. Mr. Ayoub will meet us there."

When we arrive, Charles' car is already outside.

My 'host' leads me to a huge basement filled with cells and prisoners, hands me over to a prison guard, and leaves. The guard, who has a cold face and mean, arrogant look, pushes me into an empty cell.

Just as I step inside, though, Charles walks in with me, surprising both the guard and me. He's holding an envelope.

"Don't worry," Charles says. "I've got 70,000 in cash, and I'm getting you out of here."

The guard instantly recognizes him. "Mr. Ayoub," he says, "you can't be here. Please, you must leave."

"I understand you're under orders," Charles responds. "However, I'm staying with my friend, who's been unlawfully incarcerated. You can shoot me, or bring your men to drag me out by force. But otherwise I'm not leaving without Elie. There's no need to discuss it further."

The guard is conflicted. "Mr. Ayoub, with all due respect, sir, I must ask you to vacate this cell. You're someone who I hugely admire and—"

"Listen," Charles interrupts. "I have the cash needed to solve the problem. There's no point to keeping my friend here just because the complainant isn't in the mood to receive his money."

"It's not my place to decide this," the guard says.

"Then call General Jamil al-Sayyed. He can decide," Charles challenges him.

The guard blushes from confusion. He looks really

worried about fucking with someone as influential as Charles. He decides to take Charles' advice and goes off to make the call, leaving the cell door wide open.

Ten minutes later the guard appears with his phone stretched to Charles. "It's General Sayyed," he says.

"Are you serious, Charles?" I can hear the General's voice say. "You're my friend, my very close friend," Sayyed goes on, "but you can't do this. You have to get out immediately."

"Be kind, my dear friend. You know me well enough to realize nothing on earth will make me abandon a colleague in crisis...and especially when he's innocent."

The General *does* know this, and softens his tone. Still, he tries for 15 minutes to change Charles' mind. "You're obstructing justice, which is a crime. I urge you to leave my prison."

"Please, stop lecturing me about laws," Charles says with an ironic tone. "We have what's due, all in cash, to solve the entire problem."

"Charles—I don't have the authority to release him."

"Right," Charles says, laughing. "You have the authority to choose judges, ministers, and deputies, but *this* is outside your authority. Okay, Elie and I will just sleep here until someone with enough authority can get us out."

Sayyed is completely silent for a few moments. He sighs deeply, then says, "Listen to me. I can't get him out. This is bigger than you and me, Charles."

Charles suddenly realizes the General isn't bluffing.

This is much more serious than either he or I suspected.

Charles thanks Sayyed for the information and hangs up. The look on his face is not good. If this is bigger than the General...

But Charles isn't someone who gives up easily.

Even though it's now past 3:00 am, he calls President Emile Lahoud.

Unfortunately, the officer who answers refuses to wake the President at this hour. Nothing Charles says budges him. Charles has encountered someone as stubborn as he is.

Charles then proceeds to call several ministers in the cabinet. They all apologize, but tell him they can't do anything.

Charles now confides that he called the Prime Minister while waiting for me to arrive. But Hariri told him very bluntly that he doesn't want to have anything to do with me.

We're at an impasse. For a moment, even Charles looks defeated.

So I decide to tell him about Las Vegas.

Charles is a well-known high roller in Lebanon's casinos. When I describe the Bellagio, the Venetian, the Paris Hotel, the MGM, the streets, the lights, and the women, Charles seems to forget we're in a cell. He's fully taken by my stories about the most unusual city on the planet.

"You've gotten me so excited that I want to fly to Vegas right now," he says. "I'm going to gamble on one last attempt, Nakouzi."

He takes out his phone and asks me to be

completely silent.

The ringing goes on for about two minutes before someone answers.

"Yes, brother Charles," I hear a voice say. "Are you okay?"

Charles stands up immediately. "I so apologize for calling you at this hour. I need a big favor." With that, he walks out the cell so I can't hear what else is said.

I have no idea who Charles is talking to. The conversation goes on for five minutes. Then he hangs up and returns. "If we're not out within the next 10 minutes, then we're staying her for a while, my friend. Otherwise, we'll be flying to Vegas soon."

Six minutes later, the guard shows up again. "You're free to go, gentlemen," he says politely.

And just like that, we're free.

At 7:00 am, Vincent comes to the police station. He takes his money and drops the charges.

I beg Charles over 20 times to tell me who the hell got me out.

"I can't say," he says, chuckling. "I gave my word. And you know me and my word!"

Until now I assumed that if I stayed away from drugs and prostitutes, the authorities wouldn't be able to do anything to me because of my clean record.

Now I realize that my debts create a serious vulnerability.

My loans exceed $300,000. I have no idea where to come up with that kind of money if my other loan sharks get pressured like Vincent.

I explain the situation to Charles. He talks it over with Michel at MTV.

Two weeks later, the two of them co-sign a bank loan that covers the $300,000, taking care of the crisis.

I'm still in enormous debt—but now it's to a bank. I no longer have to worry about getting swallowed by sharks.

With my financial problems are solved, I decide to get even more aggressive in my show. They have nothing they can possibly hold against me except my words.

And for my words, yes, I am completely ready to go to jail.

A few weeks after the incident, Chantal gives birth to Gio.

In the hospital's waiting room, there are perhaps more than 50 friends and relatives; the whole Nakouzi's mini-militia is here.

I am waiting outside, smoking like a chimney. My cousins sound even more excited than I am.

Chantal's doctor has decided that she'd rather do a caesarian section, which could take around two or three hours in the operation room.

Finally, the nurse informs us that *our* baby is born. "The baby is in the shower room," she tells me, "and we're waking up his mother. They're both healthy and okay," she comforts everyone.

However, I am the only one allowed to enter the room, where another nurse is giving Gio his first shower. He's shouting, crying, and kicking left and right, as she rolls him between her big hands.

The nurse cleans him, and then she rolls a fluffy towel around him and combs the little black hair on his head.

Gio shouts hysterically non-stop. The nurse puts

him in my hands and leaves us alone in the room.

From the first second he grabs my finger, he magically calms down. It's like he knows already that these hands he's touching for the first time would turn into claws if anyone or anything tries to harm him. He knows it, the little Gio.

"See, he already knows that you're his daddy," the nurse, who comes back in the room, says, smiling at me. "It's okay, Daddy," she adds warmly, "you can let those tears out. I have seen every kind of man crying in this room," she says. "I will give you some time alone with your son now." She leaves the room again.

"My son," I repeat the word after her, and some tears come out. I don't think I am articulate enough to describe the intensity of those minutes.

Somehow, this little angel has already turned me into a coward. He's five minutes old, and I am already thinking that I should perhaps stay away from trouble.

Somehow, I feel like I lost my freedom forever; something that I haven’t even felt in the prison cell. I stare at Gio's little cute face. Is this how our children are supposed to make us feel when they're born?

In my next episode, I announce the news to my viewers. I have absolutely no idea why I need to make a declaration to the entire world that I now am a father.

XXII
Déjà Vu

In April 2002 Albert Moukheiber, a 92-year-old deputy in the Metn district, passes away. An interim election must be held soon to replace him. A crazy idea occurs to me.

"Why don't you run for that seat?" I ask Michel. He was born in the Metn district and he's eligible to run.

Michel laughs at me, but I press on. "Think about it. The country needs successful and visionary people like you. And your family has a history of being in politics."

In fact, Michel's uncle and namesake has been a minister or deputy for over 30 years. Michel Sr. is a powerful man with the final word on many sensitive political matters. Some have described him as a godfather who'll grant any favor to allies, but also a shark who mercilessly devours opponents.

Further, Michel Sr.'s son Elias Murr is the Minister of the Interior.

To hold such power, Michel Sr. and Elias maintain close ties with the Syrian authorities, defending the occupation as being necessary for Lebanon's stability. My boss Michel turning MTV into the voice of the opposition has created an enormous rift in the Murr family.

"It's not for me. You know I'm terrible at diplomacy," Michel points out. "But I'll tell you a secret—my father is considering running."

Gabriel Murr is also a highly respected figure—a self-made man who's built a fortune from his expertise as an engineer, and then from MTV. Since parting ways with his brother, Gabriel's been thinking about redefining the Murr name in politics.

When Gabriel declares his candidacy, everyone's surprised. But the key opposition figures in the district almost immediately endorse him.

Michel Sr. is simply outraged. He's the political voice and figure that represent the Murr's family. And it's very well known that he usually has the final saying in this particular district. He usually names the candidates, who should win and who should lose. Therefore, he decides to teach his brother Gabriel, who stands bluntly against his political agenda, a tough lesson.

Michel Sr. can't run for the seat himself, since he's already a deputy in the parliament. Furthermore, he nominates his daughter, Mirna, for the seat, promising to humiliate his brother politically. The two brothers become official opponents.

As a well-established and Syrian-backed politician, Michel Sr. starts out 70 points ahead in the polls. We have only a month to close the gap.

"I need two to three hours of prime time every night until the election," I tell Michel. "I swear I'll set the country on fire in 30 days."

"I believe you," Michel replies.

"You know what?" Khalil says. "From the bottom of my heart, I hope we lose. Because if we win the election, we'll lose the network."

"They can't do anything to us," I assure him. "The Americans are nearby now, and with them are the winds of change. Soon they'll be knocking on the doors of Iraq and Syria, ushering in a new era of democracy. The US won't allow the shutdown of the only Arab network in the region that preaches free speech and human rights night and day. Are you out of your mind?"

"Oh yeah, I forgot about the winds," he says sarcastically. "Sometimes I feel like you're totally detached from reality, Nakouzi."

I just shake my head. Khalil always worries too much.

Michel transforms Murr TV into his father's campaign headquarters. MTV's 500 employees are young, fresh, and enthusiastic helpers to the campaign. The network is suddenly one big family.

Every night I urge my viewers to vote. I hold live debates where my guests break all the rules. I report on corruption scandals, trying to provoke citizens to exercise their national duty.

It motivates some. We soon get in 200 young activists as volunteers. But we need many, many more to even dream of beating Michel Sr.

It's hard to get past a pervasive feeling that no one can change anything. If my viewers don't believe they can make a difference, we're sunk. From previous experiences, many people believe that their voices don't count anyway, and it is really hard to motivate them, as I start to realize.

Two weeks from Election Day, Gabriel is 40 points behind his brother. That's better than 70, but still a huge gap. Michel Sr. has all the money, power, and influence he wants from the Syrians. Working for us are enthusiasm, hope for the future, and the truth. Are those enough?

Many doubt it. But I deeply believe we can win this fight. We just need the right knockout punch.

That's when I have another idea. I go to Michel and Khalil, and tell them two words: "Michel Aoun."

"What about him?" asks Michel.

"He's how we win. We get him to endorse Gabriel."

"That's a nice thought," says Khalil. "Except for the past 13 years Michel Aoun has urged his supporters to boycott any election supervised by an occupational force, remember? He considers the current government unconstitutional, and believes endorsing a candidate would be legitimizing the election process."

"You're right," I say. "At first I thought we could motivate his base through logic and truth, but I was wrong." Aoun is actually like a god to his followers. Without his loud and clear blessing, they'd rather go fishing than vote.

"The polling data is clear," I go on, "Our only chance is to fly to Paris and convince Aoun how critical it is to get his endorsement."

The next day all three of us are on a plane. It's been only six months since we aired the extraordinary interview with Aoun, so I'm hoping that's still fresh in his mind.

We employ a big pot of coffee and nonstop talking. Aoun listens carefully. Our enthusiasm puts him in tears three times.

When we finish, he asks, "Do you have your camera and crew?"

"I can bring them here almost immediately," Michel quickly replies.

"Let them come," the General says. "I will endorse your father like I have never endorsed anyone before."

I don't dare believe it until the cameras are on and he begins. Within five minutes Michel Aoun's made a speech that I feel sure will inflame tens of thousands of his supporters.

Michel arranges for the speech to air that night. When we arrive back in Beirut the next day, over 1,500 volunteers have already joined the campaign.

We're 10 days away from the election, and the excitement is intense. Because of Aoun's endorsement, everyone is now taking this battle seriously. No one knows what will happen.

Finally, the big day arrives.

The morning starts with discouraging news. Gabriel is still 15 to 20 points down in the polls.

I cross fingers that a certain number of people are lying to the pollsters to ensure personal safety, but will come out and vote from their hearts.

We set up extensive live coverage, ready to capture any attempts at election fraud. I'm on the air for 14 hours straight. By evening, I'm running on adrenaline.

At 7:00 pm, multiple news sources report that the numbers are very close.

One hour later, more than 10,000 of our supporters are celebrating victory outside the MTV building.

That exhilaration fades when the Ministry of Internal Affairs declares the results too close to call and announces a manual recount.

As soon as I hear the statement, I realize two things.

First, Gabriel received the most votes. We won!

Second, the authorities are going to tamper with

the results to make it seem we lost.

The opposition holds an emergency meeting at midnight, warning against what seems to be an obvious attempt to change the numbers. Many take to the streets in protest.

I'm on the air, urging an immediate recount to avoid a rumbling volcano in the country from exploding.

Then Khalil takes me aside for a minute. He hugs me warmly. "The Prime Minister just called Gabriel. He congratulated him officially. We won, you fucker. *You* won, you son of a thousand bitches!" We hug, both with tears in our eyes. More than 70,000 voted that day; it's an all time record in the district. We have beaten Michel Sr. by 17 votes.

Soon after Michel Sr. gives his concession speech to his thousands of supporters. "Congratulations to the opposition for having Elie Nakouzi, who brought this victory for them!" It makes the headlines of many newspapers.

The victory couldn't be sweeter. I'm euphoric.

I even win $25,000 from bets I made with fellow journalists and politicians before it started. Nouhad Machnouk, the Prime Minister's Senior Advisor, bet me that we'd lose by more than 20,000 votes. No one truly believed that we could beat the 'Maestro', as they refer to Michel Sr. Well, we did it.

The authorities couldn't dream of him losing.

The celebrations last for a whole week. Thousands of supporters and activists come to the MTV building every night to congratulate the newly elected deputy. Sometimes they hold me high on their shoulders, as if I was the one who was elected.

Weeks later I call Michel Sr. His secretary can't believe it when I tell him my name. "Elie Nakouzi? *The* Elie Nakouzi?"

"Yes. Elie Nakouzi himself," I reply gently.

His tone changes from polite to ice cold in seconds. "Let me check if His Excellency is here."

Thirty seconds later, Michel Sr. answers. "Nakouzi, what can I do for you?"

"Good morning, Your Excellency," I answer. "You can invite me for a cup of coffee. I'd like to visit you in your office."

"But of course," he answers quickly. "Do you want to come by tomorrow afternoon?"

"Definitely."

The next day, Michel Sr. invites me to sit on the leather coach of his huge office.

"It has been a great privilege and honor to be your rival," I begin. "I'm here to apologize for all the personal insults with which some of my guests attacked you. I never approved of them, and I never will. Politically, I disagree with everything you say. But I believe in clean fights, and at times there were punches below the belt—"

"You don't have to explain," he interrupts. "I know you're a decent young man, and I truly don't blame you for being blinded by the hypocrites who call themselves the opposition," he says, chuckling. "Those crooks jump to the other side only when the Syrians refuse to sponsor them, so don't let them trick you. As for my brother, he's just a puppet they're using—a puppet who owns a TV network.

"But I congratulate *you* for what you were able to do," he says more cheerfully. "I'll definitely hire you to run my next campaign," he jokes.

"My price has become very high," I say, smiling.

"Sure, sure," he agrees.

"All right." I stand up, ready to leave. "I just wanted to make sure there are no hard feelings, now that everything is over."

"Over?" he says, laughing. "Hardly. It's just started, son! It has only just started." And with that, he walks me out the door, leaving me to wonder what he means.

Michel, Khalil and I agree to cool down attacks on the authorities for a few months post-election. There's no need to appear to be a sore winner. Besides, after President Bush includes Iraq in his Axis of Evil and implies he's eying Baghdad, everyone's talk shifts to speculating what America will do next.

I believe that if US troops liberate Iraq from Saddam, there will soon be no dictator left standing. I never pray, but I call some religious friends and ask them to pray on my behalf for this to happen.

And just when things seem to be going our way, Gabriel Murr makes a serious blunder.

Lebanon's President Emile Lahoud decides to take a tour of the Metn district, and he doesn't include Gabriel during the visit. It's a bit insulting, but of no real consequence. Gabriel is too inexperienced to understand how to play the political game, though, so he responds on the air with an entirely out-of-proportion personal attack against Lahoud. He concludes with, "Tomorrow when your visit is over, Mr. President, it will rain, and all those pictures with which you decorated the walls and roads will only fall down on the ground, where they will block our sewers."

It's an act of personal disrespect. Such things are tolerated in countries with free speech. But in Lebanon, a deputy speaking this way about the President can be considered a challenge to the authority of those in power. If Lahoud was looking for an excuse, Gabriel just handed it to him.

The next morning I receive a phone call from Charles Ayoub. "I have bad news," he tells me. "My friend General Sayyed has informed me that police are on their way to MTV to shut it down."

Charles and I immediately head to MTV, calling Khalil on the way. When we arrive, just as Charles said, over 100 police officers are already surrounding the building.

We finally convince the Colonel in charge to let us inside.

Dozens of confused employees are milling around Gabriel's office, which is on the top floor. The soldiers have asked everyone to clear out so they can shut the building down. No one knows how to react.

I make my way through the crowd until I find Michel and Gabriel. They look shocked and lost.

The Colonel comes up to our floor and repeats his instructions: "By judicial decree, each of you must clear out your office and leave."

Gabriel starts arguing with him.

"I'm just executing a court order," the Colonel replies.

"I have immunity as a deputy!" Gabriel declares.

"Not anymore," the Colonel responds.

He's right. Someone from our staff comes over to

say it was just announced on the news the election results have been nullified. Gabriel Murr has been stripped of his victory.

Michel Sr. knew what he was talking about when he said it wasn't over yet.

This is bad. Very bad.

Over the next couple of weeks, the White House, European governments, human rights organizations, and thousands of activists decry the resolutions. And hundreds of Lebanese take to the streets to defend our network and freedom of speech.

But the international community's opinions are simply ignored. And Lebanon's protesters are beaten viciously until they give up.

At first I'm in denial. I tell myself it's only a serious warning. I can't accept that they'll actually shut us down permanently and piss off 1 million Christians.

Then it comes out that the shutdown has been blessed directly by Syrian President Bashar al-Assad. That means only one thing—it's irreversible.

I switch to hoping America won't let Syria get away with this.

However, America does nothing beyond expressing disapproval.

Our fellow journalists do nothing either. Only Charles Ayoub, a man who disagrees with most of MTV's political positions, shuts down his newspaper for 3 days in solidarity. No one joins him—not even our so-called allies. It is so hard to believe all our media colleagues are swallowing this.

The protests fade away.

Eventually everyone accepts the decision.

And life goes back to the way it was before, as if nothing had happened.

I'm bitterly disappointed. Whenever Khalil warned me about this, I assured him that people would respond by turning the country upside down in waves of protests that would never end. Yet only a few hundred protested, and it took only a couple of weeks to brutally beat the resistance out of them.

The network that once defended all those who had no voice is now sealed in red wax. It's forbidden to go near the building, as if it's a crime scene.

Our little revolution is over.

And silence has settled back on Lebanon.

MTV's shutdown is a terrible blow to political expression. But on a more mundane level, it means over 500 of the most talented TV personnel in the country are now jobless.

I expect most of the technicians will be okay. Other networks will compete to hire them.

But I believe there's no chance anyone will hire me as a political host again. Who in their right mind would take on a broadcast journalist instrumental in shutting down *two* TV networks?

My phone abruptly stops ringing.

Even Khalil's phone, which is almost always active, stops ringing.

The next three months pass by very slowly. Meanwhile, bills—for the mortgage, the car, various loans, and more—accumulate quickly.

I receive a call from my landlord about overdue payments. He wants me to find a solution before Christmas. Otherwise he'll "have to act," as he puts it.

Just in case I don't feel sufficiently defeated, a few weeks later armed men show up at my apartment at 4:00 in the morning.

Chantal and I wake up terrified by violent knocks on the door. "Open up! Open up right now!" a loud voice shouts over and over. I jump out of bed and run over to the door. "Who is this?" I ask.

"Open the door immediately, or we'll break it down and take you by force," the voice answers.

"I'm not opening it unless you say who this is!" I know the law. The police aren't allowed to invade a home before 7:00 am unless there's a terrorist suspect or dangerous criminal inside.

I call Charles, the only influential friend I have, and ask his driver to wake him up urgently. I quickly explain my situation. "I'm coming right away," Charles replies.

At this point my entire building is awake. I can see the lights turning on in nearby apartments. The armed men are still shouting, and it sounds like they're completely losing their patience.

I hear one of them say, "We're breaking in if you don't open the door!" Less than a minute later the door is struck very hard, repeatedly. It's soon wide open.

In seconds, 15 armed policemen are inside.

The first thing they do is drag me by my shirt and throw me into the hallway. Instead of taking me down in the elevator, they decide to drag me down seven flights of stairs. I have no idea how many hands are pushing and dragging me at the same time. All I can hear is the voice of my 2-year-old son Gio crying. Nothing else.

Twenty-five minutes later, we arrive in front of a

police station, and they push me out of the car.

A captain with a couple of stars on his shoulders is waiting for me. His men drop me in an interrogation room with him and leave. Before he can say even a word, though, we hear voices outside the door.

It is Charles' voice, and we can hear him talking to the president. "Mr. President, in the name of our friendship, I ask you to stop this charade immediately…"

After a few seconds there's is a knock at the door. Charles enters the room without waiting for the officer to invite him in. He holds out his phone to the confused captain and says, "Mr. President would like to speak with you."

The captain doesn't even argue. He stands up immediately and takes the phone. "Yes, Mr. President," he says with respect. He remains silent for two minutes and then replies, like a robot, "Yes, Mr. President, immediately," and he hangs up.

He fills out a couple of papers quickly, apologizes for the behavior of his police officers, and lets me go.

Later, I find out that the entire arrest was ordered by the minister of interior, Elias El Murr. Elias couldn't forget some of the insulting remarks made about Michel Sr., his father, on my show, so he decided to humiliate me as payback. However, the President—who is also Elias' father-in-law—was convinced by Charles that shutting down the network is enough of a punishment, and overrode Elias' order.

Word about the incident quickly gets around. Later that day Pierre Gemayel calls to check on me...and shares more bad news. "I hate to tell you this during the dark days you're going through, but I heard someone powerful is saying, 'If Nakouzi tries to wash dishes in a restaurant, it will be closed down.'"

"Great. I won't waste my time by applying to jobs that include dish washing then." I chuckle, trying to pretend I am still strong and intact.

I never realized how much energy it takes to pretend that you *still* have it together when everything's falling apart.

It is painful to see that life is continuing normally for my former competitors. I can't tell if I am actually jealous or angry with them; it is both probably. If I knew of another colleague who was being thrown in the garbage, I would fight for him until the last breath. Yet, no one is mentioning my name or MTV anymore.

I fully remember what Wardeh once said about the headache I was bringing to my table with this entire journalism thing. I could have been a lawyer, an engineer, or an accountant… no, definitely not an accountant, but whatever… anything else could have brought more peace of mind and stability.

In these tough days, I learn that only 2 percent of those I think are real friends actually are. I blame myself every boring morning. I spend my days playing Solitaire on my laptop. Taking Xanax is the only way I can get relief from the stress.

I can't believe I screwed my life the way I did. I brought this on myself and things could have been way better. I live on small loans from some old friends here and there. No one believes me when I say I'm going to return every penny. I honestly can't blame them.

I am perceived as the guy who already shut down two TV networks. Who, in his sane mind, is going to hire me?

How do people get second chances? I have no answers.

I listen to Ziad Rahbani's music every night and silently let go out those tears before they are trapped inside, once again.

XXIII
A Dinner With A Sheikh

Then, one afternoon, someone remembers me: Jean Louis Kordahi, the minister of communication that I hosted instead of Bassel Fleihan, the economist that prime minister Hariri was trying to promote. Of course, Jean Louis has no idea about the circumstances leading to that episode; however, he still feels grateful for the support and the popularity that being on my show brought him.

In turn, I appreciate that Kordahi never agreed with the unlawful decision to shut down MTV. He is still one of the closest men to the president, but his political influence is very limited.

"I have an important guest for dinner that I would like you to meet," he says quickly after hello.

"Who?" I ask.

"Waleed Al Ibrahim," he answers. "Who?" I ask again. "Sheikh Waleed Al Ibrahim," he repeats the name with confidence. "Surely you've heard of him. He's the owner of MBC!"

"Who hasn't heard of - MBC? I just didn't know who owns it."

"Well, I helped Waleed obtain his satellite broadcasting license in Beirut in only a few days. He's grateful because the bureaucratic process usually takes months. Waleed is launching an Arab news satellite channel in the near future. When he told me about it, I thought of you. Why don't you come to dinner tonight and meet him? The man owns a media empire, and I know you're jobless. You've got nothing to lose."

"Well, I...I..."

"Listen," Kordahi says with understanding, "I'm aware you're not a great fan of the Saudis—"

"Exactly," I reply.

"But Waleed isn't a typical member of the Royal Family. He's intelligent, educated, successful, and modest. I'm sure you'll like him. Anyway, think about it and call me back."

Middle East Broadcasting Center, or *MBC*, is the most popular public access satellite network for Arabs. It attracts over 150 million viewers and has no serious competition. MBC specializes in entertainment, though, with only one nightly news program. From my perspective, it's fluff. Plus its news coverage focuses on the Gulf and Saudi Arabia, while my whole universe is Lebanon. I don't even watch MBC.

My first instinct is to call Minister Kordahi back, express gratitude, and decline his kind invitation. I can't imagine a place for me on a network owned by a Saudi prince.

However, I decide to first ask Khalil, who common friends are starting to call him Google now. He simply knows something about everyone. I've heard him talking about MBC many times before. He must have heard something about this 'prince'.

As I suspected, Khalil has Al Ibrahim's résumé memorized from A to Z. "First, he's a Sheikh, not a prince," he informs me.

"Whatever," I say. "What do you know about this Sheikh?"

"In brief, he's planning a major expansion of his media empire—a news channel that'll compete with Al Jazeera."

Al Jazeera launched in 1996 as an all-news network for the Middle East, and it's quickly become the main source of news for millions of Arabs.

Based in Qatar, it has a policy of attacking Arab regimes and glorifying extremists it calls Jihadists, with Osama bin Laden being its #1 star. Arab viewers fed up with their governments flock to this message.

"The Saudi royal family understands the danger of letting this go unchallenged," Khalil continues. "Their upcoming network will eventually counterbalance Al Jazeera's propaganda. The Saudis have earmarked half a billion dollars for it and selected Waleed to put the whole thing together. He's already achieved tremendous success with MBC, so he's the logical choice."

This, according to Khalil, is the essential raison-d'être of the new project.

For reference, King Fahd of Saudi Arabia married Waleed's elder sister, Jawhara, in the early 70's. She is the king's last official wife, and by far, his favorite. But most importantly," my friend adds, "she gave birth to Abdul-Aziz, who is the king's favorite son, and supposedly, the man behind some of Waleed's family wealth."

Before he finishes his little report, Khalil makes sure to mention how powerful Waleed and his brothers are in Saudi Arabia. "Meeting Waleed is a rare opportunity," he continues. "This Sheikh is barely seen with anyone, anywhere. He is discrete and out of the spotlight. Only a small entourage of closely trusted confidantes can reach him."

"Can you imagine me working for this man?" I ask. "Absolutely not," Khalil replies immediately, laughing. "But it won't hurt for you to meet him. Just go," he concludes, and hangs up.

From Khalil's description, I picture Waleed as someone who's inherited all his success with no real effort. It doesn't matter whether he's officially a Sheikh or a prince.

I call the Minister back and thank him for his kind gesture. "But I can't see any reason for my presence at this dinner."

"Listen, he's not the kind of Sheikh you've heard about," he repeats again. "This man is different... I know your head, Nakouzi," he jokes, "and if he was an asshole, I wouldn't have invited you. But, anyway, it's up to you. You stood by me in tough political times, and I hate to see a friend in crisis," he finishes, without insisting a lot.

I pause, consider my options, and take a breath. "I'll be at your place at 9:00," I say.

"I am so glad that you changed your mind," he says very warmly.

At nine sharp, I stand on the minister's doorstep, despite my usual habit of tardiness.

Kordahi receives me warmly and leads me in to meet his guests, who are already sitting at the dinner table having drinks. "We haven't started yet," the minister says as we enter the room.

The first surprise is that the Sheikh looks much, much younger than I expected him to be. Khalil didn't tell me he is in his early 40s. He is wearing a pair of jeans and a very casual smile on his face; it makes him look easy to talk to. I had imagined him to be in his late 60s with an arrogant face and attitude. He salutes me gently. His voice is a little weird, but another surprise distracts me.

Next to him sits a young woman whose veil can't hide her charming traits; she is beautiful and elegant. Saudis usually never expose their women at private dinners or public events. He simply seems modern and relaxed. It's not very often to meet a classy, polite Saudi prince or Sheikh in Beirut lately. This Sheikh looks really different!

Across from him sits Ali Al Hedeithy, MBC's general manager. And next to him sits his beautiful, young wife.

"A glass of vodka would be good," I tell my host, who asks me what I would like to drink. It's not perhaps the wisest choice to 'impose' alcohol on the minister's table; however, I want to make sure that I am not perceived as someone who's ready to compromise his habits for a job.

The table is full of every kind of Lebanese food that one can imagine, and it is all-homemade. From the taste of the Tabbouleh, one can clearly feel the hospitality that the plates have been cooked with. The mood is cheerful and comfy.

"Nakouzi," the minister says out of nowhere, "have you heard about the news channel that Sheikh Waleed is about to launch?" He opens the main subject that he has invited me for. "You've decided to call it Al Arabiya News Channel, it that right, Sheikh?"

He turns toward Waleed, involving him in the discussion. "Inshallah (God willing)," the Sheikh replies with modesty.

"Who hasn't heard of it?" I reply. "The talk about

the new channel is all over; it's starting to compete with Al Jazeera, even before it's on-air," I drop Al Jazeera's name, showing him that I know a little about what is going on. "Have you set a date for the official launch yet? The news about Iraq is getting serious."

"We intend to launch by the end of 2003," he says. "It's a huge project and there's a lot to be done. But Inshallah, we will meet the deadline."

"You might have to launch it sooner," I say, and Ali smiles. "Funny you should say that. We're just back from a visit with a certain Arab president who said exactly the same thing," says Ali.

"Smart man," I comment.

"I don't know," Ali says with a sly smile. "If I tell you which one, you might revise that statement."

"Let me guess," I get it quickly. "Bashar el Assad?" I ask.

Waleed and Ali both burst out laughing, knowing exactly how most Lebanese feel about Syria's dictator. But, we all realize Kordahi can pay a high price for any laughter involving el Assad in his home, so we let the joke die.

"Yes," Waleed says, steering the conversation back to safe territory. "el-Assad told us that the war on Iraq is inevitable, and no matter what Saddam Hussein does to avoid it, Bush has made up his mind to overthrow the regime."

"To liberate Iraq from a tyrant is more like it," I say with a smile, hoping the Sheikh won't be offended.

"If I were you, I would be a little more cautious about using such words," he says. "But caution isn't your strong suit, from what the minister tells me." He says it in a way that makes it sound like flattery.

"Elie specializes in angering politicians," the minister comes in the discussion. Waleed smiles. "When politicians agree to dislike a journalist, then he must be doing something right."

"Oh, trust me," the minister continues, "if this is the scale, then you're sitting with the right guy." Waleed nods in approval, as if he has heard my story.

I can sense Waleed and Ali have never seen me on TV, but they were courteous enough to act as if they have. And they've obviously learned about my role in the MTV shutdown.

"What's next for you?" The Sheikh asks me. "Someone in the country has decided that there should be no *next* for me. So, I am still trying to figure things out; I have some good offers, here and there, that I am currently studying," I lie straight in his face.

"I am sure this new American network is one of them," he replies, buying the story. "Yeah, yeah," I nod in total approval. I have no idea what he is talking about. "Al Hurra, you mean?" Kordahi asks him.

"I don't know what they've decided to call it, but it's officially announced that it would be funded by the American congress," Ali interjects.

"Which will kill it before it's born," Waleed comments, "but not for pro-Americans like Elie," he adds with a big smile.

I smile. The Sheikh seems to have gathered this about me also. "Would you blame someone like me if he chooses New York over Tripoli, or Los Angeles over Tehran?!"

We have obviously established a good connection,

the Sheikh, Ali, and I.

"You know, Sheikh," I shift to a serious tone, "being pro-American is an accusation that I have never denied. On the contrary, I feel flattered by it," I say bluntly. "American collaborator," Ali jokes.

Apparently, my pro-Americanism doesn't annoy them.

The conversation continues a little more seriously. The more he talks, the more successful and sharp this young Sheikh sounds.. This guy knows media and the TV industry very, very well.

Even more importantly, he understands Arab audiences—their needs, their desires, their tastes, their likes and dislikes. He's a true expert.

Of course, he has not been tested in the world of politics, which is a completely different from entertainment.

Somehow, I am starting to feel lucky for being invited to this dinner. There are legions of actors, singers, journalists, and other celebrities stalking this Sheikh for an opportunity to appear on his highly watched network or to even meet him for five minutes. Therefore, to be invited to a dinner party with Waleed Al Ibrahim, especially in the midst of my current jobless situation, starts to sound like an unparalleled opportunity.

This Sheikh intrigues me, and somehow, the idea of working for him doesn't look as horrible as before. Yet, his news channel won't start for at least a year, and by that time, I will be completely broke, if not in jail, for failing to pay back the enormous debt my extravagant lifestyle created.

Waleed seems to like me and vice-versa. But, I

need someone to put me under contract, not just enjoy my company.

As if he has read my mind, Kordahi makes sure that no one is eating anymore, then he stands and says, "Excuse me, ladies, but I have to steal Sheikh Waleed and Elie from you for five minutes," and he asks us gently to walk with him to his office.

Kordahi escorts us to his office, where he asks his maid for three double espressos. Then, he gets straight to the point. "Waleed, Elie is like a little brother to me, and he's going through very tough times after the MTV shutdown." Kordahi hands a large cigar to Waleed after he lights it for him. "This man here," Kordahi continues, patting my shoulder, "is one of the bravest, most honest, and most loyal journalists I've ever met."

The minister catches the blush that I can no longer hide, he turns to me: "I'm not saying it to make you happy, Elie. It is simply the truth." He turns back to Waleed and continues. "This man stood by me when all the political sharks wanted to devour me. This is something that I'll never forget. If you think you have any vacancy for him, especially on the news channel that you're launching"

"Of course, of course," Waleed interrupts warmly. "I will ask Ali to exchange numbers with Elie, and he will contact you soon," he tells me. "Consider this a personal favor to me," Kordahi follows up.

"Done," Waleed says decisively, "you don't have to ask twice, Jean Louis," he reassures him again, using the minister's first name, which makes it sound more official somehow.

"Ali will speak to you soon," he tells me after I

exchange numbers with his manager. I leave Kordahi's house with a million thoughts.

Although Waleed's promise appeared heartfelt, I know that nothing is official until I sign on the bottom line. There is no way of knowing how long it will take to hear back from Ali. Moreover, they are very famous for meeting so many faces at night that they forget all of them in the morning, as well as the huge promises they may have made the night before.

My feelings are all mixed up as I drive back home, but at least, I have something to wait for.

The Sheikh and I parted ways with a warm handshake and what seemed like an informal job offer, I comfort myself when Ali doesn't call the first week. But why didn't he give me his direct phone number? Didn't I impress him enough to make a deal on the spot? The negative thoughts start to screw with my head.

A couple of weeks pass with no word from Waleed or Ali, but I still have hope. "He must be very busy traveling from country to country, jumping from meeting to meeting," I say to myself.

An entire month passes with no word.

Two months later, I have completely forgotten about him.

The daily Xanax pill loses all efficiency. I take two, and still, there is nothing to put me to sleep.

I have a family: a wife, whose childhood was so insecure and heartbreaking. Her father threw her, her four siblings, and their mother in the streets without a penny in their pockets when she was still very young. She struggled with her twin sister to feed the family and couldn't wait until she had a house that she could call home.

Gio, my son, is barely two years old now; I also have no idea what is waiting for him either.

It is depressing. Just a few months earlier, I was walking the streets with my head high, thinking I was a hero of freedom. Now, all I see are looks of pity as people keep asking me, "What's next?"

"I am still studying some offers," I reply like a parrot. I am so tired of this sentence that I want to print it on my forehead to stop people from asking. "What's next?" One of my favorite questions becomes so nightmarish now that I can't stand to hear from it anyone, even my own family. It's only a terrible reminder that I am jobless with no prospects: a loser, in more accurate words.

Finally, I come up with a more practical solution. "If you don't want people to ask you questions, avoid seeing people: easy and practical," I decide. Thus, I stop going out. I seclude myself in my house, hardly seeing anyone or getting out anymore.

Ziad Rahbani is strongly present in my life again; nothing makes me cry except his music. Like always, his tunes pull out all the heartburns and defeats that I am sensing, right up to my eyes. I'm grateful for the release, as otherwise I fear suffering a heart attack. I'm only 33, and it's too early for heart attacks.

The 20 pounds that I tried hard to lose in the past just melt off. Anxiety is the best diet you can ever prescribe to someone who is failing to lose his extra weight. It works like magic.

There are simply no nails left on my fingers to chew. I guess I have to find a new hobby to waste time.

My life has gone from non-stop action to utter boredom. Bottom line: it is dark, painfully dark!

I overcome the Sheikh and his news channel. I initially was never convinced that I wanted to work for a channel that could potentially promote the Saudi agenda, anyway. If, in Lebanon, I was deprived from saying what I wanted, then what would it be like to work for a Saudi Sheikh?! I convince myself it is best he never called.

XXIV
D.C. vs. The Desert

Finally, a ray of hope appears. An old friend, Mouafac Harb, is appointed to run Al Hurra, which everyone refers to as "The network funded by the American Congress."

After 9/11, the Americans decided to fund a channel that promotes democracy, human rights, liberty, and freedom to the Arab world. However, the real mission of Al Hurra is to improve the image of the United States in the eyes of Arabs. Finally, the Americans have realized that freedom is the answer to this stricken area, not allying with dictatorships, I tell myself.

Anyway, liberty, freedom of speech, and freedom of elections—these are all the words I like to hear the most. And fortunately, as soon as Mouafac is appointed, he remembers me.

Mouafac is a famed American-Lebanese journalist. He started his career at America's ABC News, where he became a successful investigative reporter and producer. After making a name for himself in the United States, a local TV station in Beirut offered him the position of CEO. He ran the network for two years, and then returned to the United States.

Mouafac heard about the MTV shutdown and how I was attacked afterwards. When he calls me, he wastes no words, "Do you want to come to America?"

"Of course, I do," I answer without hesitation. "Are you kidding me?"

"Fine. Prepare yourself to fly to Washington D.C. in the next couple of weeks. I will take care of your visa and call back soon," he says.

He makes it sound so easy. "I already have a visa, and in two weeks you may find me in a hospital," I say. "I am broke, threatened, followed by armed security flunkies, and afraid things are going to get even worse. If you really want to help, get me out of here tomorrow morning. Don't give me this two weeks shit. I can't stand one more minute."

The next morning, I am on a flight to D.C. via London.

"Welcome to the United States," the officer says.

"The land of the free," I reply like an idiot. However, it feels okay to be an idiot. *I am in the United States, and people have the right to be stupid if they want*, I think. While I head to the cab, I start singing, "Freedom... Freedom." I can hear the taxi driver laughing at me from inside his cab. "Do you need help with your bags, Sir?" he jumps out of his car. "No, my friend, no. I am here with no luggage, no baggage, and no history," I smile. "Just freedom?" he references the song I was singing. "Freedom, at last," I sigh.

As soon as I reach my hotel, and even before I check into my room, the receptionist delivers a small note with a smiley face on it, "Waiting for you in Four Seasons Hotel; a cigar with a good cognac is the best treatment for oppressed souls... hurry! Mouafac."

I join my friend in the fancy Four Seasons Restaurant. We drink and talk for three hours. Mouafac tells me about his big plans to change the entire Arab nation.

"Al Hurra won't be ready to broadcast for another 12 months," he says, "but it's already starting to hire staffers. I can start processing your employment papers in the morning."

Everything Mouafac says sounds perfect—especially the timing.

But, then he comes to the pay. He shocks me by the low salary that Al Hurra has set up for its senior producers and anchors. "But this is even less than half what I made at MTV," I exclaim.

"I know," he nods, "but in Beirut, you're a star... Here, nobody knows you."

"You know me," I point out.

"Sure, I do," he smiles, "but here friendships and personal feelings don't count. There are unbreakable rules. Everything has to go through a strict committee that's supervised by another committee, which is also supervised by an even stricter committee, and so on," he laughs.

Mouafac makes it clear that this is not a decision that he can change.

It is disappointing, but there are no other options. Besides, it's America, the land of opportunities and dreams. I convince myself to be content.

Before signing any contract, I have to pass a security clearance since the job is governmental, as Mouafac explains. Then, I have to fill out some bureaucratic forms and long applications for immigration, as well. I have to fly back to Beirut to stamp my new visa at the American embassy before signing my contract, which is the law for newcomers.

Anyway, within four days, I finish all the

procedures and am ready to fly back to Beirut, stamp my visa, pack up Chantal and Gio, and get back to the United States.

A whole new life is about to start. A whole new beginning from scratch. Yet, I feel a little gloomy, especially after Mouafac tells me that Lebanon is not the priority for the newly born network. "Lebanon is just a small spot on the Arab map," he says, "and Al Hurra is a pan Arab channel; so, you better expand your area of interest a little bit," he recommends.

Chantal is more excited than I am; she starts to pack up even before I tell her about the details. She sounds like the happiest person on earth when I call to inform her that I took the job.

At the security check at Dulles airport, the officer is checking and flipping my laptop when my phone starts to ring incessantly. It seems important because it is a private number. But it feels inappropriate to answer it while the officer is still doing his procedures. The phone doesn't stop blinking, though. The officer tells me it's okay to answer it.

"Hello," I say in a hurry before the caller hangs up.

"Where are you, Elie?" the familiar voice asks without saying who it is. "Waleed here," he says. It's very crowded around him, and I can barely hear him. But I am finally able to explain to him that I am at Dulles airport leaving to fly back to Beirut.

"Why don't you join me in Dubai instead, since you're at the airport," he suggests surprisingly.

"Well, I wish I could, but I just took a new job with Al Hurra, and I need to stamp my visa and get back here very soon," I apologize gently.

"But, I thought we shook hands. Did you change your mind?" he sounds a little disappointed. "We shook hands, right! But, you know, it has been a while since we talked, and I thought you were the one who changed his mind," I half joke. "Not at all! It's just that these couple of months have been crazy. But anyway, even if you took a new job with them, I still insist that you join us in Dubai for a couple of days," he repeats the offer and then explains. "We are launching Al Arabiya News Channel officially, and I'd like you to come and collaborate with me. I will let Shareef call you in a minute to take care of all your booking details, see you soon!"

"But—"

"No buts," he ends decisively.

Thirty seconds later, Shareef, his assistant, calls. Three hours later, I am in a first-class seat on British Airways in a luxurious chair, heading to Dubai via London.

"There is nothing to lose," I tell Chantal, who doesn't sound very happy when she hears about the change of plans.

In Dubai, I am received like a real VIP. Shareef and Feeras, another assistant of the Sheikh, are waiting at the VIP lounge. It takes less than five minutes for the security officer to bring back my passport stamped.

Two luxurious brand new Range Rovers are waiting outside to take me to my hotel. On the way to the One & Only Royal Mirage luxurious resort, Shareef informs me that the Sheikh is expecting me for dinner at 9:30 pm, which leaves me with five hours to rest and prepare myself.

I am shocked by the extravagant suite, which is usually given to VIP and heads of states. Knowing how expensive these kind of exclusive resorts in Dubai are, I assume this room is no less than $1500 a night. Of course, I expected something decent; however, I didn't know the Sheikh thought this highly of me.

I wish Mouafac could see this hotel room that his competitor has booked me, compared with the one Al Hurra had.

The first thing I do, of course, even before taking a shower, is call Khalil, who is expecting me in Beirut. He is happily surprised that I have an additional offer. All I talk about with him is the suite I am in. I describe it in detail and promise to update him about the serious news after my meeting. “I just adore living in luxury,” I tell my friend. “Me too! Enjoy it my friend, you deserve a little fun. You really do,” he replies sincerely.

The phone rings as soon as I hang up. It is Ali al Hedeithy. "How was the trip?" he asks. "Thank you, I really do appreciate the meet & assist at the airport," I say. "Oh, don't mention it," he says politely. "The driver will pick you up at nine, and we'll have dinner with Sheikh Waleed and some important guests. Then, we'll take it from there," he informs me.

On my way to the restaurant, I can't stop looking at the high towers left and right. The city looks clean, well-organized, and shiny. Hundreds of new infrastructure projects are launching, and everyone is expecting Dubai to set an example of how to build a city out of sand. However, even with all this, it still looks like it has left its soul somewhere. It is like a big parking lot. "Nothing like life-filled Beirut." I shake my head. I am a little jealous of all the construction, though.

We reach the luxurious Fairmont hotel at 9:30. The value of the cars that are parked here can build seven libraries, I think to myself.

Feeras is already in the astonishing lobby waiting for me. He guides me to the second floor and hands me off to Sean, a distinctive young British man who is the manager of the stylish restaurant where the Sheikh and his guests are already seated in a private dining room.

When Waleed sees me coming, he stands up politely, smiles at me, and opens his arms like we have known each other forever. "Welcome," he says, "I am glad the Americans didn't take you away from us yet." He sounds cheerful and in a very good mood.

The guests are already standing, and it's very obvious that this Waleed is somehow different than the one I met in Beirut. He's wearing his Saudi traditional dress with the "Ghutra" on his head—the traditional scarf that Saudis wrap around their heads.

This time, he has much bigger aura. I salute him warmly and gently ask everyone to sit down.

"Let me introduce you all to Elie," he looks toward his guests.

It's clear that everyone at the table has high respect for the young ‘n bright Sheikh.

When he speaks, they all listen attentively without interruption. "To those who have never seen him on TV before, this guy was a real headache for both the Lebanese and the Syrian governments. He just had talks with Al Hurra TV in D.C., but we're taking him back," he says with a smile, but also a determined tone. I love his introduction about me: brief, but straight to the point.

A few guests recognize me, and the others have no idea who the hell I am; however, I realize they are still showing interest in me because the Sheikh is showing his admiration of me.

"Just before you arrived," says Waleed while looking at me, "we were discussing the inevitable war on Iraq; yet, many think this is not going to be a promenade for your friends, the Americans," he chuckles. "I simply disagree. I believe it will," I reply with a confident smile. "And how long do you think it will take before they take over Baghdad, if the war happens?" he asks me. "Not more than one month," I answer with full confidence, as if I am Donald Rumsfeld, the US secretary of defense. "Oh, come on," one of the guests interjects. "Iraq has the fifth strongest army in the world," he says. "This is gonna be another Vietnam for the United States. I even heard there are more than 5,000 suicide bombers to protect him," he continues.

"Even if he has a million suicide bombers," I chuckle, "do you really believe that Saddam Hussein is gonna defeat America?"

"Of course, I do," he says excitedly.

Waleed is enjoying the debate that divides the table between objections and approvals. I can feel that he likes the controversy I am creating and how everyone is quickly getting involved.

He doesn't seem to mind my obvious opinions in favor of the United States, and I feel really comfortable expressing my political beliefs freely.

The discussions go on and on; some of the guests are getting nervous by my stance, and they start to repeat empty slogans they have memorized from newspapers, hopelessly trying to impress.

Waleed intervenes to cool down the heat and asks, "Let's presume the Americans overthrow Saddam, then what? Do you think Iraqis are ready for such a democratic change?"

"If they're not ready yet, they will be soon. Freedom is not only a right but, somehow, an emergency. We have been dragged down for a thousand years behind civilization because we never believed we were ready," I finish my lecture.

"You will be surprised how *not* ready Iraqis and Arabs are," one of the Egyptian guests comments. "Freedom will lead only to chaos; Iraqis need someone as tough as Saddam, and perhaps tougher, to control them," he concludes. "I don't agree," I say in a clear attempt to end a conversation that is not leading anywhere.

Frankly, I don't give a damn about the guests and their political theories; it is obvious they are only trying to impress the Sheikh. Some even start to flatter the wisdom of the Saudi king, despite the fact the man has been in a deep coma for years, even though it is obviously irrelevant to the subject; yet, they think that is probably the only way to get Waleed's attention.

Of course, I don't open a lip when it comes to the king; this is a very sensitive and *sacred* subject. I am fully aware of this and know that Saudis never swallow criticism or any kind of joke about their king and the royal family, so I stay away from unnecessary opinions.

The time exceeds one in the morning, and there will be no business talk with the Sheikh tonight obviously. This time, he catches me sneaking at the bar away from us. He whispers in my ear. “I see you’re interested in another war tonight," he points out to the extremely stunning lady that has been diverting my attention for the entire evening, laughing. "Oh, yeah," I admit instantly. "We can talk business tomorrow," he says with a sincere tone, "just go. Enjoy the rest of your night. I will see you tomorrow."

I slip out silently amidst the hot political debate, which is still at its peak, and head towards the bar. I order my vodka and stand next to her. She looks so dangerously sexy that I am not sure she will even acknowledge me if I try speaking to her.

The woman smiles at me, though, and holds her drink up. "Cheers," she says, "I am Sabrina."

"Cheers," I smile back. "I don't think I remember what my name is anymore. You know you have eyes that can do that, don't you?"

I flirt with her. She's a Korean-Uzbekistani mixture, she tells me.

She's irresistible and she knows it. "Are you here in business?" she asks. "You mean 'here' at the bar… Yes," I reply, and she smiles. She's irresistible and she knows it. "No, I mean in *Dubai*. Are you in *Dubai* for business or pleasure?"

"Oh, both. I always mix business and pleasure."

"Everyone says it is wrong to mix—"

"Everyone is wrong," I interrupt her. "Would you buy a product if you knew it was produced without pleasure?" I ask her. "No," she replies, after thinking about it for a second. "I have just been offered a big deal," I say, bragging, even though the Sheikh hasn't offered me anything yet.

"Congratulations!" she says cheerfully, "It is

worth a celebration then." She asks the bartender to fill two glasses with champagne.

Her smile is intoxicating, too much to resist, and her scent can make someone easily lose their mind. "I hate champagne," I say after taking a sip. "Do you have a better way to celebrate?" I ask.

"Of course, I do, but my kind of celebration needs a less crowded place. Cheers," she says, laughing, and clinks her glass with mine.

I'm confused. *This smart, classy woman can't be a hooker*, I think. *Or is it just that I don't want her to be? It'll be disappointing if she gets paid to seduce so effectively.*

I try to convince myself that I am, perhaps, her Brad Pitt; however, the mirror behind the bartender doesn't show a Brad Pitt. So, she must be a prostitute, the journalist in me concludes.

“Do you know, uh, a less crowded place for celebrations?” I ask her with a reluctant tone. I am just hoping she doesn’t mention money. She looks at her watch and thinks about it for a second, then says, “look, it’s usually 1800 a night, but for you, I will make it 1200.”

“Oh,” I say, disappointed like hell, “that’s a very good offer really, but I, uh, I don’t, you know,” I stutter, “I don’t pay for sex… I mean, don’t get me wrong, I have nothing against you or what you do… and I don’t judge you, of course,” I blather.

“It’s okay, it’s okay,” she interrupts me, “ but with me, it’s not sex you’re paying for,” she whispers, “it’s the journey.”

“Well put,” I smile, “but I don’t think I can afford

such 'journeys' at the time being," I say politely. "However, I thank you for the huge discount. 600 dollars is a lot—"

"It's dirhams," she explains. "1200 Dirhams makes around 300 US dollars," she enlightens me.

"Oh, *okay*," I answer.

That's half the cash I have in my pocket. Sabrina's 'journey' starts to look so tempting. "Why the discount, though?" I ask. She smiles. She starts to say something but changes her mind. "What?" I insist, "tell me," I say. "Well, after 1 am, it's so hard to find anyone, you know. Everything closes down by 2:30 am in Dubai, so—"

"I understand," I nod.

With a bottle of vodka in me, I forget all the promises I've made to Chantal. Sabrina is too ravishing even for a married man to pass up.

"Shall we leave?" she asks, "Where are you staying?" She goes on. "At the Royal Mirage," I reply. "I should have charged you in US dollars," she bursts with a cute laughter. And we leave.

I wake up at 3 in the afternoon with a terrible hangover; I am someone who usually doesn't make promises, fearing to break them. And I have just broken a big one that I have made to my wife two years earlier, when she gave birth to our Gio.

I am not here for one-night stands; I've had lots of those in my life, and most of them ended badly. I need to get my mind back on track.

I already gave my word to Mouafac and Al Hurra. And in my world, one's word counts more than a signature on a contract.

Besides, Al Hurra is funded by the American

congress, and it doesn't take a genius to realize that the Saudi royal family is potentially funding Al Arabiya News Channel. All things being equal, I much prefer working for the United States.

Before we parted dinner last night, Waleed told me to meet him in his office at 5:00 pm. I decide that I'll thank him very warmly for his invitation and VIP treatment, and then apologize for not being able to accept his offer. At least, this is the plan.

Ali calls at seven instead of five, apologizing gently for the delay. "The meeting has been moved to eight," he tells me.

Ali sends a driver to pick me up and take me to the newly launched Dubai Media City. It's where MBC is headquartered and Al Arabiya News Channel is located. MBC moved its entire operation from London to the United Arab Emirates when the ruler of Dubai, intent on transforming the city into a media center, made the network an offer it couldn't resist.

In the lobby of the extravagant MBC building, I meet a very dear colleague and friend, May Chidiac. She is one of the most famous faces on LBC, and she has been also invited to celebrate Al Arabiya's launch. She has been offered a juicy contract to join the network and move to Dubai.

“I apologized for not taking it,” May whispers in my ear. “I just can't live outside Lebanon,” she explains quickly before she leaves.

I meet with Waleed at 8:45 pm in his ultimately elegant, extravagant office on the fifth floor in the MBC building. His office is simply bigger than the three houses that I have lived in, merged!

He's in his formal Saudi attire and looks a little grumpy, as if he's heard bad news. He's still polite and respectful, though. I don't mention anything about my night before, and neither does he ask. I wait for him to open the discussion.

"Would you like to see the building?" he offers, after he finishes a couple of quick phone calls.

"Sure," I answer, and we leave his office.

My reaction to Al Arabiya News Channel boils down to one word: "Wow!" The cameras, the lighting equipment, the editing rooms, the footage library—everything is world-class. And the newsroom studio: Wow, wow, wow!

I'm deeply impressed by all this brand new cutting-edge technology. When I compare it in my head with what Mouafac showed me of the facilities in Washington D.C., I feel embarrassed for Al Hurra.

"Come on," Waleed says, "let's go talk over dinner. I am starving." Then, he sends his driver away and throws the keys of his stunning white Mercedes toward me. "Would you like to drive her?" he asks. "I'd like to reside in *her*," I joke. He still looks too formal. But he finally smiles.

Al Arabiya News Channel is officially launched, and there are more than a thousand guests hosted by MBC in Dubai to celebrate the event. He nods left and right, throwing kind smiles at the guests who are congratulating him on the big launch of his news network. He looks like he only recognizes half of the faces; however, he smiles courteously to everyone, pretending that he knows them all.

It is such a big celebration, and I am guessing the

Sheikh wants to create a big buzz, showing al Jazeera, the main competitor, that he's going all in.

On the Sheikh's main table, though, it's a different crowd tonight: some journalists and writers, actors, anchors and many, many Arab celebrities. Waleed insists, again, that I sit right next to him.

A couple of hours pass by, and just like the previous night, the conversations are mostly focused on politics.

They must cost thousands of dollars, these dinners, I think as I look at the table. Caviar, oysters, seafood...

After a couple of hours, dinner is concluded, and I am invited, with only 15 or 20 VIP guests to Waleed's private function.

"After that dinner in Beirut, I asked many politicians about you, and no one other than Minister Kordahi recommended I hire you," Waleed says bluntly. "Even your Lebanese prime minister advised me against it. He has nothing personal against you, but he said you're trouble," Waleed smiles and pauses, waiting for a response. I just continue to listen. I have no comments.

"It seems to me," he continues seriously, "having many politicians on your back can only mean one thing: you're a good journalist. And this is exactly why I am ignoring all the warnings and making you an offer."

"Pissing off people, especially politicians, is what I do best," I tell him. "However, I just gave my word to al Hurra and—"

"Did you sign already?"

"No."

"Then, nothing is set in stone yet. Anyway, let's

postpone the business talk until later. I will tell Ali to make an official offer, and we'll discuss it afterwards.

"Tell me," he says, shifting the conversation, "what did you really hear in D.C., behind the walls, about the war in Iraq?"

"All I can tell you is that it's gonna be quick, really quick," I answer very decisively.

"How quick do you mean?" he asks, showing interest.

"Three weeks. Maybe a one month."

"Is this based on information, or is this just your analysis?"

"Both," I smile, giving him a blink.

Of course, I have no information whatsoever, but who will sue me, or my imaginary source, for my vodka-induced predictions? The Sheikh obviously thinks I am someone who knows a lot. Why the hell would I tell him that I have no idea at all except what I read and see in the news? That's just ridiculous.

"Including the capital, Baghdad?" he asks, still curious.

"Every inch," I confirm. "It will all collapse very fast."

We discuss the war on Iraq for half an hour.

"And, what do you think of my newborn baby, Al Arabiya?" he shifts the conversation.

"I am impressed, Sheikh. I truly predict a huge success," I answer sincerely.

We talk about his ambitious plans. "This network will not only be a credible source for the news. It will *make* the news," he says.

Waleed has spent a lot of time in the UK and

United States and even graduated from an American university. He's clearly inspired by the western approach to news. "I don't want to ever be perceived as another Al Jazeera," he tells me.

"You want to be the CNN of the Arab world," I suggest.

"More like the BBC," he corrects me.

This man knows what he's talking about. And above all, he's got a clear vision on how to fight extremism and, as he refers to it, the "violent Islam." Osama bin Laden and Al Qaeda are at the top of his hit list.

"By the way" he remembers, "Ali will have your offer ready by tomorrow afternoon."

"Is there any possibility I can work from Beirut?" I ask bluntly.

"Listen, Elie," Waleed says gently, "I will talk to you like a friend now. May I?”

"Of course,"

"I know that you're still hurt from the way MTV was shut down. It was not fair, and I totally agree with you; it is total injustice. However, I advise you to put all this behind you now, this revenge thing you still have in your head, obviously." He throws a smart smile.

He knows he got it right. That is exactly what I had in mind when I asked him if I could work from Beirut. He's a smart man.

"Look," he says in a friendly tone, "you gotta broaden your horizons; this entire universe is not only about Beirut, Ghazi Kanaan, and the Syrian Intelligence Services, you know." He pauses. His words remind me of what Mouafac told me. I have heard the same remark from two experts in one week. Maybe they're right.

"Yeah, you're right." I agree, and swallow half of my vodka in one shot.

"We will come up with a solid, strong pan Arab show that you'll host from our headquarters here in Dubai." He adds, "Take a break from Beirut for a couple of years, I say. After that, who knows what will happen?" he concludes with his usual warm smile.

Next day, Ali calls at 5 pm and invites me for a cup of coffee in his office. He asks about my offer with al Hurra network.

“15,000 US dollars,” I lie to him, “plus the extra benefits, like housing and transportation,” I say. I don't think he buys it, but he pretends to. “We’ll double everything they offered you,” he hits me straight, “take it or leave it,” he smiles at me. "Listen," he continues in a serious tone, "Waleed likes you and he believes in you. Trust me, do your job well, and you'll have yearly bonuses that will equal or sometimes double your official income." He hands me an envelope that contains the full contract for me to review.

I draw my poker face immediately, not showing Ali that I am overwhelmed by the offer; however, I am about to jump from my seat. This could fix my entire life back. It’s a game changer. Yet, I ask for a couple of days to show it to my lawyer.

I can’t wait until I reach my room. I read the contract, clause by clause, and I quickly decide that I need no lawyers to advise me. 360,000 dollars yearly pacakge is a lot more than I have dreamed about in my life...

The next day, I call Waleed and ask to meet him in his office.

"So, what have you decided?" he asks.

"There is only one thing I have to talk to you about."

"Shoot," he says.

"After I left Ali's office, I read a clause in the contract—"

"What is it?" he interrupts. "This is a standard contract."

"I know, but it says I have to work from 9:00 am to 5:00 pm. I really don't function that way. After all, I'm a journalist, not a banker. Sometimes I'll be at the network for 24 hours straight if that's what a story requires. But—"

"That's it?" he asks smiling. "Done! We'll remove it. You have the freedom to check in and out whenever you want. What else?"

"Well, it also says I have to report directly to my supervisor before setting up the episodes; who exactly is my supervisor?"

"I am," he answers. "You'll report to me personally. Will this work for you?"

"Of course, definitely."

"Anything else you need to think about?" he asks.

"I guess not," I answer quickly.

"Then, let's shake on it." He extends his hand, and we shake warmly.

"I am going back to Beirut tomorrow," I say. "I will inform my wife, pack our things, and move here. It's not easy, you know. I have to find a new house, furnish it, and get a car," I explain. "It's a whole new life that we're talking about, and there's a lot to do."

"Nah. That's very easy," Waleed says. "You can do all this in one week."

"One week? Are you kidding me?"

"Even less; here's my suggestion," he says excitedly. He calls Feeras. The latter shows up with a big smile on his face. He looks like he's waiting for the Sheikh to ask him a question or a favor. It somehow makes him feel important apparently.

"Feeras?" the Sheikh asks. "How long will it take you to find a nice apartment for Elie and his family on Sheikh Zayed road?"

"Forty-eight hours, your Highness," Feeras answers without hesitation.

"And how long does it take to furnish it fully?"

"It's Dubai, Sheikh. People usually furnish from IKEA. It takes 24 hours." He laughs.

"Good," Waleed nods. "And a car?"

"Oh that? We can do that in 15 minutes," Feeras confirms.

"Great, then. You should get yourself a BMW. The 7-Series are beautiful," he tells me before he continues with Feeras. "I want you to take care of all this for Elie: his residency, his house, car, family's tickets, and visas... everything," he tells him gently. "And you have one week," he finishes.

"Done, Sir!" Feeras answers respectfully, and leaves the office.

"So go to Beirut," my new boss tells me, "and come back here in one week. Ten days maximum."

"Sheikh," I say, "my problem is not finding a luxurious apartment on Sheikh Zayed... and I fully agree that the 7-Series is stunning. But I have to remind you that I have been jobless for quite some time now, and I don't have a good relationship with savings accounts, in general, so—"

"You don't have to worry about that," he interrupts, "I'll tell HR to provide you an advance on salary to keep you running." He relaxes back.

The next day, I sign the contract, go to Ali's office in the afternoon, and drop it off. I don't want anything to change my mind.

Hours later, an employee from the finance department informs me that the Sheikh has given him instructions to transfer 75,000 dollars to my account as an advance on my salary. “You can pay them back in very small installments, as per the Sheikh’s orders. Are these enough, or do you need more?” he asks me. “More than enough, actually.”

Feeras books me a ticket to Beirut—first class, of course.

My new boss wants me back in one week, 10 days max. He wants me to settle down in Dubai as soon as possible and start working on a new show. "No matter if it takes six or eight months to launch," he told me. "It's important that you start immediately working on it."

I totally agree.

When I arrive home in Beirut, Chantal is far from thrilled about the dramatic change of plans. Just 10 days ago, I'd promised her a life in America. She's not a fan of Dubai or the Saudis.

"This man is different," I tell her. "He's not the typical kind of Sheikhs you have in mind, you'll see."

I tell her about Dubai and how amazing it has become; I talk about the salary, the potential bonuses, the apartment, the car and the salary advance, which will close a good chunk of our debt. Of course, I don't mention anything about the 'Bars' I have been hanging around in Dubai.

"The man works only at night, though," I prepare her. "That's the only negative thing about him," I say.

Chantal is highly skeptical; she doesn't buy it. So, I make an extra effort to convince her that with Waleed, it's pure business.

"He doesn't fool around," I confirm in a serious, serious tone. Chantal doesn't argue much about it. "You always do the right thing," she smiles. "Let's do it!"

However, it turns out she finds it impossible to pack up everything and tie up all loose ends in 10 days. "I need 2-3 months, minimum," she says. "Fly back to Dubai, since your new boss needs you. Gio and I will follow when I've taken care of everything here."

Khalil is harder to convince, though.

First, I describe the trip: my suite at the Royal Mirage, the VIP treatment, the lavish dinners, Sabrina, and mostly, the offer.

I also tell him about how sadly pathetic al Hurra appears compared to Al Arabiya News Channel. However, he still thinks I am making a terrible mistake by choosing a Saudi network. "No matter how you switch it around, you'll somehow be working for the Saudi establishment... And trust me, my friend, you can't work for them," he insists, regardless of the number of times I tell him that Waleed is really, really different.

"I have spent enough time in London, and I have met more than a hundred Sheikhs like *him*, and they're probably the best people in the entire universe, don't get me wrong," he says with his usual sarcasm, "but you, especially you, can't work with them, Nakouzi." He laughs. "Do you think he'll let you make episodes and statements about democracy, freedom, elections, and human rights?" he asks. "They have none of these in the Kingdom; wake up!" he says.

"This Saudi is different," I repeat. "He has spent half of his life between New York and London. Plus, the job is in Dubai."

"This Saudi is responsible for promoting the only existing theocracy on the planet," my friend corners me. "I can't believe you have chosen to work for the Saudi government," he says again.

"He's not the Saudi government," I argue, but he doesn't listen.

"Look," he says, "nice buildings don't make successful networks and you know it. At al Hurra, it's less money, right, but you'll be allowed to fight for freedom, democracy, liberty, and all those causes you screwed my head with for years—"

"I am tired of warnings, threats, phone calls, and accusations," I interrupt my friend. "Losing friends, shutting down networks, and taking two Xanax pills every night to sleep. And most importantly, I am tired of being in the red and in debt all the time. All for what? For freedom and liberty? Freedom my ass. With this prince, I can be a prince. And that's what I will do. Perhaps I was not designed to be a journalist," I finish my speech.

“He’s a Sheikh, not a prince,” Khalil insists to remind me.

“Sheikh, Prince… who cares? I will return one day, though, when the Syrians are out," I conclude. "Meanwhile, I will live."

XXV
A Real Prince

I still have five days before I leave Beirut. Just the idea being out of Beirut kills me, but I pretend to everyone that I can't wait before I leave. It's so untrue.

Anyway, Waleed shows up in Beirut surprisingly, three days before I leave for Dubai. He calls me after he lands and asks me to join him for dinner in downtown Beirut. He doesn't give me too much information, but it seems like there is something big that brought him suddenly to Lebanon.

And the hell if I am not right. It's his nephew, prince Abdul-Aziz Bin Fahd, who has decided to visit Beirut, for a couple of days.

I've heard hundreds of stories about Abdul-Aziz but, have no idea what he looks like. As a favorite son of King Fahd, he's one of the most powerful men in the Saudi Kingdom. I call Khalil to learn more. "He's one of the richest men on earth," my friend informs me. "There are around 60 tycoons at the level of Waleed, including Lebanon's Prime Minister Rafic Hariri.", who consider the likes of Abdul-Aziz as one of their primary sources of wealth."

When Waleed introduces me to his nephew, I'm surprised. The Prince is a young-looking 30. I salute him politely, and he gently invites me to join the table, which is located in the center of the restaurant. In addition to the 12 waiters circling around the prince, his men are spread out at the other tables. There are nearly 100 in his entourage.

At the Prince's table, however, there are only around 15 guests. I recognize two Lebanese deputies and several top newspaper journalists. The prince is interested in hearing what these experts think about the Iraqi war. He starts with the first journalist. This one answers quickly.

"The Americans are committing a huge mistake," my colleague says. "This is not a promenade, your highness. They might occupy the entire nation of Iraq, but it will take years to reach Baghdad. Saddam and his thousands of Republic forces, plus more than 25,000 suicide bombers, will fight to their last breath." The prince appears to lose interest before the man has even finished answering.

The prince asks another journalist what he thinks. "The Iraq war will be another Vietnam for America—if it even happens!" he says. "This talk of war is only for show. Saddam will end up signing a deal with the Americans." The prince doesn't look impressed with this guy either.

We continue to go down the table, each guest expressing dire consequences for the United States. Then Abdul-Aziz turns to me.

"My Uncle Waleed tells me you've just come from Washington D.C. and may have some information. What do you think?" He looks at me with interest. Everyone else at the table follows his lead.

"It will be 20 days, your Highness, or maybe 15," I say, sticking to the story I first told Waleed.

The looks on the *experts'* faces don't agree with me at all. They must think I am naive or something. But the prince shows interest in what I just said, so everyone pretends to appreciate my statement. "As for what my colleague said about a deal between Saddam and the Americans? No, it's not going to happen," I say with great confidence. "Your Highness," I continue, "when the Americans spend more than $100 million of tax payers' money to launch an Arabic TV channel, they're not joking," I repeat the sentence that Mouafac Harb told me when I was in the States. "I agree," he nods, "but this doesn't mean that Saddam will not fight." He's all focused on me now. "Saddam will run away like a cockroach; these dictators will surprise you by the cowardice they hide underneath all their ferocity," I say and smile.

Naturally, no one agrees with me on this; and perhaps I'm exaggerating. However, I love provoking these pundits who think they know it all.

The prince loses interest in the conversation and stands up. Abdul-Aziz grabs Waleed by the hand, and they both walk a little away from the table. They stand for a couple of minutes murmuring and whispering. Then, the prince leaves the place with all his men.

Waleed returns and whispers something in Ali's ear. Then, he looks at me and says, "Give any of our drivers your address, and have him pick up your passport," he smiles. "Prince Abdul-Aziz is leaving to Jeddah in one hour, and he asked me to invite you to come over with us." I can tell from Waleed's tone there's no point in arguing. It's an invitation one can't refuse.

Two hours later, we are on one of Abdul-Aziz's private jets: a Boeing 777, especially for his entourage. The prince himself is on a different 777 that is ahead of us. Obviously, he enjoys privacy when he's above 38,000 feet in the air.

At the royal palace, Prince Abdul-Aziz sits, and around him there are at least 60 princes and Sheikhs, who all look as wealthy and powerful as Waleed. These princes, who are famous with their huge entourages, are, themselves, the entourage now.

This is probably one of the wealthiest circles not only in Saudi Arabia and the Arab world, but also in Europe and the United States, where they invest billions of dollars and own properties worth hundreds of millions.

It occurs to me that I've quickly jumped from being jobless and broke to joining the inner circle of some of the wealthiest men alive.

Among the crowd of Sheikhs, one of the men I'm surprised to spot is Saad Hariri, who's dressed just like a Saudi prince.

He notices me, too, and doesn't seem to like my presence. I guess it's embarrassing for him to be seen dressing and acting like a Saudi royal by a Lebanese journalist especially when his father, Rafic Hariri, is Lebanon's prime minister.

I get the impression the princes and sheiks don't really enjoy sitting around Abdul-Aziz for days on end. But, it seems they all need his approval to make their big projects happen.

The prince never drinks alcohol, and it's not allowed in his royal palace. I hear a lot of grumbling from some of my contacts about how frustrating this is.

For six days, we sit around the prince. Every time the prince speaks, everyone around him listens intently.

It's amusing to watch a 30-year-old prince having such an immense influence over these rich and powerful men.

I'm bored to death! But it's obvious that in the prince's world, *he* decides when a visit is over, not the guest.

A week passes, and the rituals are pretty much the same. Every day, we sit around the prince, doing absolutely nothing at all except eating, chatting, drinking coffee, and smoking. Other than that, I have nothing to do except to watch the Emirs praying. They never miss one prayer; they look so reverent when they pray. *What the hell do they tell God five times a day? And isn't he bored from listening to the same words over and over again?* I think to myself.

I tell my boss that I need to leave. "I would love to stay, Sheikh, really, but there's a lot to do, you know, moving to Dubai, the show, the house, the car..."

"I understand," Waleed answers,.

At night, Waleed waits for a convenient time, and we both approach his nephew. He explains to the prince that I have some urgent business in Dubai. "He's got a show that he's starting soon, Your Highness." Abdul-Aziz is his nephew, but still, my boss addresses with respect.

"What a shame," the prince replies. "Can't you stay for a little while more?" he asks kindly.

I apologize sincerely to him, explaining how I would love to stay, "but work, Your Highness. I have a lot of work," I tell him with a sincere face.

"May Allah be with you, then," he says. He looks toward Mohamed, a gentle young Sheikh who's always around him. "Please take care of Elie."

Waleed insists I go straight to Dubai and wait for him rather than return to Beirut. "I'll be joining you soon."

Finally, Mohamed drives me to the airport and walks me directly through security. I don't even have to check in or be searched. After all, I'm a guest of the royal palace.

Mohamed escorts me into the plane. Just before we say goodbye, to my surprise, he gives me an elegant black sports bag he's been holding the whole time.

"This is from Prince Abdul-Aziz," he whispers. "Just a simple thank you gift for visiting. Enjoy the trip." And he leaves before I can even reply.

I sneak a peek inside the bag to find it is full of $10,000 packs. There are 10 packs. It's $100,000. I want to jump. My perception of the Prince quickly improves; he is a very interesting man and his habits don't disturb me at all. I wish I were invited here every week.

The first thing I do when I reach my suite is call Waleed and thank him and his nephew for the enormous gift.

"It's a little gesture," Waleed says. He doesn't even bother to talk about it. He confirms that he's coming to Dubai in three days.

I call Chantal to update her. "Wow, a $100,000!" she says. "Let's give it all to the landlord," she suggests immediately. However, I decide to send him $50,000, which covers what's due to date and a bit more. Just like that, the nightmare of losing my home is gone.

With the rest of the money, I pay off other debts—of which there's no shortage. But I haven't even started working yet. "In a couple of months, I might be able to take care of our entire mortgage and all our other loans," I tell Chantal.

"I'm sure you will," she says. "Once you're inside

someone's life, it's hard to get you out," she adds, giggling. "Is that a compliment?" I ask, half joking. "I don't know," she replies. She sounds so cheerful.

Three days later, as promised, Waleed returns to Dubai. The dinners and gatherings resume naturally. I am always invited to the Sheikh's gatherings, as if I were among his best and most trusted friends.

Even with his high-level status, Sheikh Waleed must navigate very complex relationships among the Saudi royals due to the sophisticated and varied interests that connect them.

In one month, I get really close. I'm the only employee who's always around Waleed, as if I'm one of his close buddies. I quickly develop a reputation for being a VIP with continual access to his ear.

As a result, even some executive managers start calling to ask me for favors. It can take some of them many days to get to speak to the Sheikh by phone. Sometimes he doesn't show up in his office for 2 weeks.

With my new boss, I am surrounded by luxury. I buy a new 745 BMW. I live in a luxurious hotel, with limitless access to food, restaurants, bars, etc… all-inclusive, just like I have fantasized about. All I am expected to do is send my bills to the executive office. I am appreciated and spoiled like I have never been.

Waleed has turned my life upside down. I thought that it only happens in movies. I thought the white knight on the white horse only appears in little girls' imaginations.

XXVI
Liberation, Occupation, & In Between

Meanwhile, in the outside world, all the diplomatic initiatives to convince Saddam to leave power have failed. No one doubts any longer that war is coming.

While my feelings about Saddam within the context of the Middle East are complex—at times he was helpful to Lebanon as a rival to Syria's President Hafez al-Assad—the bottom line is he's an evil tyrant, and I'll be glad to see him go.

I just hope the Americans don't change their minds about toppling him like they did at the end of the first Iraq war. I never understood why the United States withdrew at Saddam's gates, leaving the freedom-loving Iraqis who cheered the troops to the brutality of Saddam's revenge. Saddam and his two sons arrested, tortured, and killed thousands of those who embraced the Americans. I believe this time will be different, and I'll be watching!

Lebanon is hardly ever mentioned in the news, as little has changed there. The Syrians still control everything. They're tense, however, as there's no telling what will happen to the status quo when American F-16s enter the picture.

Finally, George W. Bush gives Saddam a strict ultimatum. He has 48 hours to leave Iraq. Otherwise, military operations will be launched.

Still suspecting that Bush is bluffing, Saddam declares he'll fight. He promises his people he'll defeat the

Americans in "the mother of all battles" and send U.S. soldiers back in coffins.

Two days later, the Iraqi dictator discovers George W. Bush meant every word, and the war begins.

On CNN, Al Jazeera, and Al Arabiya News Channel, millions of viewers around the globe watch Operation Iraqi Freedom as it officially launches. The skies of Iraq are lit up with explosions bigger than I've ever seen before.

At Waleed's dinners, there's absolutely nothing to discuss but the Iraqi war. Like usual, I refer to it as liberation, while most of the Sheikh's guests call it an invasion. This difference alone fuels many debates.

I stick to my prediction that the coalition will reach the gates of Baghdad quickly. "The south of Iraq will fall in a couple of days. Saddam has oppressed the Shiites in the south for decades, so they'll probably fight side-by-side with the Americans. Baghdad will probably take 10 to 15 days," I predict, inflaming those who expect an endless conflict.

Yet, 15 days of fierce fighting pass by, and the Americans are still fighting in the south in the region of Um Qasr, the first Iraqi town on the Kuwaiti border.

I watch the news, and I can't believe what is going on. Some of Waleed's guests are starting to make fun of my previous predictions.

"The Americans can't even cross the little town of Um Qasr," announces Iraqi Information Minister Muhammad Saeed al-Sahhaf. He promises American troops more hell if they approach the capital. "They will be barbecued on the gates of Baghdad."

But just five days later, the Iraqi army collapses. In fact, it's during al-Sahhaf's daily press conference to update dozens of international reporters that TV viewers first see American tanks enter Baghdad. Minister al-Sahhaf looks back and spots American troops crossing the main bridge toward the city. He cuts off his press conference, dashes to his military car, and disappears. The many colorful promises he made about defeating the "American insects" become jokes laughed at all over the world.

It's over.

U.S. troops enter the capital, and Iraqis greet them with rice and flower petals. The victory isn't good only for the United States and Iraq; it's also helpful to me. In the eyes of Waleed and his colleagues, I'm not just the pro-American anymore. I'm someone who's *connected* and knows what's really going on in the world. Even Prince Abdul-Aziz, recalls that I got the Iraq outcome right, as one of his close associates informs me.

The truth is, I was unbelievably lucky to guess right. But when some suggest I have a secret pipeline into the CIA, I only mildly deny it. I like the reputation, somehow.

I am now often asked about what is going to happen next. "Look at Japan, look at Germany. That's what will happen to Iraq," I answer, based on nothing but my knowledge of history.

I talk about Iraq as if it is my life's work, even though I have never visited it in my life. All I know about Saddam and his regime is pretty much what everyone knows from the press. Still, I give lectures and everyone listens.

Although Al Arabiya News Channel was not fully ready to launch on-air, Waleed was smart enough to grab the moment. A war is perhaps the best time to launch a news channel. I believe my smart boss did the right thing. During Saddam's reign, there was no media allowed in Iraq, so the Iraqis have no loyalty to particular TV brand. The network to win the Iraqis' hearts first will establish a base of millions of viewers in one of the richest countries on the planet,.with the potential for huge revenues.

As for al Hurra, it is so stuck in bureaucratic procedures that it entirely misses the big event. That leaves CNN, Al Jazeera, Al Arabiya News Channel, and a new channel owned by Abu Dhabi to compete for the virgin soil.

The competition is happening without me, however.

I wake up at noon, watch some news, call my wife, play some Tennis, and set up myself for the evenings. Waleed is always out of Dubai now, taking care of his various investments around the globe. However, I live like a Sheikh.

As for my show, I am not in a hurry. My boss isn't either. On the contrary, he thinks I should take my time before starting a new one. I don’t really object.

I finally rent a three-bedroom apartment on Sheikh Zayed Road, the central street in Dubai. My wife and child are due to join me in a month or so.

I will return to full family mode, then. I keep confirming to myself.

As I watch the news and see the U.S. Marines on the streets of Baghdad, I remember when I first saw them in Beirut. They were sent to protect us, and we threw rice and flowers on them, too. I envy the Iraqis. I can hardly wait until all our dictators collapse, one after the other, until the domino effect reaches Syria's al-Assad.

Only then will I return to my country. When I see the Syrian soldiers running away in their underwear, just like the Iraqi soldiers that Saddam used to terrorize 25 million of his citizens, I will go home.

The time will come one day, I tell myself, *and these marines will kick you out like rats from my Beirut*. Sometimes, it's almost a lullaby I use to put myself to sleep.

A month after the liberation, things start to get a little chaotic in Baghdad. "It's all expected; there's no magical cure that can fix all the diseases in one month," I argue.

But things even grow worse in the next weeks. Doubts start to arouse here and there. The democratic political process looks harder to launch than anticipated. Stories of revenge and murders quickly make their way in the headlines.

To me—and many millions alike—a great deal rides on the successful launching of democracy in Iraq. If millions of Arabs watch their fellow Iraqis acquire freedom and dignity, they'll inevitably ask for the same privileges. I feel strongly that making democracy work in Iraq will eventually ignite a revolution.

However, the stories coming from Iraq point in the opposite direction. As the resistance and explosions escalate, the situation appears to be deteriorating.

Words like Sunni, Shiite, and Kurd that were never used before start to surface in all the news bulletins—sectarian speeches from here countered by sectarian speeches from there. It feels just like what happened in my country 30 years before. This is how it usually starts.

Above all this, some Iraqi politicians are calling the United States occupiers now, especially when the search for weapons of mass destruction come up with nothing. If there are any weapons of mass destruction, the coalition should have located them by now.

But, who cares? I personally don't care. What is done is done, and all that matters now is the future. Will the neighboring tyrants learn something from all this before it is too late?

I have many scenarios in my head. I can't wait until the Americans move toward Syria, freeing my broken Beirut. I wonder if this is going to happen soon. It's just a matter of time, I conclude decisively in my head.

In the news, the explosions in Iraq are now the headlines; the situation is seriously deteriorating.

However, in the Dubai-located hotel's bar, there are three new sexy ladies who've just arrived from Ukraine. They insist to call themselves 'models'. I am simply in another world.

Two of the girls wear standard smiles. But, one of them, named Svetlana, looks arrogant and barely hides her annoyance. Naturally, she's the one I fixate on. I don't know why, but I am in the perfect mood to be an asshole. I look at right in her eyes and ask with clear sarcasm, "How much would it cost to take all 3 of you to my Jacuzzi tonight?" I say, sounding exactly like a rich son of a bitch.

Svetlana doesn't answer. However, the other girl interferes. "1500 dirhams each," she says, keeping the smile on her silly face. "Done," I say immediately. I ask the bartender do the reservations. “I need a suite with a big Jacuzzi,” I tell him.

20 minutes later, I have three stunning women in my Jacuzzi; however, it’s exactly at that point that I have realized it’s not women that I am missing in my life.

“What do you do exactly?” Svetlana asks out of the blues, hoping to interrupt the sudden silence that has hit me. “I am a journalist,” I answer, respectfully this time. “Oh!” she says.

She probably thinks I am a paparazzo who follows celebrities to clubs and parties. *Can I blame her?* I think to myself. *What is she supposed to think?*

"Anyway..." I jump out of the water and put a fluffy white robe on. "I am leaving for Iraq next week," I say and sit on the couch to finish what's left of my vodka. "That is the new story I'm covering," I add.

"Iraq?" all the ladies look interested now.

"Yup," I say.

"But there are lots of explosions and shit happening there," Svetlana says and gets out of the water to join me on the couch.

"Yes, there are, but that is where journalists are needed, right?" I smile at her. She becomes much friendlier after that. “Would you please leave?” I ask the women gently, putting 5000 dirhams in cash at the table. “No, it’s really okay,” Svetlana takes the initiative before the other could take the money. “You don’t have to,” she offers. “Please take it,” I insist. And they all leave, happily surprised from the easy money they got, I assume.

The first thing I do when I wake up the next day is call Waleed. "I want to go to Iraq," I tell him. "I need to talk to you about this without the presence of any vodka in my system."

"I was gonna ask you to join me. I am going on a trip to Cannes, Nice, and perhaps Ibiza on my private boat," Waleed laughs out loud. "It's painfully tempting, but I have made up my mind," I insist.

"I am coming back to Dubai tomorrow. We'll talk about it." Clearly, he doesn't take it seriously.

But, later, he realizes that it's no joke. "I will host the first *live* weekly talk show from Baghdad; I have some great ideas. I will come up with something good."

Waleed finds it hard to believe, at first, but then he becomes enthusiastic about it. "You're crazy," he says and shakes my hand. "Done," he says, "go."

Sometimes in life, all it takes is a naked woman in a Jacuzzi to wake you up. Svetlana reminded me that I am a journalist. Her sarcastic "Oh" when I told her what I do has ignited me.

I enjoy this life, this unlimited luxury, this safety, and this peace of mind Waleed has provided. But, the past few months have been like a vacation to me. And somehow, I feel useless and bored. I have never thought that one could have enough of that kind of luxury life. I always believed rich people only pretend that their lives are empty. It must be true in some cases, I learn.

I am not rich, yet, but I can already feel how things would be if I have no dreams to pursue.

In a hurry, I inform my wife, my family, and my close friends that I am leaving for at least six months.

I realize Iraq is a very dangerous place right now. I'm not worried, though. I know in my bones this is the correct course for me. I also have in mind that despite years of numerous threats and predictions of terrible consequences, I've survived intact.

XXVII
A Meeting With Voldemort

There are several countries that border Iraq. I assume I can enter through Saudi Arabia, Jordan, or Kuwait. When Waleed's assistant is nailing down the details of my trip, however, he learns that I've waited too long. The borders between other countries and Iraq have been shut down, with just one exception: Syria.

Moving to the explosions and violent chaos of Iraq is one thing. That does not bother me. But stepping foot in Syria terrifies me.

When I hear about this, I go straight to Waleed, who's in his office. "There's a problem," I say. "I'm absolutely committed to doing a show from Iraq. However, I can't travel through Syria. I have a history with the authorities there, and they have long memories. Frankly, I'm afraid they'll kill me."

Waleed laughs at me.

"What are you talking about? You're with Al Arabiya now! No one dares or is *allowed* to kill you.

"Listen," he continues, "if you're worried about being in Iraq, just tell me. I'll totally understand if you made a decision in haste. There are many others shows you can create. You really don't have to do this if you don't want to."

I shake my head. "I swear to you, I'm not at all scared of being in Iraq. But I'm very scared of traveling there through Syria."

"If this is truly what you're worried about, let me

put your mind at ease right now. I'm calling Khaled."

Khaled is Waleed's older brother, who I've met every time he's visited Dubai. The owner of numerous luxury hotels, Khaled's even richer and more powerful than Waleed.

"Khaled lives in Syria," Waleed tells me as he's dialing, "and he has huge investments there. When he needs anything from a Syrian official—hello, Khaled? Listen, guess what? Elie needs to go through Syria to get to Iraq. Yeah, he's not afraid of the war; but he's scared of Ghazi Kanaan!" Waleed laughs again. I get the impression Khaled is equally amused. "Yeah, I know! Sure, sure. I will tell him."

"Khaled will make sure that you'll be taken care of. Trust me, if there's 1% risk, my brother wouldn't have insisted that you come," Waleed assures me.

"And what if Ghazi Kanaan is holding a grudge on me? What can Khaled do then?" I ask my boss. "Are you kidding me? Khaled can reach President Bashar el Assad in five seconds," he explains.

"Don't worry about Ghazi Kanaan, Elie," Waleed adds, "my brother can bring him to the airport to receive you if you like," he chuckles.

"No, no, no! I definitely don't want Kanaan to receive me anywhere," I answer quickly.

Actually, I begin to relax. I know Syrian officials love to be bribed, and Saudi royals love to solve problems by throwing money at them, so it's a perfect marriage. I assume Ghazi Kanaan is receiving millions of dollars from the Saudis. *He wouldn't do anything to jeopardize his bank account?* I comfort myself.

The next morning, I fly to Damascus. All I have to

do is sleep there for one night and then first thing in the morning take a plane across Syria to the Iraqi border. There will be a driver waiting for me on the other side to take me to Al Arabiya News Channel's newsroom covering the war.

I arrive in Damascus in the afternoon. Two men wearing Syrian Intelligence uniforms meet me and say, "Mr. Nakouzi, welcome. We've been sent to take care of you and get you whatever you need." They get my passport stamped immediately and walk me through the red tape in minutes. Then they drive me to the only 5-star hotel in the city, the Sheraton.

After I'm settled into my room, I call Waleed and tell him what happened. "Yes," he says, "Khaled asked some people to take care of you."

So, I've been treated like a VIP, and now I'm in a big luxury suite. I'm finally starting to relax.

And then I'm struck by paranoia. Syria is an iron-fisted police state. I remember stories about it planting cameras and microphones everywhere. *Getting me to relax could be part of the plan. I must not do or say anything that will appear bad on video.* I think

Then it escalates.

Suddenly, I feel like a lamb being softened up for slaughter. *It doesn't matter what I do! I fell into a trap. They have total power over me now.* I start running scenes from *The Godfather* and *Scarface* in my mind. *Someone's going to knock on the door, smile, and shoot me in the head.*

As my blood pressure rises, I tell myself, *Whoa! You're going crazy! You're in a beautiful hotel room, and everything's happening according to plan. Just take it easy, and all will be well.*

At that moment, the phone rings.

With my nerves thoroughly on edge again, I pick up. "Hello?"

"Welcome, dear guest," an elegant, silky, almost whispering voice says on the other end. "How is it possible that I have a celebrity, Elie Nakouzi, in our lovely city and he doesn't get in touch with me?"

"Who is this?" I ask.

"This is Ghazi Kanaan. Welcome to Damascus, dear guest."

I'm speechless. More precisely, I'm petrified.

"Did you think you could come to Syria without visiting me? Did you seriously intend to come here without passing by and sharing a coffee with me? Oh, what a disappointment."

This is the first time I've ever heard Ghazi Kanaan's voice. I'm speaking to the bogeyman I've feared since childhood. I can barely breathe.

"You know," he continues, "I want you to relax. I want you to go have a good dinner tonight. Consider Syria your Lebanon and Damascus your Beirut. Enjoy a wonderful evening. At 8:30 tomorrow morning, I'll send two cars that will bring you to my office. I will have to issue you a special license so you can cross the borders," he explains.

Finally, I get back my voice. "I don't want to bother you. I don't—"

"Oh, no, not at all," he interrupts. "It's no bother for a guest like you. You're important to someone very close to my heart. And by the way, I don't need Khaled to tell me to take care of you. You are already a very dear guest."

What choice do I have? Call Waleed and scream about Ghazi Kanaan asking we share a coffee together? "Okay," I say.

"Good," he replies and hangs up.

I have no idea what just happened. Why is Ghazi Kanaan talking to me as if he's my uncle? If there's anyone in my life upon whom I've wished death, it's him. He's the man responsible for the death of thousands of my people, who presumably orchestrated the assassination of Bashir Gemayel, and who screwed our lives with fear. It was under his explicit direction that we were stabbed, shot, and bombed.

Of course, I have no better feelings toward Syria's late President Hafez el Assad and its current President Bashar el Assad, because the murders flowed from their orders. But Kanaan is the monster who planned and executed the details of the violence. Regardless of who my country elects, Kanaan was for a long, long time Lebanon's actual ruler in terms of power, and as far as I can tell, his only wish for my people is obliteration.

My earlier spark of paranoia erupts into a blaze. This is how serial killers handle their victims in the movies—polite, gentle words, followed by torture and a knife or a bullet.

And I'll be face to face with this real-life mass murderer in the morning.

I don't know if I'll even last that long—my heart is pounding so fast that I am afraid it will stop.

I don't touch my suite's food or drink a drop of its water. I fear they might be poisoned. I am being totally irrational and I know it, but I can't just stop this paranoia.

I try to go to sleep but toss and turn all night. I keep replaying Kanaan's soothing, gentlemanly voice in my head. I now remember it fits with how both his friends and opponents have described him. "He never shouts," I've been told. "He never even raises his voice. He does everything with utter calmness."

Apparently, there's no need to shout when you have the power to wipe away tens of thousands of lives with a whisper.

At 8:30 on the dot, the phone rings. I'm informed the cars Kanaan promised are waiting for me.

I couldn't sleep, so I already have everything packed. I check out from the hotel and spot two black Mercedes Benzes. They have opaque windows preventing anyone from seeing inside.

To my surprise, there are around six bodyguards by the first car. They're blocking the road and not allowing anyone to get near them or me. Everyone at the hotel is looking at me, clearly wondering, "Who the fuck is this guy to need so much security?"

I'm directed to the second car, where I get in the back. As we travel to their headquarters, I flash to gangster movies where someone is being *taken for a ride*.

When we arrive, an elevator takes me up to Kanaan. I walk into his waiting room and approach his male assistant. But before I can utter a word, Ghazi Kanaan jumps out from his office. "Elie Nakouzi, the star is here!" he exclaims.

I reach out my hand to shake his. He ignores this, choosing instead to hug me warmly. Then he kisses me on the cheeks three times, Lebanese style. "Welcome, welcome, my dear guest. My dear guest, welcome!"

"Thank you, thank you!" I answer with a very calculated smile.

Fuck you, fuck you, and fuck you. I spent my whole life fearing and hating you! Now I'm supposed to kiss you, fucker? Do you think the expensive suit you're wearing can hide the monster that lives inside you, you fucking criminal? I'm thinking,

He walks me into the office and tells his assistant in a rude tone, "No phone calls. I have an important guest and want to chat with him uninterrupted. Send us coffee and water quickly, but otherwise don't disturb us." Then he closes the door, invites me to sit, and takes the power position behind his desk.

"Were you really worried about coming to Syria?" he begins.

"To tell you the truth, yeah. I was a little concerned that you might have a problem with me."

"Seriously?" he asks. "I might have a problem with you? Are you kidding me? I don't understand this."

"Well, we haven't had the best relationship through the years. There were some disagreements, some criticisms of policies..." I choose my words very carefully. "So I had reason to think you might misunderstand some of my positions and maybe hold a grudge."

"Hold a grudge?!" The demon that East Beirut mothers use to scare their children with into behaving shakes his head at me and sighs with parental disappointment. "Oh, you Christians. President Hafez el Assad, and now his son Bashar, have tried to protect you for the past 30 years. They're the only guys who defended you against the extremists. But no matter what we do for you, you turn against us."

He's talking about regimes that slaughtered or drove away nearly half the Christian population of Lebanon.

"You know, President el Assad used to tell me all the time, 'Take care of the Christians, Ghazi. These are the water in our vast Arab desert,'" he sighs. "God rest his soul," he shakes his head, remembering. "He spent years defending the existence of your people, and every time you had the chance, you'd turn him down," he lectures with a philosophical tone.

I just smile and politely say, "I'm sorry, but I have a slightly different point of view."

"I know, I know. They filled your head with slogans of 'Syria is against you, Syria is the enemy.' But can you mention even one incident that gives you cause to say *I* hold a grudge against you?"

Despite my fear, this is too much for me to hold my tongue. "Come on, General. MTV was shut down. Isn't that a grudge?"

"What? MTV? Do you think I shut down MTV? Really?" He laughs.

I give him a look. "It could never have been shut down if the order hadn't come from you."

"That's very entertaining, but you have things upside down," he replies. "I'm the one who defended your network, kid."

I'm shocked. He sees this and smiles at me as if to say, *That's right, you're an idiot.*

"It's your president of the republic who closed down your TV network," Kanaan tells me, "after that idiotic statement that Gabriel, your boss, had attacked him with. Yet, I advised him against it. He's still alive. You can ask him yourself. 'Leave them alone,' I said. 'They're just toothless dogs barking in the night. They don't have the power to do any harm.' God knows how hard I tried to sway him back."

"Truth is," he goes on, "I have held your president twice from shutting your network down," he shakes his head. He sees the disbelief on my face, so, he explains.

"Look, I was totally against shutting your voices down. Somehow, you were the living proof, in front of all the international community, that we cherish democratic values and free speech?" He pauses.

I'm stunned again. I expected Kanaan to treat me like a hated enemy. Instead, he's thanking me for being an impotent puppet that helped make him look good to America and the world.

"Here's some more truth," he continues. "I always recommended that *you*, Nakouzi, stay on MTV to keep attacking us, cursing us, and saying whatever you wanted—even mentioning my name more than a few times.

"When you went to Paris, I didn't take the time to watch your show, but I read the reports on it. Quite honestly, it didn't bother me at all," he confides.

"And when Gabriel Murr won the deputy position, there were many who wanted to take revenge. Why do you think there were no consequences? It's because I defended him, and I defended you. And now you say I closed your network?"

Could it be true? I ask myself. Or is he just fucking with my mind? I hate to admit it, but what he's saying makes sense.

"That's enough about MTV. Now, you think I hold a grudge against *you*? You personally? The reason you're not rotting in jail, or perhaps even dead, is because of me. Remember that restaurant you owned?"

"Yes," I say. When I had money, I owned two percent of a fancy late-night restaurant. It was a classy place to bring friends, colleagues, and guests of my show.

"Your *Lebanese* Intelligence Services wanted to plant drugs there and then get you locked away for life on coke and heroine charges. I said no. Not because I love you," he explains with obvious sarcasm, "but, I remembered that Saad Hariri, the son of your prime minister, is a frequent customer there, and planting the drugs might appear as an attack on the prime minister. So, I asked them to find another way to deal with you. You made some people really angry, you know," he says with a friendly tone.

"Then," he briefs, "they turned up to your bad debts and finally threw you in jail. But you were saved by a guardian angel—and his name is Charles Ayoub."

Again, he's stunned me.

"You remember Charles, don't you?" Kanaan asks.

"Of course," I say. "He's my great friend."

"Remember the night you were arrested? How do you think you got out of jail? Charles called me and begged for your life!"

I'm staring at him, listening carefully to every word.

"When you were locked up, Charles called everyone he knew with influence. So, who do you think he finally reached at 4:00 am to get you out in five minutes, or was it two minutes?" He chuckles, triumphant.

"Yeah," I reply, "around six minutes." I feel like my head is about to explode.

"Thank your guardian angel, then, because I only did it for him. I also warned all the security agencies to never touch you without informing me first. I knew it would break Charles' heart if they harmed you, or God forbid, if they killed you. And I usually don't break my dear friends' hearts... Say hello to Charles for me, whenever you talk to him," he finishes his lecture. "And ask him about what I just told you, if you have any doubts, dear guest," he adds, looking very satisfied from the look on my face.

I'm dumbfounded.

I don't need to ask Charles anything. Everything Kanaan is telling me fits. A lot of mysteries suddenly make sense.

Kanaan takes a sheet of paper out of his notebook. "Look, I'm going to write a sentence, and I want your signature. Will you do this for me? You're a journalist, and journalists are fair."

He writes, “I, Elie Nakouzi, admit that Ghazi Kanaan was never unfair to me,” and puts my name underneath.

"You are a reasonable person, right? Will you sign this for me?"

"Yes," I say, my mind reeling. "Definitely." And I sign.

"Are you convinced? Or are you scared?" asks the butcher of Lebanon, as I sit in his headquarters.

"No, I'm convinced. If I was scared, I wouldn't have signed."

"Yeah," Kanaan replies, "I know. You're a hero." And he smirks.

I suddenly think, *what the hell did I just do? I've made a horrible mistake. He could use this signed statement in any number of ways to undermine me.*

Kanaan stands up. "I'm going to sign your papers now. And after I stamp your passport, I'm going to send two generals to make sure you arrive to Iraq unharmed. I've been asked to make sure you get there safely, and I will make 100 percent certain that happens."

Kanaan signs and stamps all my official documents.

Then, he takes the sheet of paper I signed and rips it in half.

He folds what's left and rips it in half again, and again, and again, and again, until it's in small pieces. Then he throws the pieces in the garbage.

"Go on, " he says. "Iraq is going through a lot of changes. Go do good work and be a fair journalist. And tell people how we received you in Syria."

"Yes, sure. I will," I say.

Kanaan calls in two 4-star generals. "Take care of my dear friend," he tells them. "Spoil him, and get him to Iraq with no problems."

"Yes, sir," they reply.

Almost to himself, Kanaan adds, "Once he's past the border, he's not our responsibility anymore."

A chill passes through me. But I manage to get out, "Thank you."

I leave Ghazi Kanaan's office with his generals.

Kanaan's generals personally drive me to the airport. I arrive without incident, and they inform me that two of their soldiers will meet me when I land to drive me straight to the border.

While flying over Syria, the shock of my encounter with Ghazi Kanaan starts to wear off a little, and I begin to digest what just happened.

True to his word, Kanaan never physically harmed a hair on my head.

But, with a subtlety I never dreamed he had, he successfully murdered my image of who I am.

During all the years I was on radio and TV battling Syrian oppression, I thought I was a hero risking his life against a brutal regime intent on silencing me. I liked the way I perceived myself, but not anymore.

Now I realize that regime never felt threatened by me for a second. I was a propaganda tool who helped the thugs of Syria appear tolerant.

I always believed I was lucky or somehow imagined myself invincible. But now, I realize that my freedom, my safety, and very life, maybe, were gifts from a devil that I always considered my worst enemy. *What a crazy, crazy lesson!*

It is probably the worst timing to learn this truth, especially that I'm about to plunge myself into a war zone. *And what if I don't have a guardian angel there?*

We finally reach the borders. The Syrian soldiers stamp my passport quickly, especially when they see the official note that is attached to it, signed by Ghazi Kanaan, himself.

On the other side, a man waves his hand. "Mr. Nakouzi," he shouts, pronouncing my name in a funny way, "Mr. Elie Nakouzi," he shouts again, louder this time.

I wave back to him as I approach the Iraqi soldiers. He runs toward the checkpoint and explains to the officer that I am with Al Arabiya News Channel, even before I can say hello.

"Welcome to the free Iraq," the soldier greets me. And he stamps a temporary entry visa.

"I am Wissam," the chubby guy who was waiving at me introduces himself. "I am your driver," he says gently, and takes my three bags.

He walks me to his car, and we shake hands warmly after he loads the luggage in his trunk. He's strong, but he sounds nice and warm. "Take us to where the action is, please," I say, smiling at him.

"It's going to be a long trip," Wissam says as we get in the car.

"Safe long trip?" I ask him.

"That is in the hands of Allah Almighty," he smiles, turns on his engines, and we head toward the capital, Baghdad.

The streets look tired, old, and, some, filthy. This country was under heavy siege for 12 years, and it is not hard to notice that it needs a lot to heal. I mean, a lot!

The heat is around 600 degrees perhaps. Fahrenheit or Celsius? When it's that hot, there's absolutely no difference.

"*You didn't want to enjoy the luxurious hotels, the amazing infrastructure, the super malls and towers*," I start to blame myself the more we go inside the Iraqi cities. *"No, idiot. You wanted to come here, instead. Good for you!*" I am literally shouting at myself now, inside my head, of course.

After eight hours of nonstop driving, Wissam

wakes me up from my last nap, perhaps the eleventh. "Here we are," he says, after he parks in front of an old, four-story building. "This is the office," he points at the hotel that Al Arabiya News Channel rented to run its news operation.

I get out of the car and stand there, staring at the *headquarters*.

"Oh, fuck me!" I say, not in my head this time, though. I can see Wissam trying to hold his laughter. I look at him; I insist.

"Fuck me!"

****

End of Book I

To Be Continued in Book 2:

Caves Within Castles

Made in the USA
San Bernardino, CA
05 May 2014